CHILDREN'S HUMAN RIGHTS AND PUBLIC SCHOOLI[illegible]

CONSTRUCTING KNOWLEDGE: CURRICULUM STUDIES IN ACTION

Volume 5

Scope

"Curriculum" is an expansive term; it encompasses vast aspects of teaching and learning. Curriculum can be defined as broadly as, "The content of schooling in all its forms" (English, p. 4), and as narrowly as a lesson plan. Complicating matters is the fact that curricula are often organized to fit particular time frames. The incompatible and overlapping notions that curriculum involves everything that is taught and learned in a particular setting *and* that this learning occurs in a limited time frame reveal the nuanced complexities of curriculum studies.

"Constructing Knowledge" provides a forum for systematic reflection on the substance (subject matter, courses, programs of study), purposes, and practices used for bringing about learning in educational settings. Of concern are such fundamental issues as: What should be studied? Why? By whom? In what ways? And in what settings? Reflection upon such issues involves an inter-play among the major components of education: subject matter, learning, teaching, and the larger social, political, and economic contexts, as well as the immediate instructional situation. Historical and autobiographical analyses are central in understanding the contemporary realties of schooling and envisioning how to (re)shape schools to meet the intellectual and social needs of all societal members. Curriculum is a social construction that results from a set of decisions; it is written and enacted and both facets undergo constant change as contexts evolve.

This series aims to extent the professional conversation about curriculum in contemporary educational settings. Curriculum is a designed experience intended to promote learning. Because it is socially constructed, curriculum is subject to all the pressures and complications of the diverse communities that comprise schools and other social contexts in which citizens gain self-understanding.

Children's Human Rights and Public Schooling in the United States

Edited by

Julia Hall
D'Youville College, Buffalo, New York, USA

SENSE PUBLISHERS
ROTTERDAM / BOSTON / TAIPEI

A C.I.P. record for this book is available from the Library of Congress.

ISBN 978-94-6209-195-5 (paperback)
ISBN 978-94-6209-196-2 (hardback)
ISBN 978-94-6209-197-9 (e-book)

Published by: Sense Publishers,
P.O. Box 21858, 3001 AW Rotterdam, The Netherlands
https://www.sensepublishers.com/

Printed on acid-free paper

TABLE OF CONTENTS

CHRISTINE E. SLEETER

FOREWORD

By the time this book is published, I will be a first-time grandmother. My grandson, the child of a racially-mixed (African American and White) father and a White (German American) mother, will be growing up and attending school in a large urban area. His family will give him an abundance of love and care; I have no doubt about that. What will happen to him when he goes off to school is far less certain. Although very few (if any) parents and grandparents do not want school to nurture their children and grandchildren intellectually, socially, and personally (allowing for varied conceptions of what that might mean), as yet we lack a system of legal protections for the human rights of children and youth as well as a shared moral commitment that supports children's rights.

Children's Human Rights and Public Schooling in the United States, edited by Julia Hall, offers a sobering and critically important analysis of what happens to many children when they enter school. The case studies reported in the book's chapters are contextualized within a nexus of two opposing movements: a movement to recognize and support the world's children and youth as full human beings upon whose wellbeing our collective future rests, and a movement to restore the hegemony of capital and its ruling class. As Hall clearly explains in the book's Introduction, a global movement to recognize human rights of children culminated in 1989 when the United Nations adopted the Convention on the Rights of the Child, then again less than a year later after the Convention had been ratified by a majority of the world's nations. At first glance, those in this country might be puzzled to learn that despite our rhetoric about human rights, the US is one of only two member countries (the other being Somalia) that has yet to sign on to this document. To understand why it has not, and why its failure to do so is a huge problem, we must look to the other movement that was occurring simultaneously.

The US economy in 1989 was in the midst of a crisis. The post World War II economic boom had stalled out. The term "stagflation" had been used through the 1970s to characterize the evident economic stagnation combined with inflation. As Harvey (2005) explains with reference to that time period, "Discontent was widespread and the conjoining of labour and urban social movements throughout much of the advanced capitalist world appeared to point towards the emergence of a socialist alternative to the social compromise between capital and labour" (pp. 14-15). Indeed, labor movements forty years previously had managed to shift the distribution of wealth in the US and other capitalist nations in a way that afforded working class people a larger (although still small) proportion of the economic pie. Social movements of the 1960s and early 1970s attempted to expand access to a larger share of the pie for people of color and women.

Rapid growth of several Asian economies in the 1980s threatened US global hegemony. A stock market collapse in late 1987 precipitated gyrations in US economic growth, inflation, and unemployment. The "solution" to these economic problems, hammered out earlier in various conservative think-tanks and universities, most notably the University of Chicago, was neoliberalism, or the reassertion of private capital and unregulated markets, and the alignment of government to the needs of private capital. By the 1987 stock market collapse, neoliberal economic strategies had been pioneered internationally (beginning with Chile under the dictator Pinochet) as well as within the US. Significantly, as Harvey (2005) points out, management of the New York fiscal crisis in the 1980s "established the principle that in the event of a conflict between the integrity of financial institutions and bondholders' returns, on the one hand, and the well-being of the citizens on the other, the former was to be privileged" (p. 48).

Hence, when the United Nations opened the Convention on the Rights of the Child for signatures, the US was already in the process of being actively re-tooled in the opposite direction – away from human rights and human welfare, and toward consolidating the reign of private capital accumulation. I would add that rapid diversification of the US population escalated this shift, as White people increasingly viewed the growing proportion of families of color as "welfare cheats" and criminals whose children must be contained rather than educated. It appears that White economic elites have been able to use racial prejudices successfully to convince a large bloc of voters to oppose spending on social programs including health and education, even when such programs would benefit their own families (see Bunch, 2010). Indeed, by 2012, the Pew Research Center (2012) found that while support among Democrats for domestic social programs had not changed between 1987 and 2012 (about two-thirds agreed, for example, that government should "help needy people, even if it means going deeper into debt"), support among Republicans for domestic social programs plummeted (dropping from 39% to only 20% agreeing with the same statement).

It is in this context that drawing attention to the rights of children in US schools is crucially important. As Hall points out in the Introduction, human rights frameworks are rarely studied in US schools. As a result, among the general public there is little awareness of the UN Convention on the Rights of the Child, and even less awareness of the failure of the US to endorse it. Even teachers generally do not know about the struggle for children's human rights or the potential of the UN to support the rights of children.

Nor does the US public have a very clear awareness of the everyday violations of children's human rights in US schools, which chapters in this book graphically detail. Readers learn what happens to children of color (immigrant as well as non-immigrant) – despite the wishes of their parents – when "solutions" to challenges they face in school come from predominantly White mainstream ways of thinking that incorporate deficit discourses about children and families who are not White or from affluent or middle-class backgrounds. Readers gain a glimpse of children who are treated as commodities for sale, and of schools treated as marketplaces for the military. Chapters offer windows into the pain and frustration children and youth experience when they are harassed, when they are "sold" dead-end routes to their dreams and aspirations, and when they are simply neglected by professionals whose charge it is to care for them.

Readers also gain glimpses that things could be otherwise. Hall, as well as other authors in this volume, stresses the potential of the UN as offering a shared platform from which to work for the welfare of children. Polakow shows how nations that have worked to address poverty have significantly reduced child homelessness. Books, in her analysis of cuts in public funding for schools, shows decisions the public has made that negatively impact on schools and children, implying that the public could act differently. Indeed, throughout this volume are examples of actions that teachers, school administrators, and policy-makers took that could be done differently.

This important book, then, serves not only as a call to the US to ratify the Convention on the Rights of the Child, but more fundamentally to develop a moral commitment to support the health, education, and well-being of all of our children. Currently we lack that moral commitment. Julia Hall and the contributors to this book challenge us to become a better society, one that gives the highest priority to the welfare of its citizens, and especially of its future generations. This is what I want for my own grandchild and for everyone else's children and grandchildren as well.

REFERENCES

Bunch, W. (2010). *The backlash*. New York: Harper.

Harvey, D. (2005). *A brief history of neoliberalism*. Oxford: Oxford University Press.

Pew Research Center (2012). *Partisan polarization surges in Bush, Obama years*. Washington, DC: Pew Research Center. Retrieved from www.people-press.org

JULIA HALL

CHAPTER 1, INTRODUCTION

School Children in Serious Need of Rights

The United States tends to portray itself as a human rights leader. In certain areas, the US may have a better track record compared to other nations. However, human rights concerns are confronted everyday by people in this country, including children. The purpose of this volume is to bring attention to the fact that against the backdrop of neoliberal expansion, serious human rights violations are taking place among children in the US. The daily struggles among groups of school children in the US are specifically considered, such as children sorted by race, homeless children, transient children, child refugees, children as targeted by traffickers, and/or child migrant workers. As the economy continues to constrict, more and more young people find themselves struggling to grow up on these razor thin margins of survival. Given current economic arrangements, such margins are widening. The definition of "children's human rights" as understood in this analysis is taken directly from the UN Convention on the Rights of the Child [CRC]. "Childhood" is inferred in this document as anyone under the age of 18. The premise behind this convention is there are significant vulnerabilities related to childhood that require a special set of protections. Such vulnerabilities include a lack of emotional and psychological maturity and susceptibilities related to ongoing physical development. Importantly, instead of being viewed as the focus of concern for the state or private interest, the CRC portrays the child as the subject of rights (Ensalaco & Majka, 2005).

Here I place emphasis on ways in which the CRC *could* be used to serve more effectively the needs of the most vulnerable populations of school-age children in the US and elsewhere. Schools could be the very place where children come to understand they have rights. As vulnerable members of society, all children require the knowledge they are the subject of particular rights and assurances. Unfortunately, many children do not get this information. Instead the protections stated in the CRC and the realities of the lives of so many are often worlds apart (Ensalaco & Majka, 2005). Human rights abuses are a common feature of life for children not just in the southern hemisphere, but in rich northern democracies that claim to take the high ground regarding human rights (Harvey, 2003; Kloby, 2004). To this end, the struggles experienced by schools and children in the US must be understood as shaped by local dynamics (including forms of resistance), and as contextualized within much larger geo-political arrangements. It makes sense therefore that the CRC and other international human rights frameworks be examined and used to reshape the structure, organization, and culture of public

J. Hall (ed.), Children's Human Rights and Public Schooling in the United States, 1–16.

schools in the US and abroad. Public schools also must be places where these documents are studied and discussed at length.

Unfortunately, the US has a peculiar relationship with the CRC. In 1989, the General Assembly of the UN adopted the CRC. The moment the convention was opened for signature in 1990, it was swiftly signed by 61 member nations. More countries have ratified the CRC than any other human rights treaty in history – 192 at this writing. In fact, the CRC is the most widely and rapidly ratified human rights treaty in existence. However, only two countries, Somalia and the US, have yet to ratify this agreement. Somalia is currently unable to proceed to ratification as it has no recognized government (Ensalaco & Majka, 2005).[1] With the refusal of the US to ratify the CRC, at present the convention lacks international credibility. This reality has weakened the efforts of those who advocate for children's human rights as a political concept, both worldwide and in the US (Human Rights Watch, 2012). In order to position the CRC as a powerful tool in the fight for the human rights of children, in this chapter I pay attention to the structure and history of the convention, as well as its strengths and weaknesses. The problematic relationship the US has with the CRC is also explored. I begin with an investigation of some of the major structural flaws built into the UN in general (Ensalaco & Majka, 2005; Kloby, 2004). My belief is something strong can be built from these points of weakness – something that truly protects children.

In an economy increasingly shaped by neoliberal reform, the conditions for children everywhere are deteriorating. Market logics supported by transnational bodies, networks, constituents, and policies – such as the UN, the World Bank/IMF, the WTO, and the World Economic Forum and the World Water Forum – bear out such outcomes (Goldman 2005, 2006; Goodman, 2011; Kloby, 2004). This economy helps shape policies and interaction in all spaces, including public schools in the US. When it comes to schools children are often silenced further by the gutting of school budgets, unequal funding, racial sorting/segregation/violence, sexual harassment, military recruiting, targeted cuts to ESL and special education programs, and overall privatization. Given their vulnerabilities, for children to have any chance to succeed there must be a significant shift in thinking among the public. The CRC must be debated in the US, including a discussion of it problems and promise/potential. The US must ratify an improved version of the CRC, live up to it, and other nations must too. As a crucial step, the US public needs to get behind this objective. Public schools could be the forum where these conversations begin. Regrettably, many are unfamiliar with this convention and/or are unaware of its existence. Arguably little is also known in the US about some troubling structural realities which govern the UN in general.

---

[1] The US did ratify two optional protocols to the CRC in 2002. These select protocols are related to 1.) the prohibition of child soldiers and 2.) the prohibition of the trafficking of children, child prostitution, and child pornography (Human Rights Watch, 2012).

BRIEF BACKGROUND ON THE UNITED NATIONS

The name "United Nations," coined by US President Franklin D. Roosevelt, was first used in the "Declaration by United Nations" of January 1, 1942, during WWII, when representatives of 26 nations pledged their governments to continue fighting together against the Axis Powers. An early version of the UN was the "League of Nations," an organization conceived in similar circumstances during WWI, and established in 1919 under the Treaty of Versailles "to promote international cooperation and to achieve peace and security." The League of Nations disbanded as a body after failing to prevent WWI. The gradual acknowledgement of the scope of Nazi human rights atrocities resulted in public momentum for a creation of a world-wide human rights protective body – the UN. In 1945, representatives of 50 countries met in San Francisco at a conference to draw up what would be known as the UN Charter, or mission statement. The UN officially came into existence on October 24, 1945, when the Charter had been ratified by China, France, the Soviet Union, the United Kingdom, the US and a majority of other signatories. The Charter was adopted by the General Assembly of that body on December 10, 1948 in Paris. The headquarters of the UN is located in the environs of New York City (Donnelly, 2003; Ensalaco & Majka, 2005; Kloby, 2004; Mahoney, 2007).

In terms of structure, the UN General Assembly is made up of representatives of each member nation, presided over by an elected Secretary General. These representatives of member nations also comprise the various committees, sub-committees, councils, and commissions. These smaller groups report their activities at general assembly sessions (Kloby, 2004; Mahoney, 2007). The formal and informal norms of these structural arrangements emerged out of a particular history. The US emerged as an economic powerhouse in the mid-1940s as the economies and infrastructure of many other industrialized nations were devastated by the war. At the time, the US wielded more power than it ever had before among the international community, and thus was able to exert tremendous influence over the formation of the UN, including its structure. Both at its inception and today, nations with the largest economies and militaries result in the loudest voices at the UN (Kloby, 2004).

The Security Council is arguably the most powerful UN committee, with the stated responsibility for "international peace and security." Its power and activity has increased over time, and now extends to military operations, imposing sanctions, deploying election monitors, and mandating arms inspections. The Security Council is comprised of 16 member nations, with five of those nations holding the position of permanent member [P5]. The P5 members include the US, the UK, France, Russia, and China. The remaining members serve two year terms and are voted into their position by the larger General Assembly. As it is well known among critics, one of the key problems with the way this body functions is "the veto." While all 16 members vote upon a potential resolution, any one of the P5 members has the authority to veto it, thus blocking any action (Goldman, 2005; Kloby, 2004; Mahoney, 2007; Power, 2007).

During the Cold War, the Security Council as a whole was viewed more favorably among many in the west. There was a special appreciation for its work in protecting populations from human rights abuses under Soviet-style communism. Between 1946 and 1989, the P5 cast 199 vetoes. As Security Council votes are public record, after the Cold War, many critics were assessing voting patterns and determining they had less to do with protecting human rights and more to do with ensuring corporate growth as related to particular national interests. At this juncture, in order to cut down on a traceable voting record, the P5 cleverly imposed the "hidden" veto. The formal use of the veto has diminished dramatically over the last few decades. With this strategy, decisions are now most often agreed upon in advance in closed door informal consultations, rather than in open meetings and votes. This allows more freedom for the P5 to pressure other members of the Security Council. The P5 can convince other council members to shift their position so actions do not have to go to vote, or if they do go to vote, the record shows consensus or avoidance of the veto in the form of abstention. This gives the impression to the international public that the council functions with some equilibrium in power without any record of what has been said during closed door negotiations. The P5 members continue to use the hidden veto to further various economic goals (Kloby, 2004; Power, 2007).

Based on how it is structured, the US exerts extreme influence over the UN. The position of the US as one of P5 of the Security Council gives it the power to block any resolution made by the larger body through the veto or hidden veto. Many assert historically the US has used the UN when it suited its interests and ignored it when it disagreed (e.g. Kloby, 2004). For example, over the past few decades, in terms of its more public wars, the US has disregarded UN denunciation of its invasion of Grenada, Nicaragua, and more recently with the latest invasion of Iraq. The US also continues to go against General Assembly sentiment regarding its embargo of Cuba. Along with other countries, the US owes the UN a few billion dollars in back dues and peacekeeping contributions. Because of this, the UN has had to cut funding to health, education, and democracy initiatives. In being under-resourced, the UN has had to escalate its dependence on the military strength of the US in peacekeeping missions. This results in peacekeeping efforts being dependent on the wishes of US interests (Harvey, 2005; Kloby, 2004; Power, 2007).

Still, the UN has managed to do some good work through the years. The end of apartheid in South Africa in part came about due to highly vocal UN censure. UN public pressure was also central in ending the domination of Namibia by South Africa. The UN moreover sent badly needed food aid to Haiti after the recent earthquake. These are just a few examples. Nonetheless, as a body, the unequal power built into the UN has resulted in a corpus of action that appears to protect markets over human rights. For instance, over the past few decades the Security Council P5 decided not to intervene during the impending genocide in Cambodia, Rwanda, Bosnia, and Sri Lanka. In all of these cases (with the exception of Cambodia), US military satellite feeds were most likely recording and displaying the mass slaughter in real time, so the excuse of not being able fully to understand or know about these realities is implausible. In the case of Cambodia, while the satellite technology was not in existence at the time, there was an abundance of field and infrared camera evidence. The UN instead turned its back on these countries as they each had some things in common: very few natural resources (either to begin with or left after colonial rule), and not mainly populated by Christian Europeans (Harvey, 2005; Kloby, 2004; Power, 2007). Added to this is the fact that certain P5 members may have deeply-rooted interests in locations under scrutiny (e.g. China in the Sudan and Russia in Syria). In these cases, the P5 and other council members broker back door deals with each other involving national interest tradeoffs in exchange for voting in particular pre-arranged ways or choosing not to go to vote at all.

Political dealings seemingly abound among Security Council activity. Under the pretext of stopping genocide, the Security Council P5 voted to intervene in Afghanistan and the oil rich country of Libya (with NATO). These countries are geographically valuable to western interests and/or supply oil to the west. While China and Russia abstained from voting to intervene in Libya, they did not veto the resolution. Non-P5 members of the council, Brazil, India, and Germany, also abstained. It was perhaps politic for Brazil, India, and Germany to abstain as they are known to be seeking permanent seats on the Security Council. Given the motives of the P5 and other powerful UN members, the lack of action regarding real intervention in genocide and other human rights abuses presently taking place in Syria, Sudan, Burundi, the DRC, the Congo, and so forth, is of little surprise. Reforming the UN as a democratic body will require much. As it stands, the P5 have the power to veto the election of any new Secretary General voted in by the General Assembly, so forging change through new leadership is impossible. Also, attempting to make changes to the UN charter would be futile, as any proposed changes can be vetoed by any of the P5 members (Harvey, 2005; Kloby, 2004; Power, 2007).

OTHER TRANSNATIONAL POLICY NETWORKS

The dispossession of so many worldwide is taking place amidst the contraction of neoliberal economics. In this arrangement, profit-making strategies are supported by transnational bodies, networks, and policies – such as the UN, military collectives such as NATO, and institutions such as the World Bank, International Monetary Fund [IMF], and the WTO. Similar to the UN, the World Bank and the IMF were formed at the end of WWII by the biggest winners of the war. The initial purpose of creating a World Bank was to loan money to countries to repair infrastructure that had been damaged during the war and to develop member countries towards capitalism. The role of the IMF was to stabilize exchange rates and to ease the process of currency conversion in this pursuit. At the time the Soviet Union posed a threat to western capitalism. To this end, encouraging "development" based on and connected to the US model of aggressive capitalism was seen as essential to building western wealth. The World Bank then and today is controlled by the world's most powerful countries, with capital raised by private investors purchasing bank bonds (Goldman, 2005; Harvey, 2005; Kloby, 2004). The headquarters of the World Bank and IMF are in Washington, DC.

From its inception, the World Bank focused on the needs of western countries. Guided by the unfolding logics of neoliberalism, lending money to "third world" countries however was soon found to be profitable, as often these countries could not pay the money back. The World Bank and IMF attach stringent conditions to their loans, or "structural adjustments," which gives them great power over borrower governments. It is also immensely profitable for World Bank investors. When nations default on loan payments, the World Bank and IMF use this leverage to pressure they adopt strict and aggressive economic policies. These countries are then in a situation in which they must privatize resources and public services and pay millions of dollars in interest without making a dent in the principal. The economic policies promoted by the World Bank and IMF today typically revolve around reducing trade barriers, cutting government, and privatizing services (Goldman, 2005; Harvey, 2005; Kloby, 2004).

The development projects the World Bank insists upon in countries that have defaulted on their loans often revolve around specific plans for easing the process of exploitation by transnationals and transporting resources out to the global market place. Such projects often constitute hiring private contractors to build roads, bridges, ports, and transportation systems, instead of spending funds on public initiatives such as building schools and providing medical care. It is also common for the IMF to devalue the local currency so exchange rates favor outside investors. Because many nations scramble just to make payments on principle, countries are spending more than twice their education and health budgets on debt service (Goldman, 2005; Harvey, 2005; Kloby, 2004). For example, Kloby asserts Lebanon spends 52 per cent of its government budget on debt service compared to 23 per cent on health and education combined. The World Bank and IMF, now major creditors to Central American, African, and some South American governments, have gained huge control over the running of the economies and natural resources of nations in those parts of the world (2004).

Over the past three decades, the poorest and most desperate nations in the world have turned increasingly to the World Bank and IMF for loans as they have no place else to go. The 1980s was a decade in which the World Bank did its largest amount of lending to "third world" nations. An outcome of this is poverty rates in these regions doubled during that time period. The World Bank provides loans to over 100 countries, and currently manages a loan portfolio of more than US$200 billion and growing. In 2003, African countries alone paid over $25 billion in debt to creditors even as some 2.3 million lost their lives to HIV/AIDS that same year. With all that money going towards debt, these nations could not invest in ways to address this impending health crisis (e.g. providing education, medical attention). This is directly a reason why the rates of HIV/AIDS infected people in African countries has sky-rocketed (Kloby, 2004). The World Bank and IMF are part of the Economic and Social Council at the UN. The UN however has little say over World Bank and IMF activity. The World Bank for instance lent money in the past to South Africa, despite the UN General Assembly resolution to cease financial support in opposition to the policy of apartheid it had at the time. The World Bank is also accused of brokering loans with repressive regimes (e.g. its dealings with the Ceausescu government in Romania) (Goldman, 2005; Kloby, 2004).

A more recent transnational body that works to expand markets is the World Trade Organization [WTO]. The WTO was formed in 1995, and presently has 145 member nations. Its power is vast as it is the first organization that can insist governments/countries comply with the trade rules (or new, more aggressive rules of capitalism) they create. There have been many angry protests of WTO actions. Major criticisms are members are not elected to the body, yet these individuals enforce rules by which countries must abide. The WTO also does not publicize what they are doing, and rules are made behind closed doors. Those rules mostly protect trade/free markets, at the expense of environmental, human rights, and worker safety concerns. The organization additionally has the authority to initiate sanctions against governments. There are moreover no policies or procedures by which people can make appeals to the body's dispute process. The WTO is so dominant it pressures governments to shape domestic and foreign policy to meet its agenda (Kloby, 2004). Given the rogue power of the WTO, the question becomes "isn't there an international body with the power to stop this arguably undemocratic, destructive power?" There is one international body whose expressed purpose is to protect such exploitation from happening – the UN (Harvey, 2005; Kloby, 2004). Given the structural realities of this body, a popular response by the UN is to create a convention.

CRC BACKGROUND & STRUCTURE

Human rights oriented treaties and conventions have a longstanding international presence. As Ensalaco and Majka (2005) explain, the Universal Declaration of Human Rights [UDHR] was the first international statement put forth on human rights in 1948. It makes, however, only minor mention of family and children. Subsequent frameworks reflected this absence. Both back then and in the years to come, many argued the special needs of the child required immediate and serious address. For decades, UNICEF, certain NGOs, and some children's human rights groups were drawing attention to the rising numbers of children in the southern hemisphere who were dying of malnutrition and disease, from the lack of clean water and adequate sanitation, and from the effects of poverty and displacement from war. Although the seeds of these dehumanizing conditions are firmly rooted in the colonial past, such arrangements continue to be sustained by contemporary neoliberal policies and interactions which favor the "opening up" of markets. World Bank/IMF debt in the southern hemisphere throughout the 1980s played a major role in deepening the deplorable conditions of many children's lives in those regions. During that decade, as mentioned the numbers of children in sub-Saharan African countries who were infected with HIV/AIDS began to gain worldwide press. The staggering percentages of children who received little to no formal education, were coerced to fight as soldiers, and were exposed to other forms of abuse and exploitation were likewise starting to get some western mainstream media attention (Ensalaco & Majka, 2005; Kloby, 2004). Such sentiments were ironically coalescing during the same time period in which neoliberalism was expanding as an economic doctrine.

The UN was in a situation in which they were compelled to do something. The action was typical – to draw up a convention – hence the development of the CRC. During its creation, there were those who thought there was no need for a convention on the human rights of children because the topic was somehow "covered" in the UDHR. Still, momentum in favour of a separate convention was growing. The result, according to the UN, is a document designed to protect the development of child, while taking into account the diversity of cultural values and traditions. The standards and articles in the convention were negotiated by governments, NGOs, human rights advocates, lawyers, health specialists, social workers, educators, child development experts, and religious leaders from all over the world over a 10-year period. The UN purports the convention reflects the principal legal systems of the world and acknowledges the specific needs of developing countries (Ensalaco & Majka, 2005).

The CRC is an international treaty that recognizes the human rights of children. In this document it is argued children must be provided with conditions for participation in family, cultural, and social life in keeping with their ongoing development. It is thought that as subjects, children are entitled to special care and safeguards by reason of his/her views. Structurally, the CRC contains 54 articles covering a range of topic areas. In article 1, children are defined as persons up to the age of 18 years. Article 2, thought of as the non-discrimination clause, designates all subsequent articles apply to children everywhere, regardless of gender, culture, social class, family structure, ability, or language (Ensalaco & Majka, 2005). Subsequent articles consider a range of autonomy, development, and protection standards. These standards include "the rights and responsibilities of parents; the best interests of the child; non-discrimination; the child's right to life, survival, and development; protection from harmful influences, abuse, and exploitation; respect for the views of the child; and the full participation of the child in family, cultural, and social life" (Ensalaco & Majka, 2005, p. 12).

The CRC recognizes a comprehensive list of rights and state obligations. These state obligations require all children have access to services such as primary education and health care; have room to develop their personalities, abilities, and talents to the fullest potential; have the chance to grow up in caring environments; and are informed about and participate in achieving their rights (Ensalaco & Majka, 2005; United Nations, 2012). As Ensalaco and Majka explain, articles 2 through 4 define what is meant by these "state obligations:"

> States incur the fundamental obligation to "respect and ensure" the rights set forth in the CRC, "without discrimination of any kind," taking into account "the best interests of the child" and the "rights and duties of his or her parents" or of others who have legal responsibility for the child. States also incur two sets of actionable obligations … First, states are obligated to "undertake all appropriate legislative, administrative, and other measures for the implementation of the rights recognized in the present Convention."

> Second, "with regard to economic, social, and cultural rights" states are obligated "to undertake such measures to the maximum extent of their available resources, and where needed, within the framework of international cooperation." (2005, pp. 14-15)

Thus, while the CRC places the primary obligation for the progressive realization of children's rights on the states themselves, its underlying premise is the survival, protection, and development of the child as part of the reach of the international community. In article 3, the CRC understands these obligations as also the responsibility of "competent authorities" in each state specifically when it comes to issues of child safety and health (Ensalaco & Majka, 2005; United Nations, 2012).

As articulated in the CRC, states must provide standards for children to receive the basic requirements needed for survival – including access to potable water, nutrition, health care, labor protections, and primary education. States should also ensure children have knowledge of their rights, and that these rights be fulfilled based on the maturing capacities of each child. Only two articles in the CRC, 28 and 29, are directly related to education. In these articles, it is declared all children should receive a free primary education. While there are no specific provisions for schooling beyond the elementary level, overall the articles in the convention address the special needs and requirements concerning children up through the age of 18 who come from economically challenged backgrounds, culturally marginalized groups, and refugee groups. Also, children with disabilities and those who come in punitive contact with the justice system are provided with safeguards. As outlined in the convention, all children have the right to protection from physical and mental violence and mistreatment (Ensalaco & Majka, 2005). It is also explained that schools be free of violence, and that school discipline be based on the dignity of the child (United Nations, 2012). It becomes immediately obvious there is incongruence between these specific state responsibilities outlined in the CRC and the realities of life of so many children everywhere, including in the US and within its public schools.

STRENGTHS AND WEAKNESSES OF THE CRC

An obvious strength of the CRC is that it exists. The CRC is a single code of ethics to which ratifying countries have consented. It is a unifying moral compass meant to guide policy and actions of agreeing countries in terms of respecting and preserving the human rights of children. There are however many notable weaknesses to this convention. The CRC is a declaration, rather than as a treaty, and as such, it has a non-binding nature. Given the existence of the CRC and the number of the countries that ratified it, there should as a result be very few human rights abuses experienced among children anywhere in the world. Unfortunately, nations that have ratified the document do not have to abide by it as there are no real sanctions or penalties for not living up to the agreed upon articles. Ratifying nations, rather, are simply supposed to agree to uphold the promises made in such agreements (Power, 2007). The UN contends the CRC reflects the principal legal systems of the world and the specific needs of developing countries. When scrutinized, the document though seems to represent a western, capitalistic, Judeo-Christian perspective. For example, it promotes a protection of individual rights and excludes collective rights. The convention also for instance can be seen to violate Confucian virtues of obedience, order, and respect for authority, and the notion that at times one must limit the rights of the few to the benefit of many (Ensalaco & Majka, 2005).

Another weakness of the CRC is many in the US at least have not heard of it, despite its international role. In fact, many children do not know they are the subject of specific rights to which they are entitled. There are reasons why the UN, the UDHR, and the CRC are not studied in US public schools and openly discussed in mainstream media. Citizens would likely be upset their country has not signed it and is routinely violating this document at home (e.g. hunger, homelessness, poverty) and abroad (e.g. postcolonial practices such as western companies exploiting child workers). They might learn their country is perhaps not a human rights leader. In other western countries in which there may be more attention put on the UDHR and the CRC in public discourse, there seems to be little understanding among citizens of those nations that their countries are also regularly in violation of this document. The UN makes many promises on its website and in all its documents, including the UDHR and CRC, yet so many human rights abuses take place every day around the world (Ensalaco & Majka, 2005; Power, 2007).

THE CRC & THE US

Why has the US not yet ratified the CRC? The answer from the UN website (2012) reads as follows: "… As in many other nations, the United States undertakes an extensive examination and scrutiny of treaties before proceeding to ratify. This examination, which includes an evaluation of the degree of compliance with existing law and practice in the country at state and federal levels, can take several years-or even longer if the treaty is portrayed as being controversial or if the process is politicized …." The US has had more than 20 years to scrutinize. Given this, it is perhaps accurate also to consider the US has not yet ratified the CRC for it runs ideologically against the ideology of a free-market economy. For instance, it is easy to imagine fear of international influence upon state sovereignty and the concern the state (instead of the markets) will have an invasive presence inside homes and families. Some are likely apprehensive the CRC would draw attention to human rights abuses in the US (Ensalaco & Majka, 2005; Power, 2007).

After reading the articles detailed in the CRC, it is easy to conclude the US is in direct violation of the human rights of children. Consider the US juvenile justice system as just one example. This structure is characterized by high numbers of juvenile "offenders" comprised of disproportionately high percentages of low income African American children. Due to underfunding of the courts and the related privatization of prisons, many of these youth do not have adequate legal counsel. In the 1990s, due to new transfer legislation, it became easier for juveniles to be transferred to adult courts. This means following a juvenile sentence, such children can now carry out an adult sentence. In these situations children have been known to experience overcrowding, denials of food and healthcare, as well as physical and sexual abuse. Children from culturally marginalized groups are also more likely to have longer sentences compared to others. In addition, it has been found that children as young as 13 have been given life-without-parole sentences. Children in the US can also be sentenced to death. Over the last decade, only the US, the Congo, and Iran were known to have administered the death penalty to juveniles. Article 37 of the CRC directly prohibits this (Sarri & Shook, 2004). Scrutiny of the US industrial prison complex is surely something private prison contractors who are reaping huge profits do not want to happen.

An underlying premise of the CRC is that the survival, protection, and development of the child is an obligation of the international community. As implied in the CRC, international cooperation means international aid. Numerous constituents in the US would clearly not want to have to give foreign assistance, especially as a matter of contract. To such groups it would be interpreted as giving the international community a role in shaping US policy. Others may fear ratifying may result in the country being pressured from both inside and outside its borders to act in compliance with the convention. One alarm is this could open also up the possibility of the US being held accountable for violating this agreement on an international stage.[2] While Canada, the UK, Australia, Italy, France, and so forth are countries that have proudly signed and ratified the CRC, they regularly violate the articles in the convention (e.g. children living in poverty, child migrant workers, children exposed to violence, children being trafficked). It is hard to say which is better – refusing to ratify the CRC or eagerly signing it but violating it (Ensalaco & Majka, 2005; Power, 2007). Regardless, both vantage points suggest this UN convention at the moment reflects little more than public relations posturing. Weaknesses aside, as a UN document, the CRC has at least a degree of international recognition.

CONNECTIONS TO SCHOOL CHILDREN

Clarifying ways in which US schools are in direct violation of the internationally known CRC may help draw more attention, and more interdisciplinary attention, to already existing work on education inequality. Using the CRC to conceptualize the direct violations of children's human rights as understood, on various levels, by those in many parts of the world, may help illuminate the fact that school reform driven by free market principles is hurting children and compromising their rights, including those of safety and health. Despite the use of critical pedagogy and other

---

[2] Realistically the US has already ensured it has little to fear regarding this point. The US has done much to undermine the credibility of the World Court through its indifference to rulings. This plus underfunding has resulted in its disarray and haplessness. In an effort to establish the newer International Criminal Court as a forum to try individuals accused of war crimes, the US stalled its creation until 2002, after it was granted permanent immunity from the court (Kloby, 2004).

forms of resistance among many US educators, the marginalization of students and the diminishment of public spaces have increased over the past few decades. Underfunding, inequitable resource allocation, racial segregation, privatized reforms; such as standardized and corporate curriculums/tests, charter schools, additional testing, sanctions for poorly performing cutting schools; and overall sorting in schools along in lines of social class, race, gender, and perceived disability are some of the ongoing assaults that continue to have a devastating impact on individual lives, communities, and the very notion of democracy (e.g. Kozol, 2009; MacLeod, 2009; Saltman, 2007, 2010). Given the invasive nature of neoliberal forces, it is no surprise there is a deficiency in learning going on in schools about the concepts of rights and the CRC.

While there is a developed body of scholarship related to inequity in US public schools, little of this work connects these issues to broader human rights-oriented frameworks. Existing work on human rights and P-12 public schools in the US is focused on curriculum analyses and/or curriculums and curriculum integration, such as conflict resolution and "peace studies" curriculum (e.g. Bender-Slack & Raupach, 2008; Hornberg, 2002; North, 2008; Reardon, 2002; Smith Crocco, 2007). Yet, in the US, public schooling is the one institution in the lives of children where everyone is supposed to get an equal chance to succeed. Succeeding equally requires inequities be disrupted, the learning needs of all students be addressed, and young people become equipped with ways to think critically so they can effectively engage in the concept of democracy. Children need a sustained space in which directly to learn about rights, that they have rights, and what those rights are. Taking this a step further, children should also have a say in what those rights ought to be. As the subsequent chapters demonstrate, the reality of public schooling for children in the US and the main messages put forth in the CRC seem to exist on parallel planes.

VOLUME STRUCTURE

While there are vulnerabilities specific to childhood in general, the economic arrangements that characterize life in the 21st century have resulted in growing groups of children worldwide who are forced to live on the unsafe/unhealthy margins of survival. The realities and implications for these children in the US as they experience public schooling are explored in this volume. Ten chapters follow which investigate in detail what it is like to be a child in US schools during this mature stage of capitalism. The chapters were selected as they are directly reflective of the following specific protective promises made to children in the CRC – schoolchildren as vulnerable populations; and violence, punishment, and juvenile justice among schoolchildren. The chapters purposefully bear witness to the struggles experienced by various groups of children from all corners of the US, from different regions and from urban, rural, and suburban communities. It is clear children across the nation are becoming more vulnerable to silencing and violence both inside and outside schools. Many in fact experience multiple forms of violence, from compounding symbolic and physical sources.

Reflecting the global unfettered markets firmly supported by a network of transnational bodies, in spite of formidable resistance at all levels and also local situatedness, more children are finding themselves pushed into treacherous spaces by school policies and provisions and/or lack of them. Important things are missing from schools and inside them many children have little chance to succeed. In light of the latest recession/crisis in capitalism, Valerie Polawko and Huayun Xu, for instance, explore the realities of homeless children and the growing inability of schools to reach out to this population. International migration and displacement continues as a result of past colonial policies and ongoing economic manipulations. Legislation shaped by neoliberal ideology has resulted in a massive reduction in overall state and federal funding leaving resettlement policies and education in tatters. Given the new groups that are seeking refuge in the US, Craig Centrie investigates the silencing experienced by Burmese refugee students in public high schools in a large Northeastern city. Likewise, due to funding cuts and cultural "misunderstandings," Jessica Lister and Allison Anders investigate how Burundi refugee ESL elementary students in rural Southern Appalachia are put on a swift track to special education. This has serious implications for the future outcomes of the Burundi students as well as students with special needs. Regina Rahimi and Delores Liston also look at how funding cuts result in students being less protected in schools. While the vague issue of "bullying" is now widely discussed in the education research, they explore how public schools remain places where high concentrations of sexual harassment and gender harassment among students takes place unaddressed on a regular basis.

Robust economic strategies which encourage the "opening up" of new markets for exploitation have fueled the illicit growth in human trafficking everywhere, including throughout the US. Virginia Batchelor and Illana Lane draw attention to the reality that school age children in the US are increasingly being targeted by traffickers. They consider how given the state of the economy, which put growing pressures on families, human traffickers are entrapping socially, economically, and/or psychologically vulnerable children in suburban shopping malls and on the street. Educators must be aware of this growing problem, and students must learn about this crime and how to avoid being targeted. In another example of schools and students being "opened-up" as markets, under the guise of providing free and unbiased "career counseling," Brian Lagotte details how military recruiters enter high schools using sophisticated profile techniques. As we learn, such individuals recruit aggressively but differently depending on the social class and cultural composition of the particular student population. The end result is further degrees of limitation and marginalization of so many.

While neoliberal policies are enacted in schools, students from culturally marginalized groups are being sidelined further in increasingly compounding and punishing ways. Keith Sturges uncovers how state sponsored curriculum evaluators perpetuate images of failing and uninterested Mexican American students in US schools on the Southern border. No attempts by educators in this research were found to understand the cultural ecology and exchanges of power that undergirded decision-making at the local and state levels. Carl James explains how the idea of the US "athletic scholarship" at the expense of academics has become a powerful aspiration for young working class Black male students in Canada. This research pushes the literature on black make students in sports because it considers the global power of neoliberal ideology as it asserts across national borders. For these youth, athletics is "a ticket" out of their community, and a ride to the US. Many of these Black male student athletes subscribe to meritocracy, individualism, and athletic prowess – thinking the system of racism might not be an obstacle to their education and career goals. The belief among these young men is that racism is less pointed in the US, particularly when it comes to sports. Here the role of educators, coaches, and media in shaping this thinking and sidelining of academics is critiqued.

As is emblematic free market education reform, public schools and teachers continue to lack the badly needed resources required to begin to address the growing problems experienced by students. However, instead of unwittingly contributing to a deficit model of culturally and economically dominated students in such analyses, Encarnacion Garza focuses on positive academic stories of children of Hispanic migrant workers. In so doing, he details the life journeys of successful students, despite the odds stacked up against this group in schools. The volume then ends with a call to follow the money. Sue Books contends the unequal and underfunding of public schooling in the US is in itself a violation of the basic rights of children. The practice of funding public schools largely through property taxes ensures families from different backgrounds receive something vastly different. Books provide an overview of school funding disparities today and weighs the strengths and weaknesses of the courts as instruments of reform. She lastly ends with much needed suggestions for change, which involve embracing a human rights oriented ideology when it comes to schooling.

CONCLUSION

The vulnerabilities of children in US public schools are linked to global dynamics. Taking into account meaning-making at the local level, including important forms of resistance, unsafe and unhealthy conditions in schools and in the lives of children also take shape as nested within a tessellation of transnational bodies/organizations and their responsive policy networks. At the same time, there is little critical discussion in US schools about rights. Although not often referred to in typical discourse on education and social justice, the CRC *could* be used as a powerful lens to bring into sharp focus the reality that so many young people around the world are being denied their human rights and access to learning about them (Ensalaco & Majka, 2005; Kozol, 2005). In spite of its flaws and in many ways because of them, this convention *could* be used to serve more effectively the needs of vulnerable populations of school age children in the US and beyond. Such populations include, for example, children from culturally marginalized groups, transient children, homeless children, refugee children, trafficked children, and/or children with disabilities. As the chapters to follow in this volume indicate, at this advanced stage in the development of capitalism, young people are increasingly being pulled beyond acceptable measures of safety and care.

It is hard to argue against the importance of upholding children's human rights in US public schools. Due to the Internet, social media, and easy access to digital archives, select human rights stories at times are known to become instantly viral (e.g. "fair trade," "blood" diamonds/"conflict-free" diamonds, "Kony 2012"). There appears to be a growing interest among the public in the concept of international justice, human rights, and UN activity in general. It is vital to seize this important moment and collective interest and build upon it (Hall, 2012). As US politicians (and corporate influenced history texts) claim this country is a human rights leader, it is our duty to hold the writers of the past and the makers of the present and future accountable to this ideal. When it comes to human rights and protecting people, it is important to remember many of the legal frameworks are there, such as Plessey, Brown, the UDHR, the CRC, and the Genocide Convention. As flawed as many of these pieces of paper are, we would do well to take them seriously, draw attention to them, improve upon them, and bring them to life. Schools could play a big part in this and in educating all children on their rights. Children moreover should be permitted to narrate their own needs and they should be listened to. This would first involve a genuine commitment to the value and dignity of childhood and children everywhere.

Indeed truly to ensure the human rights of children, neoliberalism as an economic doctrine itself must be interrogated. In order to solve problems in education more fully, schools must be understood as shaped by transnational organizations and policies. The structural inequities built into the UN must be called into question, along with the transnational bodies and networks which support free market policies. When it comes to children, the US must ratify an improved version of the CRC and live up to it. Other nations must too. As a first step, the US public needs to get behind these objectives. To push back successfully against the powerful forces behind neoliberal reform, educators alone cannot be asked to solve the problem. Backed by the public, a coalition of schools, government agencies, NGOs, non-profits, human rights advocates, lawyers, health specialists, social workers, child development experts, and religious leaders at home and abroad must be assembled. As the standards in the CRC were negotiated by members across these disciplines, there is already a vast and organized network of individuals who want change that could be tapped into by educators (Ensalaco & Majka, 2005). The chapters to follow exemplify the extremely vulnerable conditions of the lives of so many US school children. At stake are the basic rights of the young in the US and around the world who are straining to grow and learn.

REFERENCES

Bender-Slack, D., & Raupach, M. (2008). Negotiating standards and social justice in the social studies: Educators' perspectives. *The Social Studies, November/December*, 255-259.

Donnelly, J. (2003). Universal human rights in theory and practice, 2nd edition. New York: Cornell University Press.

Ensalaco, M., & Majka, L. (Eds.). (2005). *Children's human rights: Progress and challenges for children worldwide*. New York: Rowman & Littlefield.

Goldman, M. (2005). *Imperial nature: The World Bank and the struggles for social justice in the age of globalization*. London: Yale University Press.

Goldman, M. (2006). How "water for all!" policy became hegemonic: The power of the World Bank and its transnational policy networks. *Geoforum, 38*, 786-800.

Goodman, R. (2011). *Feminist theory in pursuit of the public: Women and the 're-privatization' of labor*. New York: Palgrave Macmillan.

Hall, J. (2012). Water is a right: A critique of curricular materials and learning experiences in schools sponsored by the transnational water utility service industry. *The Journal of Critical Education*, 3 (2), 12-35.

Harvey, D. (2003). *The new imperialism*. New York: Oxford University Press.

Hornberg, S. (2002). Human rights education as an integral part of general education. *International Review of Education, 48*, 187-198.

Human Rights Watch. (2012). *US: Ratify children's treaty*. http://www.hrw.org/en/news/2009/11/18/us-ratify-children-s-treaty

Kloby, J. (2004). *Inequality, power, & development: Issues in political sociology 2nd edition*. New York: Humanity Books.

Kozol, J. (2005). *The shame of the nation: The restoration of apartheid schooling in America*. New York: Crown Publishers.

MacLeod, J. (2009). *Ain't no makin it: Aspirations and attainment in a low-income neighbourhood*, 3rd edition. New York: Westview Press

Mahoney, J. (2007). *The challenge of human rights: Origin, development, and significance*. New York: Blackwell Publishing.

North, C. (2008). What is all this talk about "social justice?" Mapping the terrain of education's latest catchphrase. *Teachers College Record, 110*(6), 1182-1206.

Power, S. (2007). *"A problem from hell:" America and the age of genocide*. New York: Harper Perennial.

Reardon, B. (2002). Human rights and the global campaign for peace education. *International Review of Education, 48*. 283-284.

Saltman, K. (Ed.). (2007). *Capitalizing on disaster: taking and breaking public schools*. New York: Paradigm Publishers.

Saltman, K. (2010). *The gift of education: Public education and venture philanthropy*. New York: Palgrave MacMillan.

Sarri, R., & Shook, J. (2005). Human rights and the juvenile justice system in the United States. In M. Ensalaco & L. Majka (Eds.), *Children's human rights: Progress and challenges for children worldwide*. New York: Rowman & Littlefield Publishers, Inc.

Smith Crocco, M. (2007). Speaking truth to power: Women's rights as human rights. *The Social Studies, November/December*, 257-269.

United Nations. (2012). *Convention on the rights of the child*. http://www.un.org/Docs/journal/asp/ws.asp?m=convention%20on%20the%20rights%20of%20the%20child

VALERIE POLAKOW & HUAYUN XU

CHAPTER 2

Homeless Children in the United States: Dispossession and Rights Foreclosed

> In this nation I see tens of millions of its citizens – a substantial part of its whole population – who at this very moment are denied the greater part of what the very lowest standards of today call the necessities of life …. I see one-third of a nation ill-housed, ill-clad, ill-nourished. It is not in despair that I paint you that picture. I paint it for you in hope – because the nation, seeing and understanding the injustice of it, proposes to paint it out. (Roosevelt, 1937, pp. 8-9)

It is ironic that Roosevelt's second Bill of Rights, proposing social and economic rights for United States citizens, never came to pass; yet it formed a cornerstone of the Universal Declaration of Human Rights and subsequent international human rights conventions for most of the wealthy, industrialized nations of the world. However, the United States, whose exceptionalism has made it an outlier among the community of democratic nations, has consistently failed to create a platform of social and economic rights. Over seven decades later, poverty, destitution, and homelessness are stark reminders of the price of extreme injustice that Roosevelt determined to "paint out," but never succeeded where "the price of inequality" (Stiglitz, 2012) has resulted in a severe crisis of child poverty and child homelessness. For children, the politics of poverty have far-reaching physical and psychosocial consequences. Homelessness is a traumatic life-event destabilizing families and relationships, leading to social exclusion, denied educational access, and disrupted development.

In the United States the rise in family homelessness has been tied to the epidemic of mortgage foreclosures resulting from predatory lending to vulnerable buyers who, without an adequate social safety net, have lost homes, livelihoods, and health care amid a deepening recession and high unemployment. However, homelessness in the United States is also deeply rooted in an eroded welfare state, where welfare assistance, Medicaid, social and educational spending have all been cut to trim deficits in state budgets amid a national right-wing clamor to erode the role of government. Neoliberalism and its attendant trilogy of deregulation, privatization, and the shrinking of public entitlements, always hits the most vulnerable hardest; and poor children in the United States endure "circuits of dispossession" (Fine, Stoudt, Fox, & Santos, 2010, p. 30) as loss of a home

J. Hall (ed.), Children's Human Rights and Public Schooling in the United States, 17–43.

frequently means loss of the familiar – school, friends, neighborhood, and those social spaces which hold symbolic meaning and identity.

In this chapter child homelessness is analyzed both as *an* existential and material dispossession and as a violation of human rights.

POVERTY AND RIGHTS

> A commitment to protecting children from poverty is therefore more than a slogan or a routine inclusion in a political manifesto; it is the hallmark of a civilized society. (UNICEF, 2012, p. 4)

From an international policy perspective, the understanding of poverty has changed dramatically in past decades, shifting from economic income models of absolute poverty – encapsulating subsistence and survival needs – to a far more complex understanding of both material and non-material poverty to encompass agency, participation, and voice (Lister, 2004). Sen (2001) has argued that poverty needs to be understood not as a "deprivation of means" but as a "deprivation of ends" so that while material impoverishment restricts freedom and reduces life chances, it is "capability deprivation" that allows us to understand the meaning of poverty in lived social contexts where material poverty leads to social exclusion, and becomes a poverty of agency and participation. Nussbaum (2011) links the Capabilities Approach to a social justice framework, and points out that understanding poverty and deprivation must focus not only on well-being, but also on the opportunities and freedoms available to people so that the fundamental question becomes "What is each person able to do and to be?" (p. 18). The answers to such questions involve the redress of wrongs that create exclusion and discrimination, and point to public policy and the role of government in assuming responsibility for restricted opportunities and the failure of capabilities.

Yet, in the United States, poverty is constructed primarily as an individual deficit, a lack of work ethic, an attitudinal problem, and worse, a pathological disorder of single-mother families. From Charles Murray's "rotten mother" diatribes against poor single mothers in the 90's (Fremstad, 2012) to Republican presidential candidate Romney's recent contemptuous construction of the 47%, "who are dependent upon government, who believe that they are victims, who believe the government has a responsibility to care for them, … [who do not] take personal responsibility and care for their lives" (Madison, 2012), government programs and the few entitlements that remain are viewed as undeserved handouts. Support to subsistence households is decried as promoting dependency and parasitic behavior, negating freedom and the inalienable right to capital. Here freedom is constructed as a supreme individual right to *have* and to *profit*, and the right to unfettered accumulation that leads to a society of "private affluence" and "public squalor" (Judt, 2010, p. 12).

Hence a rights-based approach to housing and homelessness, premised on the human right to a minimally sustainable level of existence reframes the right to shelter as a democratic and fundamental freedom; for as Roosevelt presciently stated in 1944 " necessitous men are not free men" (quoted in Sunstein, 2004, p. 90). The right to shelter is enshrined in multiple human rights conventions, grounded in the Universal Declaration of Human Rights (UDHR) of which Eleanor Roosevelt was a prominent architect. The UDHR lays out a clear platform of 'standard of living' rights stating, "Everyone has the right to a standard of living adequate for the health and well-being of himself and his family, including food, clothing, housing, and medical care and necessary social services …" (UDHR, 1948, Article 25.1). While Western and Northern Europe and many other wealthy, industrialized countries have committed to fundamental social and economic rights for their citizens, the United States is still an outlier – lacking rights that guarantee entitlements to housing, medical care, and social services. Similarly the International Covenant on Economic, Social and Cultural Rights (CESCR, 1966), and the Convention on the Elimination of all Forms of Discrimination Against Women (CEDAW, 1979) embody the right to shelter such that "State Parties … shall ensure … the right … to enjoy adequate living conditions, particularly in relation to housing, sanitation, electricity, and water supply, transport and communications" (CEDAW, Article 14.2). However, most pertinent to the right to shelter for children is the Convention on the Rights of the Child (CRC), where "State Parties … shall take appropriate measures to assist parents and others responsible for the child to implement this right and shall in the case of need provide material assistance and support programmes, particularly with regard to nutrition, clothing, and housing" (CRC, 1989, Article 27.3). The United States with its policy of exceptionalism, has notably not ratified these (and other) important human rights conventions and trails Western nations in ensuring that children's developmental needs are met in terms of shelter, health, and child care.

When we consider the appalling record of the United States in relation to poverty, we note that children on several indices of material poverty – well-being, health, food security, and housing – face critical challenges to their development. The Innocenti Research Centre's latest report, *Measuring Child Poverty* (UNICEF, 2012) compares 35 "economically advanced" nations, and the United States ranks next to last in the percentage of children living in poverty (23.1%), sandwiched between Latvia (18.8%) and Romania (25.5%).[1] Hunger among impoverished US children is another critical impediment to healthy development and Child Trends (2012a) reports that 22% of US children under 18 live in food-insecure households, with 1% living in households with very low food security. Poverty is also racialized with disproportionate numbers of African American, American Indian and Hispanic children living in poverty (Addy & Wight, 2012). Currently 31.9 million children live in low-income households, and of that number, 15.5 million live below the federal poverty line (and only the latter are officially categorized as

[1] The Innocenti Report defines poverty (relative poverty) as the "*percentage of children living in homes with equivalent incomes below 50% of national median*" (UNICEF, Report Card 10, p. 3).

poor); and 1.5 million children are estimated to be homeless with the majority living in single-mother families (Addy & Wight, 2012; Aritani, 2009). The United States has consigned millions of the nation's children to truncated and damaged lives, scarred by acute material deficits that are the consequences of public and corporate policies that have spawned extreme inequality which says Judt, "is corrosive. It rots societies from within" (Judt, 2010, p. 21). Wilkinson and Pickett (2012) argue similarly that vast gaps in inequality are the source of "social poison" causing an array of social and public health problems in the most unequal of wealthy countries, such as we see in the US and Britain, in contrast to Scandinavia where the inequality gap is far lower.

Yet, poverty is not only resource deprivation, it must also be understood in terms of its existential and non-material meanings. Jones and Sumner (2011) propose a more comprehensive understanding of child poverty using a multi-dimensional approach – the 3-D Well-Being model that encompasses material, relational and subjective poverty. They emphasize that this model goes beyond traditional economic measures of poverty and expands on recent rights-based and social exclusion approaches – because the emphasis of this model is on both the relational and the subjective dimensions of poverty, "implying that what people feel they can do or be influences what they will actually be able to do and to be" (p. 15). The 3-D approach focuses on positive possibilities not solely on deficits. By focusing on the relational dimensions (social interactions, collaboration with others to attain goals) and the subjective dimensions (the meanings that individuals assign to their own experiences and goals they achieve), this approach also enables us to be attentive to children's experiences and perceptions of homelessness, and emphasizes their agency and participation in decisions affecting their lives. This closely aligns with key Articles of the CRC emphasizing children's voices, agency, and participation "where state parties shall assure to the child who is capable of forming his or her own views the right to express those views freely in all matters affecting the child (Article 12,1) and "the right to freedom of expression" (Article 13,1).

However, in the United States, where there is an unprecedented crisis of child poverty and homelessness, not only are the voices of children and their parents unheard, but basic levels of material poverty are so low that life for a homeless child in the United States resembles the world of the street urchins of the 1800s. How far does a country allow its children to fall before redressing the appalling living conditions of the youngest and most vulnerable? Locating the current crisis of child and youth homelessness in historical context is important in order to understand contemporary public policies and practices. In the following section, critical moments in the history of homelessness, and specifically child homelessness, are explored; from pauperism and the street urchins of the 1800s to the development of social welfare policies and the evolving concept of rights, including the right of homeless children to housing and an education.

CRITICAL MOMENTS IN THE HISTORY OF HOMELESSNESS IN THE US

During the nineteenth century, poverty and inequality were viewed as essential byproducts of the transition to capitalism and democracy. Large waves of immigrants and increasing urbanization created vast swaths of impoverishment, most visible in the squalid and teeming tenements, where immigrants were seen as potential threats to community order. Immigrants who became homeless joined freed Blacks, street children, impoverished youth, 'fallen' women, and unemployed men, all of whom made up the swelling numbers of vagrants, hobos, and paupers. The discourse about the poor was rooted in the distinction between the 'deserving' and the 'undeserving poor.' Katz points out how pauperism was constructed as a moral category, and seen as the consequence of vice, as "willful error, of shameful indolence, of vicious habits" whereas poverty was viewed as "an unavoidable evil … a condition to which many were "brought from necessity … the result not of our faults, but of our misfortune" (1989, p. 13). Constructing the dispossessed and homeless as lazy, irresponsible, and immoral served to legitimate those public policies that maintained persistent inequalities in American society (Kusmer, 2002).

During the latter part of the nineteenth century in New York, immigrants and young hobos were housed in unhealthy small dwellings, furnished with windowless rooms and communal water taps and water closets. According to the 1890 police statistics, about 5,121,659 lodgings had been furnished to serve 14,000 homeless men in that year (Plunz, 1993). In 1849 the Chief of Police reported that a total of 2,955 vagrant children under 15 years old were found; constituting 10% of the entire child population of school age (Riis, 1892). Historical records also reported notorious slums on New York streets like Mulberry Bend in the Five Points neighborhood, where "abuse is the normal condition … murder its everyday crop, with the tenants not always the criminals" (Riis, 1890, p. 61). A sanitary census of 1891 showed that 160,708 children under five were living in the tenements (Riis, 1892). In 1882, a total of 155 deaths of children were counted in the Bend, a block between Bayard, Park, Mulberry, and Baxter Streets (Riis, 1890). The experiences of children who grew up in those tenements and slums were toxic. Few babies could survive after being abandoned on the streets and child abandonment was prevalent. Of the 508 babies received by the Infant Hospital on Randall's Island in New York, 170 were picked up from the streets and the mortality rate was extremely high. Orphaned and abandoned children were also a common sight on city streets. In New York, a total of 2,968 lost children were found on the streets in 1889. Street urchins never went to school, could neither read nor write, and were frequently sent out to beg and steal. Riis describes a drunken father who states that two of his sons picked up by the police, "didn't live nowhere" (1890, p. 200). According to the Federal census of 1880 and the New York State census of 1892, more than 50,000 children between the ages of five and fourteen did not attend school. The lack of access and the lack of provisions for poor children in the public education system exacerbated the growing population of street children (Riis, 1892).

Philanthropic efforts during the late nineteenth century focused on the deplorable conditions of the street children starkly memorialized a century later by Doctorow in the *WaterWorks* where the narrator portrays the children as castoff specks of humanity, describing them as "losses society could tolerate." He writes:

> And the children, the ubiquitous children, weaving through the crowds of Broadway under no authority but their own, flashing a mop of hair or a furtive glance back, and a moment later becoming invisible, as if not air was their medium but dark river water. (1994, p. 66)

Charity organizations like the Society for the Prevention of Cruelty to Children (SPCC) and the "Fresh Air Fund" invested considerable funds in providing health care and saving abandoned or abused young children from the streets. Founded in New York Five Points District by missionary, Charles Loring Brace, in 1853, the Children's Aid Society established 21 industrial schools, 12 evenings schools, reading rooms and 5 low-cost lodging-houses to educate children (Riis, 1892). The industrial schools provided a comprehensive curriculum to train workers for the industrial economy. Children were taught gender-specific skills: housekeeping for girls and carpentry and drawing for boys. The quick expansion of the scope of the Society's industrial schools encouraged many other philanthropic efforts in the Progressive-Era, for instance, church-funded settlements like boys' clubs, which taught boys trade skills. Such organizations were characterized by a dualism of motives: the apparent benevolent aims and the underlying control to produce compliant servants, laborers, and workers as Social Darwinism and the presumed efficiency of compulsory schooling was embraced (Ramsey, 2007).

Like the charity organization movement, the Settlement House movement also took shape at the turn of the century. Hull House located on the west side of Chicago was a landmark in the history of American child welfare development. Founded by two well-educated young women, Jane Addams and Ellen Gates Starr in September 18, 1889, Hull House became "home" to many impoverished women, homeless children, immigrants, and the elderly. It also functioned as a community educational center through the delivery of kindergarten and nursery services, literary programs, cultural activities, and health care. The ideals of social justice and progressive education motivated many social reformers to expand the movement's scope and by 1910, more than 400 settlement houses were established across the country (Winsten, 2011). Settlement houses attempted to ameliorate the "social ills" caused by poverty and impacted the work of leading social welfare reformers, such as Julia Lathrop, Frances Perkins, and Harry Hopkins (Thelen, 1972; Katz, 1996). Despite the grassroots progressivism of the movement, it was primarily focused on white immigrants, and largely excluded impoverished and homeless African Americans. In the Deep South, the plight of African American homeless families was largely ignored (Greenberg, 1991). Most of the communities did not furnish shelters for blacks and in the North, the municipal shelter services that did provide minimal services were segregated.

Homelessness in the Great Depression

The Great Depression created an unprecedented population of homeless people. In January 1933, a conservative estimate based on a three-day census reported that about 1.5 million people were homeless in America (Anderson, 1933). Wanderers traveled every corner of the nation. In California, over 20,000 interstate transients were documented, according to a transient census of September 30, 1934 (New General Subject Series, 1935). About 300,000 to 400,000 impoverished Oklahomans, Texans, Arkansans, and Missourians moved to California and settled there during the 1930s (Gregory, 2004). The migration of homeless and destitute "Okies" to California and their struggles in the Dust Bowl migration have been chronicled by historians (Stein, 1973) and also by novelists such as Steinbeck (1939) in his acclaimed *Grapes of Wrath*, as the Okies struggled to find jobs, land, and a viable future amid constant loss and often insurmountable obstacles during the Depression years. Homelessness among women and children was both underestimated and inaccurately recorded by historians during this period with estimates of approximately 30,000 homeless women (Bloom, 2005; Kusmer, 2002). Anderson (1933) reported that there was at least a tenfold increase in the number of female transients during the first years of the Depression. Between 1929 and 1933, among women who headed displaced families, 70% were separated, widowed, or divorced (National Committee on Care of Transient and Homeless, 1933).

Homeless Children

During the Depression era children suffered from malnutrition, abuse, lack of educational materials, frequent moves, and constant insecurity (Evans, 2010). In the impoverished coal regions of Illinois, Kentucky, Ohio, Pennsylvania, and West Virginia, the rate of child malnutrition reached 90%. About 3 million children between 7 and 17 years left their schools and approximately 40% of older youths 16 years and older, lived on the streets (Cohen, 1996).

By the time Franklin D. Roosevelt took office in January 1933, the government lacked national programs for workers' relief, and local agencies had exhausted their resources. At least 13 million Americans were unemployed and 1.5 million were homeless (Evans, 2010). Family disintegration, homelessness, and unemployment characterized poor people's lives, with children the most immediate and vulnerable victims.

Congress created the Federal Emergency Relief Administration (FERA) on May 12, 1933 to provide relief to the destitute "whether resident, transient, or homeless" (Crouse, 1986, p. 130). The Federal Transient Program was also established with the passage of FERA targeting 300,000 transients across the country. FERA set up the criteria for identifying homeless persons or families, providing care and job services (Crouse, 1986; Katz, 1996).

During the worst years of the Depression, one out of five children in New York City suffered from malnutrition. In coal-mining regions, nine in ten children were malnourished. A kitchen in Yuma, Arizona reportedly fed 7,500 homeless boys and girls between November 1, 1931 and March 15, 1932 (Uys, 1999). In Thomas Minehan's (1934) study about 500 tramp boys and girls across six states, he describes how young girls prostituted for food, and boys stole to get shoes and clothes.

Most schools of the time cut their hours or closed their doors which led to hundreds of thousands of children being denied access to an education. During the 1933-1934 school year, about 175,000 children were out of school because schools shut down. Schools in Dayton, Ohio were open only three days a week. In the South, where racial discrimination was pervasive, Black schools were only open 146 days a year, compared to 182 days for white schools (Lindley & Lindley, 1938/1972). Many Black children could not attend schools because they lacked shoes and some had to walk 14 miles to school (Johnson, 1934; Mintz & Kellogg, 1989). In Arkansas and Mississippi, less than 5% of the African American youths were in school (Uys, 1999).

By 1938, over half of all sixteen and seventeen-year-olds were jobless and out of school (Mintz, 2004). Many experienced mental stress, insecurity, and shame. As a result, millions of youths went "on the bum." The turmoil of homeless children symbolizes the youth crisis during the Great Depression. When first lady Eleanor Roosevelt spoke about the country's children during the Depression, she claimed:

> I have moments of real terror when I think we might be losing this generation. We have got to bring these young people into the active life of the community and make them feel that they are necessary. (Roosevelt in Melvin, 1940, pp. 5-6)

After receiving thousands of letters from children and youth seeking help during the Depression, Eleanor Roosevelt played a prominent role in founding government programs for young people, including the National Youth Administration (NYA) and the youth-oriented Works Progress Administration (WPA) programs. The First Lady was not only involved in advocating for impoverished and homeless youth during the Depression, she was also a firm believer in equality and the right to an education stating, "We must equalize educational opportunities throughout the country" (Roosevelt, 1936, p. 21). And later, as part of her leadership in constructing the Universal Declaration of Human Rights, Eleanor Roosevelt argued that all "children have a right to certain opportunities for education and should be allowed to take advantage of them" (Roosevelt, 1949, p. 32).

Public Policies, Homelessness, and the Role of Government

During this period, the United States came close to mirroring some of the social democratic principles that would feature so prominently in post-World War II Europe, as children's welfare was viewed as a public responsibility. Roosevelt's

New Deal agencies marked the beginning of the federal government's involvement in promoting children's well-being. During this time, federal aid included free school lunch programs, free nursery schools, and work study programs. The federal government provided employment to millions of youths through funding programs like the Civilian Conservation Corps (CCC), the Works Progress Administration (WPA), and the National Youth Administration (NYA).

The Emergency Relief Appropriations Act of 1935 initiated the Works Progress Administration (WPA) to provide work relief for unemployed people. It was one of the best known New Deal Programs of the time. Headed by Harry Hopkins, the program replaced FERA and offered jobs to millions of Americans, who built highways, buildings, bridges, airports, and schools. It was renamed as the Work Projects Administration in 1937 (Evans, 2010; National Resources Planning Board, 1939; Blakey, 1986). The WPA also established about 1,500 emergency nursery schools for 2- to 4-year-olds of parents on the federal relief programs. By 1937, about 40,000 children were enrolled (Yarrow, 2009).

In June 1935, the federal government established the National Youth Administration (NYA), an agency under the WPA program. The NYA was created to solve the crisis of destitute, homeless, and dispossessed youth so pervasive during the mid-1930s. Work-study opportunities for high school and college students were provided as well as employment for youth who were out of school and out of work (Mintz, 2004). The NYA also focused its resources and personnel on apprenticeships, placement services, and educational camps for young women. During its eight-year operation, the NYA financially supported more than 2.1 million youths, helping them to remain in schools (Yarrow, 2009). A leading social worker of the time, Aubrey W. Williams, was Director of the NYA and worked closely with Eleanor Roosevelt to ensure that the NYA also served African American youth. He appointed African American educator, Mary McLeod Bethune, as the director of Negro Affairs. Under her efforts, the NYA program stipulated that the numbers of minority youth aided on the school aid program should be proportional to their number of the total population.

In 1935, President Roosevelt also introduced the Social Security Act, the most significant New Deal anti-poverty policy. From its inception, the Act created a two-channel welfare state with provisions for social insurance for 'deserving' able-bodied workers who were attached to the labor force, and they received social protections such as unemployment and old age insurance. Of the welfare programs, Aid to Dependent Children (ADC), Aid to the Blind, and Old Age Assistance, ADC was stigmatized from its inception, with assistance tied to the control of the conduct of its beneficiaries. ADC (which replaced Mother's pensions from earlier years), included the 'suitable home' criterion and premised aid on moral fitness, thereby excluding unmarried mothers and women and children of color in many states. The moral fitness provision served as a racialized, regulatory, and exclusionary mechanism to deny benefits to so-called undeserving recipients (Nelson, 1990; Polakow, 1993).

Many New Deal programs lost federal support during the 40s, but the advent of World War II dramatically reduced unemployment and homelessness by providing unlimited jobs in the war industries and the armed forces. The war exigencies also brought new federal support for the poor civilian population and their children. War-time child care services were authorized under the Lanham Act and by 1945 over a million young children received day care services (Steinfels, 1973). The end of the war era, heralding a time of economic growth, was also a time of expanded social welfare programs such as the G.I. Bill, which invested in returning soldiers, with incentives to enroll in higher education.

It was not until the 1960s when President Johnson declared war on poverty that large-scale investments in poverty eradication were developed as part of federal policy with bold initiatives that mirrored Roosevelt's New Deal. Medicaid (health care for the poor) and Medicare (health care for the elderly) were enacted. Public housing was expanded as was the food stamp program that began during the Roosevelt years. Many Black women, previously excluded from welfare, now gained access to AFDC (Aid to Families with Dependent Children) and enrollment rates of beneficiaries increased exponentially. Head Start, the federal early intervention program for poor children, was created amid a period of social, legal, and educational transformation. Job Corps, Legal Services and Supplemental Social Security all played a major role in the alleviation of poverty particularly for the elderly, single mothers, children, and African Americans (Katz, 1995).

The homeless population of the 1950s and 1960s was predominantly comprised of older white males living in cheap hotels, bars, and religious missions. While skid row was a symbol of the "old" homeless, the "new" homeless – women, children, and minorities – emerged toward the end of the 1970s (Rossi, 1990), as a consequence of the conservative backlash against the expanded welfare state that followed the War on Poverty in the 60s. Under the Reagan Administration, a ferocious War on Welfare was launched, and the social safety net began to unravel when Congress passed the Omnibus Budget Reconciliation Act (OBRA) cutting social spending on public housing, Medicaid, food stamps, child care, school lunches, and other nutrition programs (Katz, 1995). Given the significant increase and demographic diversity of the homeless population, Hoch points that they were like their skid row predecessors, "near the bottom of the economically weak and politically disenfranchised underclass" (1987, p. 30). The growing numbers of homeless families, typically headed by poor mothers, made up one-third of the homeless population of 2.5 million people in the 1980s (US Conference of Mayors, 1987; Bassuk, 1984).

As child homelessness increased, few documents recorded how many children and youths were homeless. The US General Accounting Office reported in 1989 that there were about 68,000 homeless children under 16 years on any given night. The National Coalition for the Homeless reported 500,000 to 750,000 school-age homeless children nationwide. In 1987, the National Association of State Coordinators for the Education of Homeless Children and Youth (NASCEHCY) documented that 57% of homeless children were reported out of school (Ely, 1987; NASCEHCY, 1996).

In response to public campaigns about the deplorable conditions of homeless families and children, the Stewart B. McKinney Homeless Assistance Act (P. L.

100-77) was signed into law on July 22, 1987. Renamed the McKinney-Vento Act after the two Congressmen, Stewart McKinney and Bruce Vento who were active in advocating the passage of the Act, approximately $1 billion was appropriated for homeless families during 1987-1988, through the provision of programs that covered areas of health care, emergency food and shelter, mental health services, alcohol and drug abuse treatment, housing, education, and job training (Rossi, 1990; US Interagency Council on the Homeless, 1991; US Conference of Mayors, 1988). Title VII(B) of the Act, Education for Homeless Children and Youth, required states to remove the barriers to homeless children's education and to protect their educational rights; thereby ensuring they were entitled to the same access to education and services provided by Chapter1, Head Start, and the Individuals with Disabilities Education Act (IDEA). Residency requirements were revised so that children could continue to attend their schools of origin through the rest of the school year, or attend the school in the attendance area in which they were sheltered – "whichever is in the child's best interests" (McKinney [§722(e)(3)A]; Polakow, 2007a; Rafferty, 1995, p. 40).

Title VII(B) was reauthorized in 1990, 1994, and 2002. New programs were included and expanded to meet the needs of homeless children that addressed further barriers to education, including residency, guardianship, special education needs, school records, absences, and transportation. States receiving Title VII(B) funds were required to gather data on the number and location of homeless school-age children, identify their problems regarding access to public education and their special needs, and to develop a systematic plan for overcoming barriers. However, the McKinney-Vento Act, designed to protect the educational rights of homeless children and youth and to ensure that they have equal access to public education and public preschool, has been persistently underfunded and compliance has been spotty and varies dramatically among the states.

In an attempt to increase the access of homeless families to HUD housing assistance, advocates lobbied for passage of HR 32, the Homeless Children and Youth Act. In February, 2012, the House Financial Services Committee's Insurance, Housing, and Community Opportunity Subcommittee passed HR 32 by a voice vote. Because of recent HUD regulations, many homeless families cannot qualify for HUD housing assistance if they are living in motel rooms or doubled up with families or friends. Rather, these families must meet complicated criteria to qualify for assistance despite the fact that public schools and other federal programs such as Head Start, the Runaway and Homeless Youth Act, and other intervention programs all recognize those living in such precarious and unstable conditions as homeless. HR 32 is pending and must yet be approved by the entire House Financial Services Committee (NAEHCY, 2012).

As we trace the threads of poverty, destitution, and homelessness across the United States from the undeserving poor of the 1800s to the discarded children of the present, it is clear that public policy *does* make a difference. Policies that have shaped and supported, or damaged and eroded, the lives of men, women, and children, clearly hit the poorest and dispossessed amongst us most heavily and most harshly. As Katz points out, "The federal government remains potentially the most powerful weapon in the anti-poverty arsenal" (1995, p. 72). Yet, poor children's rights – to housing, to health care, to education, to child care, to a sustainable and nurturant young life – have not featured prominently in either poverty policy or media discourse. At the time of writing, children's dispossession has been invisible in the 2012 presidential campaign.

HOMELESSNESS AND THE MAKING OF DEMOCRACY'S DISCARDS

Homelessness in the United States has burgeoned in direct proportion to unemployment, foreclosures, and the decrease in social spending across the states. Cuts in school budgets, social welfare services, housing subsidies, Medicaid, child care and health care have all hit the most vulnerable families, creating vast circles of dispossession: loss of jobs, loss of home, loss of social networks, deteriorating neighborhoods, and lack of access to affordable child care. As homelessness has increased so, too, have pernicious city ordinances, shrinking the public space for those who are placeless. The National Coalition for the Homeless and the National Center on Homelessness and Poverty (2009) published a joint report that documents how many cities have passed anti-loitering, anti-panhandling, and anti-camping laws that criminalize homelessness so that even sleeping or sitting on a park bench may result in arrests or fines. Homeless people are frequently targeted for 'sweeps' of public spaces where they are living, causing loss of important possessions, documents, medications, and their dignity. Ordinances against sharing food in public spaces, such as in Orlando, Florida, or against sitting or lying in specific places – all serve to criminalize homeless people's daily lives, and turn them into human discards, with little to maintain their own dignity and identity as persons

The lack of safe, affordable housing coupled with domestic violence and lack of social supports has led to a shelter crisis for children, with young children in poor single mother households experiencing disproportionate rates of homelessness. Forty-two percent of homeless children are 6 and under, and of the 1.5 million children estimated to be homeless, the largest percentage, 47%, are African-American (Aritani, 2009). In New York City alone, there are 20,000 children living in shelters, a 20% increase over 2011, as Mayor Bloomberg has cut support programs to end homelessness and priority referrals to public housing and rent subsidies ("More," 2012, p. A26). In addition, over 1.6 million children are classified as unaccompanied youth – runaways, throwaways and independent youth – who either intentionally choose to leave their family homes due to abuse and violence, substance abuse, mental illness, conflicts and sexual orientation, or are cast out with no place to go (Aratani, 2009).

For almost two decades, one of the authors, Polakow, has interviewed over 50 homeless women and children in New York, California, Iowa, and Michigan. Many of the women have fled from violent partners and violent homes; others have fled dangerous neighborhoods or lost low-wage jobs and faced evictions; others with young children in need of child care have been unable to juggle shelter and child care as cash assistance has been cut, and housing subsidies are unattainable due to long waiting lists in counties with severe shortages of affordable housing.

One of the consistent themes of the women's housing narratives has been a struggle against the 'invisible hand' of the market – rising rents, non-living wages, unsafe neighborhoods, high costs of quality child care, lack of access to health care, transportation barriers, and above all, in a now eviscerated welfare state – the lack of family support services to help them get back on their feet.

Snapshots of Homelessness[2]

Christy, a white Michigan survivor of domestic violence, whose former partner sexually abused their six-year-old son, describes how daunting the path has been to find affordable housing: "Being back in that motel was devastating for us … there's so much rejection … you know you not gonna find anything." Christy's children regularly missed school until they were rehoused in a neighborhood that she worried was not safe. Several months later, the landlord entered the apartment when Christy's young teenage daughter was there alone and attempted to sexually assault her. Christy immediately left the apartment with the children, after reporting the attempted assault, and moved to another county where she had a distant relative. The children's lives were once again disrupted necessitating school relocation and further shelter living for a period of four months. During this time her daughter received very little school support in terms of counseling.

Danielle, a married African American mother of two young sons, tells how her husband, a former military policeman, has been unable to find a job, necessitating two bouts of family homelessness in Virginia and in New York City. For Danielle with aspirations to become an attorney, the two years of constant shuttling from one unaffordable apartment to another, has caused stress, anxiety, and ongoing frustration as she struggles to find good quality child care for her two boys:

> You know, nowadays you've got to be real careful … just because someone on the block is watching kids, it doesn't mean I want them with *my kids* … and welfare don't care about that … as long as somebody's watching your kids and they got a welfare sign, you just have to go do it!

Danielle's determination to find quality care for her two children creates enormous obstacles as she speaks out publicly to demand the right to decent child care. Without child care she cannot work, and if she does not actively seek jobs – cash benefits are cut for the entire family.

For Kathy, a single African American mother, the lack of access to affordable child care led to a lost job and directly to homelessness, following an eviction for

---

[4] The excerpts from the three women's stories are based on in-depth interviews and first reported in Polakow (1993, p. 9; 2007b, p. 78; 2000, p. 4).

unpaid rent. The consequences were so serious that she eventually lost custody of her daughter, as panic and anxiety attacks in the shelter led to substance abuse:

> I had no money for day care and then I lost my job because they said I had to work the night shift and who was there to care for my daughter? So they fired me and then the eviction notice came … and soon after we ended up in a shelter and my daughter was traumatized.

What does it mean to be placeless in a society of wealth and material opulence? Clearly homelessness is a disruptive and destabilizing event in itself; but homelessness quickly spirals out of control leading to despair, depression, anxiety, fear, and severely stressing the capacity of mothers (and fathers) to parent their children. And how does it affect the child's developing being? His insecurity about moving to yet another school? Her sense of loss when the family cat has to be given away? Their disrupted security and sense of diminished identity?

Tenuous Lives

Life on the edges for women as the tenuous heads of economically vulnerable households involves constant juggling acts, making choices that often have no good outcomes. Choosing to keep an older child at home to care for a younger sick child may allow mom to hold down a low wage job for a period of time, but an older daughter or a younger sibling misses school and fails to graduate (see Polakow, 2007b). For women in fragile housing situations, one tip of the apple cart means all comes crashing down. Failure to show up for work could mean a lost low-wage job, which means that rent does not get paid and eviction looms. In other situations, life with a violent partner means choosing to stay and endure the violence with children as traumatized witnesses, or to leave and flee to a shelter which may mean a prolonged period of homelessness.

Being poor is to be disempowered – where one's choices in the best interests of one's children are subjugated to unrelenting market forces, controlled by welfare-to-work mandates that lead to a severely circumscribed set of human capabilities, limiting one's capacity to function as a full human being. Such is the lack of rights that dispossession has wrought in the United States. For those who are destitute, the "opportunity society" is buttressed by exclusionary policies of "None for You" and when one is resource-less and placeless what one 'is able to do and become,' occurs on a flat and truncated trajectory. When social citizenship rights are absent, poor women's mothering is placed at risk, distorted by punitive welfare legislation such as the Personal Responsibility Act of 1996, which requires them to fulfill mandatory work requirements in low-wage dead-end jobs, denied access to most forms of quality post-secondary education, and relegated to cheap and low-quality child care for their young children (Polakow, 2007b). The Personal Responsibility Act is an example of pernicious public policy that furthers dispossession, and eviscerates the rights of poor women as single mothers, where they are forced to "purchase their families' short-term survival by sacrificing basic rights the rest of us take for granted" (Mink, 1998, p. 133). Children have become the pawns in relentless cost-cutting in the name of deficit reduction, Hence child care, health care, housing are all commodified and the universal provisions that still do exist in most of Northern and Western Europe that create decommodifcation through social protections, are absent for poor and destitute women and their children, emblematic of what Fine terms "the uneven distribution of social suffering" (Fine et al., 2010, p. 1).

The Impact of Homelessness on Mothers and Children

What does homelessness do to women who are alone and parenting their children? It is clearly as one young mother of a two-year-old son in rural Iowa states, "a fall into hell." The emotional toll produced is part of the social poison that affects the lives of people who are resource-less. And depending on where one falls, the geography of homelessness can be determinative in whether it is an episode or whether it becomes a chronic way of being. For many poor women, homelessness is the consequence of life histories filled with danger and violence. Frequently the actual choice to flee is also a choice to become homeless. Epidemiological studies conducted by Ellen Bassuk and colleagues during the 90s indicate multiple adverse events experienced by homeless women: unstable housing histories, stressful life events including the hospitalization of self or child, loss of children to foster care, physical and sexual assaults, suicidal behaviors, substance abuse, and compromised physical and mental health (Bassuk et al., 1996; Bassuk, Buckner, Perloff, & Bassuk, 1998). Steinbock has also pointed to the risks incurred by single mothers who become homeless as a result of domestic violence, primarily the risk of losing their children to foster care. Oftentimes substance abuse may induce the loss of children (Polakow, 2007b; Steinbock, 1995).

In other situations of desperation, the lack of family and friendship networks may precipitate the loss of young children, disrupting attachments and causing depression and anxiety. For some mothers with young, adolescent boys, single sex shelters may coerce the separation; in other contexts mothers may choose not to expose their children to shelter life fearing shame and stigma and reluctantly place them with relatives instead. Barrow and Lawinski's (2009) qualitative study of mothers separated from their children points out that family preservation and unification policies intersect with problematic, bureaucratic institutional practices that promote scrutiny and surveillance of shelter mothers' behavior, but pay little attention to the terrible loss experienced by mothers and children alike; losses that fracture relationships and disrupted social worlds. Of 207 children in the study, 143 children (69%) were separated for an average of 2.6 years from their mothers, some living with kin and others in stranger foster care.

For homeless mothers whose children live with them in shelters, their parenting is frequently undermined by policies and practices that infantilize them and take away their parental autonomy. Volunteers at shelters may be young college students enforcing shelter rules – 'Lights out,' 'No smoking,' 'No loud noise,' 'No cell phone calls after 10pm' – rules that may be necessary, but also threaten their autonomy and undermine their parental authority. Barrow and Laborde (2008) cite several studies that depict how vulnerable mothers must parent along "fault lines" and how "dominant standards of mothering can become another source of injury for women whose circumstances render such standards impossible to achieve" (pp. 158-159).

A recent longitudinal study (Park, Fertig, & Metraux, 2011) focusing on the impact of homelessness on maternal health follows over 2600 low-income families for five years in 20 cities across the US. Approximately 10% lived in shelters and another 24% lived doubled-up with families or friends. Mental health, depression anxiety and substance abuse issues are far more prevalent among homeless families, and are highest for those living in shelters where one third of homeless women report depression. For the children, shelter life can be stigmatizing and a source of deep shame. Separation from a parent may be perceived as rejection and abandonment. One eight-year-old child interviewed angrily berated his mother after the family was evicted and moved into a fourth spell of homelessness, "Why does she do this to us – why can't we have a regular home like other kids – I can't go to school no more 'cos my friends will find out I'm in a shelter – I hate her, I hate her – I'm gonna run away from here" (Polakow, 2007a, p. 45).

Homelessness and Social Toxicity

When children are exposed to the unremitting stress of homelessness and chronic instability, their young worlds are characterized by what Garbarino (1995) has termed 'social toxicity.' When an accumulation of risk factors converge such as hunger, homelessness, street violence, parental substance abuse, the child's development may be severely disrupted – affecting both intellectual and socio-emotional development (see also Sameroff, Seifer, Barocas, Zax, & Greenspan, 1987). Garbarino's research (1992) conducted with children, who live in dangerous neighborhoods across the United States, illuminates how their worlds are punctuated by street violence, instability, and fear. Socially toxic environments erode children's human capabilities, stripping them of not only material resources, but relational resources and social capital. The *ecobiodevelopmental* framework pioneered by Shonkoff and colleagues corroborate the impacts of social toxicity, drawing from new interdisciplinary research in neuroscience, epidemiology, molecular biology, and genomics. Shonkoff et al. (2011) argue that early emotional experiences are embedded in the brain's architecture and that emotional development is integrally connected to both cognitive and physical development so that chronic environmental stress, including trauma and persistent adverse experiences, become toxic to the young child's developing brain.

Homelessness, and the accumulated risks, affects all dimensions of a child's environment: parenting behavior and nurturing time with their children, emotional availability, housing stability, neighborhood safety, social isolation, compromised opportunities for play, friendships, and quality early education and schooling. Witnessing and experiencing violence, chronic episodes of homelessness, the unremitting stress and anxiety of food insecurity and potential loss of home and relationships are devastating for young children with long-lasing developmental damage and adverse adult outcomes (Center on the Developing Child, 2010). Healthy development is sustained through bonding, emotional attachments, and stability of care, and as children reach school age, affirmation and engagement in intellectual endeavors, adult-child relationships, and peer friendships become vital. For homeless children, who lack autonomy and choice, their entire lifeworld is threatened by a chronic series of losses and disruptions: home, school, relationships, possessions, and more; yet little attention is paid to these shattering developmental threats as homeless children are constructed as costly, problematic, and disruptive to school routines and achievement.

Disrupted Schooling

While accurate counts of the number of homeless students are difficult, estimates indicate that 1.1 million school-age students were homeless during the 2010-2011 school year (Child Trends, 2012b). The numbers of children not enrolled in school are even more difficult to ascertain as they are part of the invisible homeless, pointing to many more thousands who are neither served nor counted. Moreover, children who are homeless also have a greater incidence of health problems and many lack up-to-date immunizations. Homeless children living in overcrowded conditions experience more illnesses such as respiratory infections and higher rates of asthma, ADHD and emotional impairments and over 50% of homeless children experience mental health problems such as anxiety and depression (Child Trends, 2012b; Duffield & Lovell, 2008).

Homeless children in school face social isolation, segregation, and persistent barriers to an equal education. The intersectional identities that many homeless children face – poor, minority, and homeless – introduce additional rights violations (Tars, 2009). In addition to racial barriers, children face barriers of *place* and *bureaucracy*. The geography of homelessness prefigures educational access, where some schools are well resourced to cope with the multiple needs of newly homeless children; and others are understaffed and unable or unwilling to respond to homeless children in their schools. In some schools, a pattern of hostility and rejection is evident. In an ethnographic Master's thesis, Felice Moorman describes the lonely classroom world of a first grade African-American homeless child, Melissa, who is consistently hounded by her teacher and marginalized in the classroom. Melissa is described as constantly sucking her thumb, lying on the floor, and is placed alone at a desk separated from the other children as her teacher states:

> I'm calling your dad as soon as we're done … after math you're going to the office … I don't want to hear from you, you never tell the truth … you do lazy man's work … you're not going to be ready for third grade …. (Moorman, 2009, p. 33)

Despite the considerable impact of the McKinney-Vento legislation in helping to secure homeless children's educational rights, the legislation remains an unfunded mandate and implementation is idiosyncratic, working effectively in some regions of a state and completely ineffectively in others. Nationwide, only 6% of states receive funding under the McKinney-Vento Act. Duffield and Lovell (2008) have extensively documented the barriers to educational access for homeless children and the challenges faced by school districts. School officials report increases in the numbers of homeless children and inadequate staff and supplies to cope with the influx of destitute families. Homeless liaisons are typically assigned part-time loads in a school district and together with shrinking community resources, schools are overwhelmed by the acute needs of homeless children who are enrolling earlier in the school year. Transportation is also a huge barrier, challenging school districts as well as families. Title VII(B) of the McKinney–Vento Act explicitly protects the "best interests of the child" so that homeless children, who may be sheltered in another adjacent school district, are permitted to remain in their school of origin for the duration of the school year, if it is determined to be in their best interests, thereby placing responsibility on the school district to arrange the cost of transportation. With teacher lay-offs and school districts cutting services, and in some cases general school transportation, children who are homeless fall through the cracks and are perceived as a drain on school resources. For children transportation may mean long commutes of two hours or more to and from shelters to their schools of origin. And friendships formed with unhoused peers at a shelter are always temporary, as children may be transported to different school districts, creating further disruptions of a child's tenuous social network.

Homeless children experience multiple disruptions in their schooling, and may be bounced around from school to school with some children attending multiple school placements in a year. Aratani reports that 39% of homeless children missed more than a week of school in a three-month period and relocated to different schools two to five times during the school year. While almost half of sheltered homeless children are in need of special education services, less than a quarter actually receive them. (Aratani, 2009; see also Zima, Bussing, Forness, & Benjamin, 1997). Residential and school instability interrupts children's learning, special education services, and engagement in school activities. It means yet another adjustment to new teachers, new peers, new curricula, and new school cultures. Homeless children perform consistently below grade level in reading and mathematics in comparison to their housed peers; they are held back to repeat a grade at twice the rate of their peers; experience double the rate of suspensions or expulsions and are much less likely to graduate from high school (Child Trends, 2012b; Duffield & Lowell, 2008; Rubin et al., 1996).

Unaccompanied Youth and Runaways

Unaccompanied homeless and runaway youth are those who have left their families of origin because of domestic violence, abuse, or who have been thrown out by parents and/or guardians and many have been in foster care for part of their childhoods. Substance abuse and mental illness are additional contributing causes of homelessness among youth. They have higher school dropout rates and are far less likely to graduate. In addition, unaccompanied youth and street runaways who drop out of high school are vulnerable to sexual violence, sexually transmitted diseases, and teen pregnancy (Aratani & Cooper, 2008; Child Trends, 2012b).

The Runaway and Homeless Youth Act (RHY) of 2008, includes four programs that target youth: Basic Center Programs, Transitional Living Programs, Maternity Group Homes for pregnant and parenting teens, and street outreach programs. The RHY programs are administered by the federal Department of Health and Human Services (DHHS) and the Act increased funding for basic center programs for emergency shelter, basic needs, and family reunification, as well as for street outreach which includes programs for assisting street youth and crisis intervention (Aratani, 2009).

Runaways and homeless youth, particularly girls, are also victims of trafficking and girls who have been prostituted are typically categorized as juvenile delinquents. Boxill and Richardson (2007) argue that this involves a "massive denial" of the widespread industry of child prostitution in the USA (estimated at between $14 and $20 million annually) and that there has been a general indifference, academically and professionally, to understanding the social and economic conditions that produce child prostitution; and the severe traumas girls have endured as trafficked and purchased commodities – through manipulation, deception, coercion and violence. Child trafficking is an international crisis that has received increasing attention by UNESCO and other international bodies, but is still largely invisible in the USA (Boxill & Richardson, 2007; Willis & Levy, 2002). Trafficked children, particularly adolescent girls, are part of the invisible, gendered, homeless population, frequently stigmatized and unrecognized as they live in the shadows of an underworld, where their bodies are expropriated and their coercive 'homes' are sites of threat and violation.

HOMELESSNESS AND CHILDREN'S RIGHTS

> Me and my mom are homeless. We got that way because my dad was abusing me and my mom … He hit me and called me stupid and retarded. He tried to choke my mom. We went to court to get help but they didn't help us. We left our home in June last year and went to stay in a hotel for a couple nights. My mom didn't have enough money to stay longer. She tried to find a shelter for us to stay in but they didn't have any room … She tried to get us into the shelter for families that have been abused but we couldn't because of me. They don't allow older boys like me to stay there. My mom kept trying to find a place for us because school was starting soon. We were in one shelter for a little while but they had a time limit so they moved us into a hotel. It was really scary because drug dealers stood around outside … When I went to school the bus would pick me up. I didn't want anyone to know where I was staying. When the bus dropped us off I waited until no one would see me and then I went to the

> hotel … The hardest part was having to move so much and stay in so many different places. We lost everything … Everywhere we went it didn't work out no matter how hard we tried. (*Testimony of Rumi Khan*, 2011)

The testimony of a young eleven-year-old child, Rumi Kahn, to the House Subcommittee on Insurance, Housing, and Community Opportunity, is iconic of how far the United States has moved away from affirming the fundamental human rights of children to stable shelter. All the crises encountered by this resilient young boy are violations of his human rights and his human capabilities. The domestic violence and abuse he and his mother experienced, the terror and loss of home, the ongoing dislocation, the fear of drug dealers, his status as a preadolescent boy which excludes him from many family shelters, the disrupted schooling, the shame and stigma, the profound sense of loss, are all part of an enduring crisis of dispossession that millions of children and their families now face in this country.

The human right to housing in the United States has had an uneven history. The Universal Declaration of Human Rights unequivocally confers that right, stating, "Everyone has the right to a standard of living adequate for the health and well-being of himself and of his family, including food, clothing, housing and medical care and necessary social services" (1948, Article 25, 1). But in 1949, the federal Housing Act modified the right to housing and as the National Law Center on Homelessness and Poverty points out, that right was scaled down to a "goal" of providing "a decent home and suitable living arrangement for every family" (quoted in NLCHP, 2011, p. 6). Goals are far more vulnerable to political exigencies, social spending cuts, and the downsizing of the social state, and as we have seen in recent times, the propagation of corporate greed and unrestricted profiteering has stripped millions of vulnerable families of the 'right' to shelter.

Under the Obama Administration there have been some serious efforts to tackle the crisis of homelessness, and in 2010, the Federal Interagency Council on Homelessness released a federal plan to prevent and end homelessness with President Obama declaring, "It is simply unacceptable for a child in this country to be without a home" (US Interagency Council on Homelessness, 2010, p. 1). The Plan commits to preventing and ending homelessness for families and children within five to ten years, in addition to ending homelessness for veterans (within five years) and ending chronic and other types of homelessness, by investing in interagency partnerships with states, local agencies, philanthropic organizations, and communities. For homeless families and children strategies outlined in the report include the expansion of low-cost rental housing, construction and rehabilitation of low-cost housing, and an increase in rental housing subsidies at the federal, state, and local levels. However, given the Congressional gridlock, the severe cuts already implemented in many states across the nation, and the constant chorus of calls for less government by the Tea Party and Republican legislators, the complicated and multidimensional problems that cause homelessness among families, children, and youth are unlikely to be addressed. The November 2012 election will be decisive in terms of policies pursued or discarded in relation to the crisis of homelessness.

The issue of rights is central to the discourse and policies that shape homelessness. The United States has been heavily criticized for its pariah status in terms of the lack of economic and social rights afforded to its citizens. Davis and Powell (2003) argue that the US policy of exceptionalism is unjustifiably based on the notion that the US is exempt because "its domestic human rights policies are universally superior to those of other nations" (p. 711).

In the past decade, grass roots organizations have mobilized against exceptionalism, arguing that poverty should be addressed as a violation of human rights, and they have attempted to link human rights violations to international law. The US Human Rights Network, which grew out of a Howard University Law School Human Rights Summit on "Ending Exceptionalism: Strengthening Human Rights in the United States" in 2002, is comprised of political and civil rights activists, organizations, and scholars. They argue that the US must be held accountable to human rights standards and norms on the domestic front, and that this encompasses not only civil and political rights, but also economic, social, and cultural rights (see US Human Rights Network).

In 2011, in response to the UN Working Group's Periodic Review, The United States under the Obama Administration, acknowledged that despite the failure to ratify CESCR, it is, nevertheless, a signatory to other Human Rights Conventions and is therefore accountable, stating "accordingly we understand the references to rights to food and health as references to rights in other human rights instruments that we have accepted. We also understand that these rights are to be realized progressively" (UN General Assembly, 2011). Yet, there has been little movement in Congress to recognize these major human rights Conventions.

The advocacy for children's rights has its critics within the United States and globally. One of the arguments is embedded in the critique of Western nations imposing democracy and liberal/individualist rights on collective and indigenous cultures where such imposition is viewed as a threat to 'traditional' structures of governance and authority (Minujin & Nandy, 2012). Yet, while it is important to understand the legacy of neocolonialism and the damage wrought, it is equally important not to romanticize the patriarchal structures that perpetuate the oppression of women and children under the guise of traditionalism. In the United States, the opposition to children's rights has also focused on the threats to family values as well as threats to national sovereignty. However, despite objections, as of 2012, 193 countries, with the exception of the United States and Somalia, have signed and ratified the Convention on the Rights of the Child.

The CRC creates a human rights gold standard against which nations must measure their 'progressive realization' of rights, their accountability to an international body, and the ensuing scrutiny of children's conditions within their own countries. This maintains a visible and ongoing discourse about children's rights. Because social and economic rights are embedded in the fabric of social policies in Europe, child poverty rates are far lower, and child well-being, child health, and housing are all considered integral to social integration and the building of a healthy citizenry. The CRC affords children three distinct sets of rights: provision, protection, and participation, which include both needs-based and capacity-based rights (Woodhouse, 2008). EuroChild, which advances a social justice agenda in relation to children in Europe, argues that poverty is still the most significant factor shaping children's well-being and educational outcomes, and that is it vital to employ a child-centered approach in understanding the impact of child poverty on children, and framing child deprivation and concomitant social exclusion through the lens of human rights (Eurochild, 2007, 2011). International measurements of child poverty and child well-being (see UNICEF Innocenti Research Centre and the LIS Cross-National Data Center) consistently point to the failure of the United States to ensure that children enjoy the 3 P's – provision, protection, and participation – considered essential for their development as young agents of their own lives. This is particularly pertinent for homeless children who are rendered placeless, resource-less and voiceless as they are forced to navigate the unstable and threatening worlds incurred by homelessness.

A right-based discourse reframes poverty as a consequence of domestic social and economic policies and macro-economic policies of globalization. Homelessness from a right-based perspective is not an individual-induced condition, but rather a violation of rights in need of redress. And because poverty and homelessness are intertwined, it is not only rooflessness and lack of shelter that damage children's human capabilities, but the ensuing toxicity of non-material forms of poverty: social exclusion, impaired development, the environmental stress and chronic anxiety, destabilized family life, and disrupted education. As Steinbeck presciently writes about the tragedy of dispossession and homelessness in the throes of the Great Depression, there are lessons to be learned:

> There's a crime here that goes beyond denunciation. There is a sorrow here that weeping cannot symbolize. There is a failure here that topples all our success. (1939/1967, p. 385)

The failure to affirm the right to secure and stable housing in the United States is iconic of our indifference to the thwarted lives and human capabilities of millions of our children. Rights are necessary to redress appalling wrongs and to delineate the geography of a more just and democratic world.

REFERENCES

Addy, S., & Wight, V. R. (2012, February). *Basic facts about low-income children: Children under age 18*. New York, NY: National Center for Children in Poverty. Retrieved from http://www.nccp.org/publications/pub_1049.html

Anderson, N. (1933). *Summary of report on homeless census of January, 1933 and February 21, 1933.*

Aratani, Y. (2009). *Homeless children and youth: Causes and consequences*. New York: National Center for Children in Poverty. Retrieved from http://www.nccp.org/publications/pub_888.html

Aratani, Y., & Cooper, J. L. (2008). The effects of runaway-homeless episodes on high school dropout. Paper presented at the *Annual Meeting in Boston for the Society of the Study of Social Problems*, Boston, MA.

Barrow, S. M., & Laborde, N. D. (2008). Invisible mothers: Parenting by homeless women separated from their children. *Gender Issues, 25*, 157-172.

Barrow, S. M., & Lawinski, T. (2009). Contexts of mother-child separations in homeless families. *Analyses of Social Issues and Public Policy*, 1-20. Retrieved from http://homeless.samhsa.gov/Resource/Contexts-of-Mother%E2%80%93ChildSeparations-in-Homeless-Families-47181.aspx

Bassuk, E. L. (1984). The homelessness problem. *Scientific America, 251*(1), 40-45.

Bassuk, E. L., Weinreb, L. F., Buckner, J. C., Browne, A., Salomon, A., & Bassuk, S. S. (1996). The characteristics and needs of sheltered homeless and low-income housed mothers. *The Journal of the American Medical Association, 276*(8), 640-646.

Bassuk, E. L., Buckner, J. C., Perloff, J. N., & Bassuk, S. S. (1998). Prevalence of mental health and substance use disorders among homeless and low-income housed mothers. *The American Journal of Psychiatry, 155*(11), 1561-1564. Retrieved from http://ajp.psychiatryonline.org/article.aspx?articleID=173102

Blakey, G. T. (1986). *Hard times and New Deal in Kentucky: 1929-1939*. Lexington, KY: University Press of Kentucky.

Bloom, A. (2005). Toward a history of homelessness. *Journal of Urban History, 31*(6), 907-917.

Boxill, N. A., & Richardson, D. J. (2007). Ending sex trafficking of children in Atlanta. *Affilia, 22*(2), 138-149.

Center on the Developing Child. (2010). *The long reach of early childhood poverty: Pathways and impacts Q & A*. Cambridge, MA: Center on the Developing Child, Harvard University. Retrieved from: http://developingchild.harvard.edu/

Child Trends. (2012a). *Food insecurity* Retrieved from http://www.childtrendsdatabank.org/alphalist?q=node/363

Child Trends. (2012b). *Homeless children and youth.* Retrieved from: http://www.childtrendsdatabank.org/?q=node/340

Cohen, R. (1996). "Dear Mrs. Roosevelt:" Cries for help from the Depression generation, and the American youth crisis of the 1930s. *New Deal Network.* Hyde Park, NY: Roosevelt Institute. Retrieved from http://newdeal.feri.org/eleanor/cohen.htm

Convention on the Elimination of All Forms of Discrimination against Women (CEDAW). (1979, December 18). *United Nations Division for the Advancement of Women*. Retrieved from http://www.un.org/womenwatch/daw/cedaw/

Convention on the Rights of the Child (CRC). (1989, November 20). *United Nations Office of the High Commissioner for Human Rights.* Retrieved from http://www2.ohchr.org/english/law/crc.htm

Crouse, J. M. (1986). *The homeless transient in the Great Depression: New York State, 1929-1941.* Albany, NY: State University of New York Press.

Davis, M., & Powell, R. (2003). The International Convention on the Rights of the Child: A catalyst for innovative child care policies. *Human Rights Quarterly, 25*(3), 689-719.

Doctorow, E. L. (1994). *The waterworks.* New York, NY: Random House Publishing Group.

Duffield, B., & Lovell, P. (2008). *The economic crisis hits home.* Minneapolis, MN: National Association for the Education of Homeless Children and Youth. Retrieved from http://www.naehcy.org/dl/TheEconomicCrisisHitsHome.pdf

Ely, L. (1987). *Broken lives: Denial of education to homeless children.* Washington, DC: National Coalition for the Homeless. (ED292897)

Eurochild. (2007). *Discussion paper: A child rights approach to child poverty.* Brussels, Belgium: Author. Retrieved from http://www.eurochild.org/fileadmin/user_upload/files/Eurochild_discussion_paper_child_rights_poverty.pdf

Eurochild. (2011). *Eurochild policy position: Child poverty – Family poverty: Are they one and the same? A rights-based approach to fighting child poverty.* Brussels, Belgium: Author. Retrieved from http://www.eurochild.org/fileadmin/ThematicPriorities/FPS/Eurochild/Position_paper_ch_pov_vs_family_pov_designed_FINAL.pdf

Evans, M. (2010). Homelessness (1929-41). In L. Daniel, K. J. Bindas, A. H. Stein, J. Corfield, & S. L. Danver (Eds.), *The Great Depression and the New Deal: A thematic encyclopedia* (pp. 321-330). Santa Barbara, CA: ABC-CLIO, LLC.

Fine, M., Stoudt, B. G., Fox, M., & Santos, M. (2010). The uneven distribution of social suffering: Documenting the social health consequences of neo-liberal social policy on marginalized youth. *The European Health Psychologist, 12*(3), 30-35. Retrieved from http://www.ehps.net/ehp/issues/2010/v12iss3_September2010/12_3_fine_etal.pdf

Fremstad, S. (2012). *The NYT and the "Disorganized Single-Mother" memo*. Washington, DC: Center for Economic and Policy Research. Retrieved from http://www.cepr.net/index.php/blogs/cepr-blog/the-new-york-times-vs-single-mothers-and-other-qdisorganizedq-people-places-and-things

Garbarino, J. (1992). The meaning of poverty in the world of children. *American Behavioral Scientist, 35*(3), 220-237.

Garbarino, J. (1995). *Raising children in a socially toxic environment*. San Francisco, CA: Jossey-Bass.

Greenberg, C. L. (1991). *"Or does it explode?" Harlem in the Great Depression*. New York, NY: Oxford University Press.

Gregory, J. N. (2004). "The Dust Bowl Migration" poverty stories, race stories. In G. Mink & A. O'Connor (Eds.), *Poverty in the United States: An encyclopedia of history, politics, and policy* (pp. 242-247). Santa Barbara, CA: ABC-CLIO.

Hoch, C. (1987). A brief history of the homeless problem in the United States. In R. D. Bingham, R. E. Green, & S. B. White (Eds.), *The homeless in the contemporary society* (pp. 16-32). Newbury Park, CA: Sage.

International Covenant on Economic, Social and Cultural Rights (CESCR). (1966, December 16). *Office of United Nations High Commissioner for Human Rights.* Retrieved from http://www2.ohchr.org/english/law/cescr.htm

Johnson, C. S. (1934). *Shadow of the plantation.* Chicago, IL: University of Chicago Press.

Johnson, P. O., & Harvey, O. L. (1938). *The National Youth Administration*. Washington, DC: US Government Printing Office.

Jones, N. A., & Sumner, A. (2011). *Child poverty, evidence and policy: Mainstreaming children in international development*. Bristol, UK: Policy Press.

Judt, T. (2010). *Ill fares the land.* New York, NY: Penguin Press.

Katz, M. B. (1989). *The undeserving poor: From the war on poverty to the war on welfare*. New York, NY: Pantheon Books.

Katz, M. B. (1995). *Improving poor people: The welfare state, the "underclass" and urban schools as history.* Princeton, NJ: Princeton University Press.

Katz, M. B. (1996). *In the shadow of the poorhouse: A social history of welfare in America* (2nd ed.). New York, NY: Basic Books.

Kusmer, K. (2002). *Down and out, on the road: The homeless in American history.* New York, NY: Oxford University Press.

Lindley, B. G., & Lindley, E. K. (1972). *A New Deal for youth: The story of the National Youth Administration*. New York, NY: Da Capo. (Original published in 1938)

LIS Cross-National Data Center. (n.d.). Retrieved from http://www.lisdatacenter.org/our-data/

Lister, R. (2004). *Poverty.* Cambridge, UK: Blackwell/Polity Press.

Madison, L. (2012, September 18). Fact-checking Romney's "47 percent" comment. *CBS News.com* Retrieved from http://www.cbsnews.com/8301-503544_162-57515033-503544/fact-checking-romneys-47-percent-comment/

Melvin, B. L. (1940). *Youth – Millions too many? A search for youth's place in America.* New York, NY: Association Press.

Minehan, T. (1934). *Boy and girl tramps of America.* New York, NY: Farrar and Rinehart, Inc.

Mink, G. (1998). *Welfare's end.* Ithaca, NY: Cornell University Press.

Mintz, S., & Kellogg, S. (1989). *Domestic revolution: A social history of American family life*. New York, NY: Simon and Schuster.

Mintz, S. (2004). *Huck's raft: A history of American childhood.* Harvard University Press.

Minujin, A., & Nandy, S. (2012). *Global child poverty and well-being: Measurement, concepts, policy and action.* Bristol, UK: The Policy Press.

Moorman, F. (2009). *The impact of homelessness on young children: Building resilience through supportive early educational interventions* (Master's thesis). Retrieved from http://commons.emich.edu/theses/230

More children in homeless shelters [Editorial]. (September 25, 2012). *The New York Times,* p. A26. Retrieved from http://www.nytimes.com/2012/09/26/opinion/more-children-in-homeless-shelters.html?emc=eta1&_r=0

National Association for the Education of Homeless Children and Youth (NAEHCY). (2012). *Support the Homeless Children and Youth Act: Help cut the red tape for homeless children and youth.* Minneapolis, MN: Author. Retrieved from http://www.naehcy.org/definitionsbill.html

National Association of State Coordinators for the Education of Homeless Children and Youth (NASCEHCY). (1996). *Making the grade: Successes and challenges in educating homeless children and youth.* Minneapolis, MN: Author.

National Coalition for the Homeless, National Law Center on Homelessness and Poverty. (2009). *Homes not handcuffs: The criminalization of homelessness in US cities.* Washington, DC: Author. Retrieved from http://www.nationalhomeless.org/factsheets/criminalization.html

National Committee on Care of Transients and Homeless. (1933). *Report on census of transient and homeless for March 22, 1933.*

National Law Center on Homelessness and Poverty. (2011). *"Simply Unacceptable:" Homelessness and the human right to housing in the United States.* Washington, DC: Author. Retrieved from www.nlchp.org/content/pubs/SimplyUnacceptableReport.pdf

National Resources Planning Board. (1939). *Federal relations to local planning.* Washington, DC: Author.

Nelson, B. (1990). The origins of the two-channel welfare state: Workmen's compensation and mothers aid. In L. Gordon (Ed.), *Women, the state, and welfare* (pp. 123-151). Madison, WI: University of Wisconsin Press.

New General Subject Series. (1935, February). *State of origin of persons receiving Transient Relief on September 30, 1934.*

Nussbaum, M. (2011). *Creating capabilities: the human development approach.* Cambridge, MA: Harvard University Press.

Omnibus Budget Reconciliation Act of 1981, P. L. 97-35, 95 Stat. 357-933 (Aug. 13, 1981).

Park, J. M., Fertig, A. R., & Metraux, S. (2011). Changes in maternal health and health behaviors as a function of homelessness. *Social Service Review, 85*(4), 565-585.

Personal Responsibility and Work Opportunity Reconciliation Act of 1996, Pub. L. 104-193, 110 Stat. 2105 (1996).

Plunz, R. A. (1993). On the uses and abuses of air: Perfecting the New York tenement, 1850-1901. In J. P. Kleihues & C. Rathgeber (Eds.), *Berlin/New York: Like and unlike: Essays on architecture and art from 1870 to the present* (pp. 159-179). New York, NY: Rizzoli.

Polakow, V. (1993). *Lives on the edge: Single mothers and their children in the other America.* Chicago, IL: University of Chicago Press.

Polakow, V. (2000). (Ed.). *The public assault on America's children: Poverty, violence, and juvenile injustice.* New York, NY: Teacher College Press.

Polakow, V. (2007a). In the shadow of the ownership society: Homeless children and their families. In S. Books (Ed.), *Invisible children in the society and its schools* (pp. 39-62). Mahwah, NJ: Erlbaum.

Polakow, V. (2007b). *Who cares for our children? The child care crisis in the other America.* New York, NY: Teachers College Press.

Rafferty, Y. (1995). The legal rights and educational problems of homeless children and youth. *Educational Evaluation and Policy Analysis, 17*(1), 39-61.

Ramsey. (2007). Wrestling with modernity: Philanthropy and the Children's Aid Society in Progressive-Era New York City. *New York History, 88*(2), 153-174.

Riis, J. (1890). *How the other half lives: Tenements of New York.* New York, NY: Charles Scribner's Sons.

Riis, J. (1892). *The children of the poor.* New York, NY: Charles Scribner's Sons.

Roosevelt, E. (1936, September). Are we overlooking the pursuit of happiness? *Parent's Magazine, 11*: 21, 67. Retrieved from http://www.gwu.edu/~erpapers/documents/articles/pursuitofhappiness.cfm

Roosevelt, E. (1949, September). Making human rights come alive. *Phi Delta Kappan, 31*(1), 23-33. Speech to the Second National Conference on UNESCO, Cleveland, Ohio, April 1, 1949. Retrieved from http://newdeal.feri.org/er/er35.htm

Roosevelt, F. D. (1937). *Second inaugural address.* Hyde Park, NY: Franklin D. Roosevelt Presidential Library and Museum. Retrieved from http://avalon.law.yale.edu/20th_century/froos2.asp

Roosevelt, F. D. (1944). *State of the union address.* Hyde Park, NY: Franklin D. Roosevelt Presidential Library and Museum. Retrieved from http://www.fdrlibrary.marist.edu/archives/stateofthe union.html

Rossi, P. H. (1990). The old homeless and the new homelessness in historical perspective. *American Psychologist, 45*(8), 954-959.

Rubin, H., Erickson, J., San Agustin, M., Cleary, D., Allen, J. K., & Cohen, P. (1996). Cognitive and academic functioning of homeless children. *Pediatrics, 93*, 289-294.

Runaway and Homeless Youth Act of 2008, P. L. 110-378. (2008).

Sameroff, A. J., Seifer, R., Barocas, R., Zax, M., & Greenspan, S. (1987). Intelligence quotient scores of 4-year-old children: Social environmental risk factors. *Pediatrics, 79*(3), 343-350.

Sen, A. K. (2001). *Development as freedom.* New York, NY: Oxford University Press.

Shonkoff, J. P., Garner, A. S., the Committee on Psychosocial Aspects of Child and Family Health, Committee on Early Childhood, Adoption, and Dependent Care, and Section on Developmental and Behavioral Pediatrics, Siegel, B. S., et al. (2011). The lifelong effects of early childhood adversity and toxic stress pediatrics. *Pediatrics, 129*(1), 232-246. Retrieved from http://pediatrics. aappublications.org/content/129/1/e232.full.pdf

Social Security Act of 1935, 42 U.S.C.A. § 301 *et seq.*

Stein, W. J. (1973). *California and the Dust Bowl Migration.* Westport, CT: Greenwood Publishing Company.

Steinbeck. (1939/1967). *Grapes of wrath.* New York, NY: The Viking Press.

Steinbock, M. (1995). Homeless female-headed families: Relationships at risk. *Marriage and Family Review, 20*(1-2), 143-159.

Steinfels, M. O. (1973). *Who's minding the children?: The history and politics of day care in America.* New York, NY: Simon and Schuster.

Stewart B. McKinney Homeless Assistance Act of 1987, P. L. 100-77, 101 Stat. 482, 42 U.S.C. § 11301 *et seq.* (1987, July 22).

Stewart B. McKinney Homeless Assistance Amendments Act of 1990, P. L. 101-645, 42 U.S.C.A. §11421-11432.

Stiglitz, J. E. (2012, August 5). Separate and unequal: "The price of inequality." *The New York Times.com.* Retrieved from http://www.nytimes.com/2012/08/05/books/review/the-price-of-inequality-by-joseph-e-stiglitz.html?pagewanted=all&_r=0

Sunstein, C. (2004). *The Second Bill of Rights: FDR's unfinished revolution–And why we need it more than ever.* New York, NY: Basic Books.

Tars, E. S. (2009, Summer). *Separate & unequal in the same classroom: Homeless students in America's public schools.* Loyola Public Interest Law Reporter.

Testimony of Rumi Khan: Hearing before the Subcommittee for Insurance, Housing, and Community Opportunity, of the Committee on Financial Services, US House of Representatives (December 15, 2011). Retrieved from http://financialservices.house.gov/uploadedfiles/121511khan.pdf

Thelen, D. (1972). *The new citizenship: Origins of progressivism in Wisconsin, 1885-1900.* Columbia, University of Missouri Press.

UN General Assembly. (2011). *UN Human Rights Council, Report of the working group on the Universal Periodic Review, United States of America* (A/HRC/16/11/Add.1). Retrieved from http://www.unhcr.org/refworld/publisher,UNHRC,,USA,4d6b6d3e2,0.html

UNICEF Innocenti Research Centre. (n.d.). Retrieved from http://www.unicef-irc.org/

UNICEF Innocenti Research Centre. (2012). *Measuring child poverty: New league tables of child poverty in the world's rich countries* (Innocenti Report Card 10). Florence, Italy. Retrieved from http://www.unicef-irc.org/publications/660

Universal Declaration of Human Rights (UDHR). (1948). *Office of the High Commissioner for Human Rights*. Retrieved from http://www.ohchr.org/en/udhr/pages/introduction.aspx

US Conference of Mayors. (1987, May). *A status report on homeless families in America's cities: A 29-city survey*. Washington DC: Author.

US Conference of Mayors. (1988). *A status report on the Stewart B. McKinney Homeless Assistance Act of 1987*. Washington, DC: Author.

US General Accounting Office. (1989). *Homeless children and youths*. Report to congressional committees. (GAO/PEMD-89-14). Washington, DC: Author.

US Human Rights Network. (n.d.). Retrieved from http://www.ushrnetwork.org/

US Interagency Council on the Homeless. (1991). *The McKinney Act: A program guide*. Washington, DC: Author.

US Interagency Council on the Homeless. (2010). *Opening doors: Federal strategic plan to prevent and end homelessness*. Washington, DC: Author. Retrieved from http://www.ich.gov/PDF/OpeningDoors_2010_FSPPreventEndHomeless.pdf

Uys, E. L. (1999). *Riding the rails: Teenagers on the move during the Great Depression*. New York, NY: TV Books.

Webb, J. C. (1935). *The transient unemployed: A description and analysis of the transient relief population*. Washington DC: GPO.

Willis, B. M., & Levy, B. S. (2002). Child prostitution: Global health burden, research needs, and interventions. *Lancet, 359*(9315), 1417-1422. Retrieved from http://www.popcenter.org/problems/trafficked_women/PDFs/Willis&Levy_2002.pdf

Winsten, P. (2011). *A century of service*. Alliance for Children & Families.

Wilkinson, R., & Pickett, K. (2012, August 5). *The poison of inequality* was behind last summer's riots. *The Guardian*. Retrieved from http://www.guardian.co.uk/commentisfree/2012/aug/05/riots-inequality-poverty-self-esteem

Woodhouse, B. B. (2008). *Hidden in plain sight: The tragedy of children's rights from Ben Franklin to Lionel Tate*. Princeton, NJ: Princeton University Press.

Yarrow, A. (2009). *History of US children's policy, 1900-present*. Washington, DC: First Focus.

Zima, B. T., Bussing, R., Forness, S. R., & Benjamin, B. (1997). Sheltered homeless children: Their eligibility and unmet need for special education evaluations. *American Journal of Public Health, 87*(2), 236-240.

CRAIG CENTRIE

CHAPTER 3

From Mandalay to Nickel City: Exploring the Changing Identities and Struggles of Karen Burmese Youth

INTRODUCTION

After independence from British colonialism in 1948, Burma, once part of the Raj system and one of Southeast Asia's largest countries, became engaged in one of the longest civil wars in the region's history. A democratic republic from 1948 to 1962, Burma experiencing the turmoil of nation state building in a post colonial world was unable successfully to incorporate its ethnically, linguistically, and religiously diverse population into one national identity, forcing hundreds of thousands of ethnic Burmese into refugee camps throughout Southeast Asia. Historically, British interest in the region was centered on its strategic position between the British ports of Calcutta and Singapore and the economic importance of Burma's extensive teak forests (Harvey, 2000). Britain was also concerned that the last independent ruling king of Myanmar, Thibaw, favored economic relations with France furthering their determination to annex Burma into the Raj. Burmese territories were annexed separately in various stages of imperialism following aggressive colonial wars. Also, the long term British colonial administration resulted in systemic destruction of villages and the exiling of large communities. The subsequent successful subjugation of the territories appears to have created a precedent followed by the later independent and oppressive Burmese government. The separate administration and ethnic favoritism in these territories may contribute to contemporary Burmese difficulties in state integration of its diverse populations.

In response to the military coup of 1962, a police state was established which increased state sponsored brutality and effectively closed Burma off from the rest of the world, renaming itself as Myanmar. From 1962 to the present, the military government of Burma has experienced many popular challenges to its legitimacy with continuing flight of its population as refuges to neighboring countries (Charney, 2009). In 2008 the ruling party promised a constitutional referendum in 2010 to a "disciplined flourishing" democracy. The Union Solidarity and Development Party won over 70% of the election results with allegations of wide spread voter fraud and increased opposition from pro democratic factions. Increased protests threatened civil war. The move to a Constitutional Referendum was also a direct result of cyclone Nargis which has been described as Burma's most devastating national disaster. With over 10 billion dollars in damages and

J. Hall (ed.), Children's Human Rights and Public Schooling in the United States, 45–69.

over 1million displaced and homeless, Burma's secretive government hindered the distribution of medical and food supplies creating additional protests and thousands more fleeing to refugee camps across the border. The government of Myanmar has been responsible for state sponsored terrorism of its ethic populations in order to curb movements for semi-autonomous ethnic zones responsible for the preservation of language and culture, as well as direct representation in government. The Karen language and ethnic group of South and Southeast Burma has been especially targeted for ethnic cleansing. Many have escaped to refugee camps in neighboring Thailand (Marshall, 2011).

On the other side of the world, since 2005, "Nickel City," a northern postindustrial metropolis in the US, has become home to over 8,000 Burmese refugees. This city has become the unofficial state capital for refugee resettlement, taking in more than 30% of the state's refugee population and the majority of Burmese refugees resettled in the state. Unofficial population tracking by local resettlement agencies suggests the actual number of Burmese refugees is closer to 12,000 as a result of child birth and undocumented internal migration. This makes Nickel City's Burmese population one of the largest in the US.

The purpose of this chapter is to explore the acculturative experiences and perceptions of Burmese refugees, particularly the youth, living in Nickel City, and to contribute to the extremely sparse and limited literature on Burmese refugee youth in general. My intention is to shed light on the lived experiences of young refugees who struggle to negotiate identities and navigate complex social institutions while adjusting to their new lives. In this chapter I argue that the transnational experiences, resettlement in socially and economically marginalized communities, and placement in a public school system ill prepared to manage their needs, is relegating the Karen youth to a future of failure. In addition, the inter-ethnic conflicts and racially charged experiences of the Karen youth are creating an early oppositional identity to particular minority groups in the US. In many instances their experiences have been harsh and very contradictory to the myths refugees typically hold of the US. In the words of one narrator: "I believe America truly understands the idea of individual liberty but doesn't really understand justice for all."

A NOTE ON METHODOLOGY

Data presented in this chapter are from field work conducted in the fall of 2011 and spring 2012 in which I explore the acculturative experiences and perceptions of several recent refugee groups, including Karen Burmese, in Nickel City. Specifically the data presented explore how Karen Burmese youth begin to negotiate their identities. Four prominent refugee non-governmental resettlement organizations were contacted whose staff provided the most recent refugee and immigrant data for the Nickel City community since the 2010 census. These agencies also provided general information on the neighborhoods which contain the largest clustering of Burmese refugees in the city.

I began this research by driving and walking through recent immigrant and refugee neighborhoods familiarizing myself with the general atmosphere of the communities. I spent time shopping in neighborhood stores and eating when possible in the recent ethnic restaurants that have rather suddenly appeared to serve the needs of the newly arrived refugee and immigrant populations. After meetings with agency staff and the establishment of trust, agency personnel introduced me to Burmese youth and their families who then later introduced me to others in their community. Together the field observations as well as the interviews have provided a broad understanding of the acculturative experiences and perceptions of recently arrived Karen people in the Nickel City region (Creswell, 2009).

Data for this chapter include field observations from Karen Burmese neighborhoods conducted intermittently over 8 months, as well as informal interviews of 7 agency staff, 15 Karen Burmese youth (ages 18 to 25), 2 Karen families, and 3 members of the Karen Burmese community that have been identified by resettlement personnel as emerging leaders. Three public school teachers who teach Karen students were also interviewed. Both resettlement agency personnel and teachers provided initial contacts for current students or former students to interview for their experiences and perceptions. All interviews were conducted in English, and in the homes of students, in the classrooms of teachers, and in the offices of resettlement agency administrators. Pseudonyms are used throughout this analysis (Creswell, 2009).

The Karen Burmese community I discuss in this research is located in the lower west side of Nickel City. The local Burmese population is heterogeneous with 3 prominent ethnicities represented, including the Karen, Chin, and Karenni, with the Karen the largest. The Karen more commonly define themselves in terms of religion – specifically, Christian, Buddhist, or Muslim. They make little differentiation between Roman Catholics and other Protestant groups that comprise the Christian community. The majority of Burmese interviewed report intergenerational Christian working class or agricultural backgrounds in Burmese villages, but all spent the majority of their lives living in refugee camps in Thailand. In fact, some never lived in Burma, spending their entire childhood in a Thai refugee camp. All 15 Burmese youth interviewed spent 7 years or less in the US. At no time during my data collection did any interviewee refer to Burma as Myanmar.

For this researched I engaged the assistance of Law Eh Soe, a prominent member of the Burmese community. He is additionally a photographer and activist in Burma. Mr. Soe is well known and respected by the Karen Refugee community and has assisted and guided me through the various language and cultural differences I encountered throughout my research. Though not Asian, I am familiar with the experiences of immigrants as a first generation immigrant myself who identifies as an Antillian from the French speaking West Indies. Throughout my life I have identified with the local Latino community and am the director and curator of the region's only Latino visual arts organization. I have lived in marginal communities my entire life though admittedly now continue to do so by choice. Like my narrators I am personally familiar with the lack of city services, and the problems encountered by my friends and neighbors who struggle to navigate often complex and sometimes contradictory social institutions. I am familiar with the graying meats, redistributed produce, and nearly expired products in my neighborhood grocery store. However, I now do so by choice whereas the narrators of Karen Burmese community explored here have little to none (Creswell, 2009).

Nickel City, a once important transportation center and urban hub connects major Atlantic cities with the mid-west through train and water routes. At the beginning of the 20th century, Nickel City was poised to be one of the most important, influential, and perhaps richest cities in the US with its population peaking in the fifties at nearly 600,000. The end of the 1950s began a gradual decline as a result of its manufacturing and industrial sector decimated by the transfer of capital to overseas industry in search of cheaper means of production. White flight to the suburbs, race riots, and forced busing of school children to satisfy federal desegregation laws of the 1960s led to the steady drain of middle class families out to other areas. The shift from rail and sea transportation to transcontinental trucking as a means to transport goods, and an unsuccessful urban renewal plan, further left Nickel City with an overwhelmingly poor inner city (Centrie, 2004). A greatly reduced tax base, marginalized poverty stricken population, and the continuing exodus of the middle class left behind emptied decaying neighborhoods with a greatly decreased population of 261,310 as of the 2010 US Census.

Today Nickel City is listed as one of the top 10 poorest cities in the county with a notably segregated population. The estimated per capita income in 2009 is $20,000 with a mean household income of $29,285, up from $24,516 in 2000. The city's total combined non-white and relatively poor population slightly exceeds half of its total population. When examined by race and ethnicity Nickel City's income disparity between cultures is described by one regional think tank as a chasm with African Americans earning $1 to every $2 earned by a white resident. The same report goes on to say:

> (Nickel City's) poverty is highly segregated and racialized. (The greater Nickel City Region) is now the fifth most racially segregated large metro in the nation; (Nickel City) is 38.6% African-American; the county is only 3.5% African-American; in the metro area, 81.4% of African-Americans and 58.9% of Hispanics live in high poverty neighborhoods, compared with 10.7% of whites; as of 2005, the poverty rate in the metro area for African-Americans was 32.3%, for Hispanics 29.8%, and for whites 8.7%.; in the city of (Nickel City), of the 18,454 foreign born people, 34.05% are living in poverty. In the metro area, of the 65,724 foreign born people, 24.97% are living in poverty with African Americans earning less than half of whites in the city.

However, Nickel City's leaders contend that the city is poised for a renaissance with the creation of a state of the art hospital sector, expansion of its higher education sector, and scientific and established artistic communities. The city's downtown is being revitalized by a young and educated middle and upper middle class population wanting to live closer to employment with access to its prominent cultural assets and increasingly attractive harbor development.

An influx of immigrants and refugees from around the world too has dramatically increased since 2000. These families are reinvigorating devastated neighborhoods on both the east and west sides with businesses to support their communities' needs and home ownership of its neglected late 19th and early 20th century housing stock. A recent news article in the City's only remaining paper reported that the Burmese community, one of the nation's largest, now composes 1% of the city's total population. Karen Burmese, along with other recent refugees and immigrants from around the world have become a significant presence in the region. However, not all refugees and their resettlement experiences are the same. Changes in the immigrant and refugee experience from past models is affected by transnationalism, the cultural capital differing groups bring, as well as the receptivity of their hosts, transnational encounters, and even the community in which they are placed.

I am introducing here the notion of social class as a significant indicator by which people interact and experience the world around them and indeed the refugee experience itself. Class as a framework to understand the perceptions, interactions with social institutions, and life outcomes, to a certain degree always been an area of investigation in the identity production literature (e.g. Brantlinger, 2003; Burawoy, Chang, & Fei-yu Hsieh, 2010; Lareau, 2003; Masey & Denton, 1993; Patillo-McCoy, 2000; Reay, Crozier, & James 2011; Torres, 2009). As argued by Weis (2012), class has gained importance in two ways. First there is the greater recognition of class as a key signifier of positionality (Lareau, 2003; Reay et al., 2011; Vincent & Ball 2006). It is as Weis (2012) argues "to be additionally understood as the practices of living – and better understood, perhaps as "the social and psychic practices through which ordinary people live, survive and cope" (Walkerdine et al., 2001, p. 27).

Over the past decade there is increasing evidence that social inequalities are widening not just on a national level but on an international level as well (Aron-Dine & Shapiro, 2006; Chauvel, 2010; Gilbert, 2003; Piketty & Saez, 2003, 2006). The middle class once an indicator of economic well being is growing smaller while poverty increases and the opportunities for upward social mobility decrease (Kloby, 2004.) Further, as argued by Weis and Dolby (2012), economic inequalities are increasing both within nations as well as between nations (Cheval, 2010; Gilbert, 2003; Piketty & Saez, 2003, 2006; Sherman & Aron-Dine, 2007). As refugees, some living their entire lives within the artificial confines of refugee camps, many find the common practices of their daily lives indefinitely suspended, often waiting for 10 years or longer to resume their lives. For many of the Karen, their entire lives from infancy to young adulthood has passed without the traditional social institutions to support socio-economic mobility.

Globalization and changes in migration patterns have altered the way in which everyone experiences contemporary society. Massive changes in communication, media, remediation, and accessible global transportation have altered the refugee experience as well, particularly as to how groups adapt to their host county. Research has demonstrated in a global context that refugees and immigrants retain strong social ties to their home countries while adapting to their host country. Burmese Karen have expressed in interviews that they have had limited or no direct communication with family or friends in their homeland. They evidence a powerful desire to return home and aid in the reconstruction of the country.

Like the interviews have suggested, recent scholarship has moved to deterritorialize place and space with an understanding that refugee experiences have become multi layered, and perhaps more importantly, ones which transcend national boundaries (Crespo-Sancho, 2012) reflecting the ways in which individuals and groups adapt and form identities. As presented here, social class is viewed as a collection of cultural resources which guide individuals, families, and even communities to interact with society along specific lines. This perspective highlights the ways in which non-material goods or resources such as ways of behaving, community bonds, and individual and collective perceptions allow or disallow access into mainstream society and transformation of such into cultural capital (Bourdieu, 1977). Capital in this sense is not strictly economic but rather attributes, possessions, and personal qualities that are exchangeable for goods, services, or even esteem which exist in many forms – symbolic, social, linguistic, and economic (DiMaggio, 1979.) In US society ethnicity, race, or national background is important and must be considered as in the case presented here. The Karen refugees are beginning a process of social critique as they interact with middle class Nickel City communities and multiple ethnicities within their own neighborhoods which represent working class and underclass groups.

In this study all 15 Karen youth describe backgrounds in which they lived in Thai refugee camps before being resettled in the US. Eight youth have never lived in Burma. Respondents were not asked to recount their experiences in Burma which necessitated their flight or their experiences in the camps in order not to re-traumatize them. However 7 individuals volunteered their general experiences while describing resettlement here in this country. All Karen youth, community members, and families narrated oppressive conditions in Thai camps with limited access to education, health care, or day to day interactions with traditional social institutions. Instead refugee camp life was expected to be a temporary and somewhat artificial life with an anticipated ending with a return to their homeland or acceptance into a host country.

Since 1984 Karen Burmese have fled oppressive conditions in Burma and sought asylum in Thailand. In their study of life in Thai refugee camps, Oh and van der Stouwe (2008) report that for Karen refugees it is extremely difficult to control the development of their societies and participation in social life in these camps:

> Officially, refugees do not have access to services provided outside the camps, nor are they permitted to leave the camps to earn an income. International nongovernmental organizations [NGOs] provide most basic and capacity-building services in the areas of food, shelter, health, education, and community services. Despite these contributions and the good intentions of

> the NGOs, the protracted refugee situation and the restrictions on refugee movement have created a deadlock situation in which it is extremely difficult for the refugees to control the development of their own society.
>
> In the six camps studied, the vast majority of camp residents share rural roots: 91.8% of the refugees come from small villages in Burma, and only 6.5% lived in towns or cities before living in camp. Since it is not possible for the refugees to work outside the camps, their monthly incomes are low, with 69.3% of the camp population earning between 0 and 100 baht (about $2.85) per month (Oh et al., 2006). These low incomes are supplemented, however, by the free food, shelter, health care, and education provided to the refugees by NGOs.

Descriptions of life in the camps were described by participants as meager. While basic needs were provided for, there was little possibility for creating a life which resembled normal for anyone. As described by one narrator, "You only live from day to day. Each day you hope that this day is the day you can find a host country that will accept you and you can begin your life."

MAKING A NEW LIFE

The Karen Burmese like other refugees apply for asylum to the host country of their choice. Deciding on a host country is often based on several factors such as the likelihood of a quick acceptance, where other members of their family have been accepted, and whether there is a large community of Karen Burmese already established. The minimum waiting period is two years, with many individuals waiting much longer periods of time, sometimes as long as 10 years. Refugees accepted by the US become sponsored by a federally-funded agency that has the responsibility of working with that individual or family during the resettlement process.

For more than 30 years, the US federal government has attempted to place refugees across the country as not to put too much burden on several states such as Florida or California as has been the case in the past. It is not unusual for refugees to experience secondary internal migration to locations they believe to be more acceptable. Their decision to migrate is often based on climate or to place themselves in larger established communities of the same ethnic group (Centrie, 2004). New groups of refugees such as the Karen, however, more often remain in the location of original settlement compared to Vietnamese or Laotian refugees of past waves. During interviews with resettlement directors I asked why that was the case and why was Nickel City home to such a large community of Karen Burmese:

> Ms. Johnson: Over the past 20 years various areas of the country have experienced considerable loss of population to warmer climates and to areas where jobs are more plentiful. This has certainly been the case here in (Nickel City). At some point the state realized to send newly arrived refugees to big cities such as New York City was really setting them up

for failure. It's just harder to live in these places and really hard if you are coming from a (refugee) camp where you have been for 5 or 10 years. There is plenty of cheap and available housing here, and it's a less complicated place to live, less expensive overall. You can get more bang for your dollar. The Karen Burmese have created a large community here. In general, I think they find the area more accepting and rather easy to manage.

Mr. Addison, from another resettlement organization, had this comment when asked why they have placed so many refugees on the west side:

> We have to look at cost of living as a major factor. The far west side and to some extent the east side are the less expensive places to live. And more importantly, we are trying to create a critical mass. It's easier for the refugees because they have other friends and family they can rely on and it's much easier for us (resettlement agencies) to deliver services.

Much of the comments by resettlement agency directors were very positive. It appeared over the several decades of refugee resettlement, changes such as federal funding and finding appropriate locations to live for refugees, particularly the Karen Burmese, was regarded as a success. Ms. France, the director of a "post resettlement agency" agreed with the comments of her colleagues from other agencies in regard to federal funding and general approaches to initial resettlement:

> Placing refugees in urban and sometimes rural areas can work well for both the refugees and the communities they settle in. In cities like (Nickel City) where there has been a major decline in population, refugees revitalize neighborhoods that are in decline and they (refugees) make big contributions to the regional economies because they're setting up ethnic businesses to serve their communities like markets for familiar food, or even a laundromat where people from the refugee communities can go to wash clothes if they don't own a washer or dryer. Cities like Utica and Rome were devastated by the loss of businesses and industry and the population decline. But these cities are rebounding and it's because of the influx of refugees and other immigrants to these communities. For a long time they (Utica and Rome) were the state's choice for resettlement but now we are replacing them as the preferred place for resettlement. We now have the largest concentration of refugees outside of New York City.
>
> CC: Can you explain the difference between a post resettlement agency and a resettlement agency? I've not ever heard this term before.
>
> Ms. France: Well, a post resettlement agency is a place where refugees and recent immigrants can go for assistance after six months. Resettlement agencies only work with clients for the first six months after they arrive. I worked for (Refugee Assistance) for several years and I

realized that most of the problems, the big problems refugees experience occur after six months. So I proposed this post resettlement agency to (Resettlement Care) and they found it to be a great idea.

CC: Can you tell me what kind of problems you are talking about?

Ms. France: Well, the resettlement agencies only help with refugees' initial resettlement problems like general orientation, finding housing, getting them into the county system etc. but after six months and once they are placed they don't have anything more to do with them. They aren't funded to do more. And most of the major problems with schools, medical attention, and translation problems, or problems with landlords don't come up until after they have been placed.

Much of what the agency directors stated sounded very hopeful and was supported by many articles written in local newspapers. Nickel City is on the verge of a renaissance and some of its recent successes were in part due to the new life refugees were bringing to socially and economically disadvantaged neighborhoods. Reporters were also positively commenting on how cosmopolitan the region was becoming, and how the influx of refugees and immigrants was beginning to reverse the decreasing population trends in the national census. It all appeared very positive for both the refugees and the region. The newspaper reporters of course are interviewing agency directors. However, Ms. France illustrates how the resettlement system is in fact flawed. Government funded resettlement agencies are not funded to assist refugees beyond six months. At the conclusion of six months, clients are listed as successfully resettled, and follow up reports claim major successes allowing for continued agency funding. Very little is known about the general health or psychological well being of refugees, or as resettlement professionals explain, the long-term quality of their housing.

Resettlement agencies try to find appropriate housing before the refugees arrive. If that is not possible, they are placed in temporary housing. Refugees are also placed in orientation classes which cover the basics of living in their new location. Such an orientation may include basic language classes in English, becoming acquainted with the city and neighborhood, learning to take the bus or subway, familiarizing the refugee with the monetary system, understanding the basic rules of crossing the street, learning to shop at a supermarket etc. One agency director comments she has been involved in refugee assistance for over 10 years and that resettlement has improved considerably:

CC: Tell about the resettlement process. You comment that it has improved, can you explain how.

Ms. Johnson: Before 2005 each refugee was provided $400.00 per person from the federal government. That amount stayed the same for a long time. I don't even know how far back that goes. That is for everything – housing, furniture, dishes, pots and pans, sheets, towels – everything.

> Since 2005 the federal appropriation is $1,800 per person which is making everything much easier. So if you have a family of 4 we now have $7,200 to get them started. You know, things have become so much more expensive. Even on the west side where we place most of our clients. You know, the west side was once a very inexpensive place to live. But now, even on the west side things have become so much more expensive. Even really bad apartments begin at $500 and go up from there.

The experiences of resettlement can create major anxieties and other barriers to accessing services. Language issues, a lack of understanding of procedures in medical establishments, and lack of finances can impede receiving medical or dental services. Post resettlement may also include housing problems, education related issues, employment concerns, and cultural clashes with existing ethnic groups in communities in which refugees are resettled. Problems such as these are commented on by case workers in resettlement agencies. Ms. Lipsky, working in housing, remarks:

> Many of the resettlement agency executive directors are not in touch with the day to day realities of resettlement. They are not in the trenches. They are mostly concerned with statistics and financing of the agencies. For example, there have been lots of problems with housing. There really isn't enough money for agency staff to investigate the condition of housing in all cases or there is an agency need to get refugees like the Karen in housing quickly. There are several cases I am aware of where Karen refugees were placed in apartments were there was no water for extended periods of time or the heating systems were not working properly.
>
> In one case, this Karen family lived next door to another Karen family who helped them. They had to go to their neighbors to take showers, get water for cooking and cleaning. It was really a horrendous situation. On my own time I helped them search for an adequate apartment because they were already documented as resettled and technically the agency has nothing more to do with them after six months. It was so heartbreaking though.

Understanding the plight of these Karen Burmese refugees can be more difficult than other refugee groups. As agency field representatives have commented and much of my field experiences mirror, the Karen are far less likely than other groups to complain, making corrections more difficult for the agencies. When asked why Karen refuges are less likely to complain, various resettlement agency personnel responded that it simply was cultural. No complaining or little complaining in fact is similar to the Vietnamese studied earlier (Centrie, 2004.) When asked about this particular point, Mr. Soung, a Karen Burmese community leader remarked: "Yes, that, true; we are not likely to complain. That is part of Burmese culture." In one field session to collect data, I passed by the home of a Karen family I had meet several weeks before. Sung, one of the Karen youth I interviewed saw me and invited me in for tea with her family. I remembered they lived elsewhere and casually asked:

> CC: Sung, you and your family have moved. Weren't you living on Albany Street not too long ago?
>
> Sung: Yes, we lived on Albany Street. But the house, it was not so good.
>
> CC: Oh, what happened? I thought everyone liked it there.
>
> Sung: Yes we did like the street. We had (a) lot of friends there. But it was kind of, you know, difficult. Many of the windows didn't close so it was very cold in winter and everyone was getting sick. My mother and her friend, too, they were cleaning and they looked under the rug and found much black mold. Then we started to look more around and find so much more of this black mold behind the wood on the walls (paneling). And my father said he thinks maybe it's because of this that we are always so sick. And then one day we don't have hot water but the landlord, he doesn't want to fix this. So, with the help of our friends, we looked for a new place to live and we found this one and we moved.

Nearly every interview contained some comment about poor housing or problems with landlords who would not repair broken or malfunctioning mechanicals. The housing in this part of the city like much of Nickel City is old, often predating the turn of the previous century. Unlike more affluent neighborhoods that boast restored Victorian Queen Ann housing, the lower west side is mostly composed of small worker style cottages, many of which are owned by absentee landlords who purchased the properties for little money, sometimes at city auctions, and who make minimal repairs.

Before Nickel City experienced large increases in its immigrant and refugee populations, the lower west side was first home to a tight knit Italian community and later in the seventies, replaced by poor Latinos/a and African-Americans who also had less agency to articulate demands for better housing. The lower west side is also a community with limited city services, few if any repairs to the city's infrastructure (such as sidewalks and sewers), few supermarkets and health clinics, along with limited public transportation, making the area somewhat isolated. The poverty rates moreover are as high as 72%. In this sense, the total impact of the neighborhood itself has a profound effect on all aspects of quality of life, and acts as a barrier to good employment, access to education, and other institutions that facilitate personal and group success. Since 1990 there is a growing body of literature (e.g. Ainsworth, 2002; Burton Price-Spratlen & Beal Spensor, 1997; Leventhal & Brooks-Gunn, 2003) which posits that the neighborhood and community in which children live has a large impact on life outcomes. Likewise, the limited resources of the community and concentration of poverty also creates tensions between groups in the lower west side. A prominent theme arising from the data are racial and ethnic conflicts which occur with some regularity.

COMMUNITY CONFLICT

The lower west side is often referenced as the melting pot of the city. It is a community which is known regionally for its diversity as well as high concentrations of poverty. More recently it is known as one of the more dangerous communities of the city, and one which is known for its youth gangs. As previously stated, the lower west side was once an Italian community which became home to a diverse Latino/a population with a large Puerto Rican majority. More recently, a large and growing African American population has resided here. African Americans, traditionally, since the mid-1900s, have lived on the city's east side. They have however migrated to the lower west side in hopes of accessing better housing and city services. Over the last 30 years most of the Italians have left for the northern communities of the city or, if they have become very successful, to the suburbs. Along with the Italian community, many businesses have left, homes were sold to absentee landlords, and diminishing city funds have left this community as a low priority while the city's revitalization efforts have targeted other areas. The very problems African American families have tried to escape on the east side have expressed on the west side.

Resettlement agencies chose the west side for many reasons such as lower rents and creating a critical mass, and anticipated that the preexisting diversity of the lower west side would make acceptance of refugees and immigrants easier. However, every Karen participant commented on inter ethnic conflicts without being questioned or prompted to do so, making racial or ethnic conflict one of the most significant concerns. When asked how she and her family like Nickel City and their neighborhood, Linn, a 19 year old Karen female, describes:

> Linn: We love Nickel City and are so grateful for the opportunity to start our lives over. Maybe now we have a future. We didn't really have a future before. But sometimes it can be little difficult here.
>
> CC: Can you tell me a little more about why it's difficult here?
>
> Linn: Sometimes when we are walking to the store or going to school … people call us names and say really bad things to us. Sometimes they tell us why we don't (you) go home. You know why we come to their (neighborhood) hood. At first I don't know what "hood" mean. Now I know, they [Puerto Ricans and African Americans] want to know why we come to their neighborhood. Most of the time I don't answer; but sometime I say we have a right to be here too. America is for all (every) body. Not just for them. Once these girls got very angry and came after us. I thought they would hit us or hurt us, so me and my brothers and sisters, we ran, ran away. This happen a lot and we are kind of, you know, scared.

A young 20 year old Karen male who calls himself Rick made this comment:

> Rick: Me and my friends, sometimes when we walk around, the other guys in the neighborhood they want to fight with us. We only walking and someone will hit us.
>
> CC: Who hits you Rick?
>
> Rick: If we go to 18th Street it could be black guys, if we walk to West River Street it's, maybe some Puerto Rican guys. Sometimes I don't know who they are.
>
> CC: Why do you think they do this?
>
> Rick: I don't know. They just don't like us. Sometime they think we are Chinese. I tell them, we are not Chinese. We are Burmese, Karen Burmese people. One guy he say, "I don't give a damn what you are mother fucker, you a chink as far as I know."

In one narration, Soo, a 21year old Karen woman explains:

> Soo: Poor Mr. Un, he our neighbor. He has six children. He walk to the Burmese food store and when he come out these men they just start beating him. He came home and his face was all bloody. They really hurt him bad and now, Mr. Soo, he is afraid to go out at night.

Depictions of harassment and general antagonism are prevalent throughout the Karen youth narratives. In one instance, while sitting in my car and packing up my notes and other materials, I witnessed a scene which I immediately wrote up as data. Four Karen youth – two presumably older teens I did not know and two younger children – were walking down Johnson Street, the main business street of this west side community. As they passed a corner grocery store they had to walk by a group of 5 young Latino looking youth:

> Latino male: Hey, you got a cigarette? (no response)
>
> Latino male: Hey, I'm talking to you! (no response). (The Latino male now starts walking after the group of Karen and throws an empty can he was drinking hitting the one Karen male in his back.)
>
> Karen male: Don't throw (anything at) me!
>
> The group of Latino males all start laughing.
>
> Latino male: Shut the fuck up you stupid fucker! Who you think you are? You're just a fuckin' Asian nigger.
>
> Karen male: Says something to the other Karen and they now just walk faster away from the scene.

This was not the only time I witnessed street antagonism between Karen youth and other US minority ethnic groups. Throughout nearly a year of data collection I saw five incidents between Karen youth and other youth groups on the west side. Not all confrontations end with the Karen youth acting in a passive manner. Thien, a 22 year old Karen male narrated the following story which previously had been told to me by one of the education directors of a resettlement agency:

> Thien: We, my three friends and I, we were students at "Neighborhood High School." Every day we went to school together and walk home together after school. We ate lunch together and we are good friends. For months, this gang of Latin guys would fight with us after school. It was getting pretty bad, you know. So I began to take a heavy piece of wood with me. I hid it behind some bushes on the school grounds before we went in and get it when we were leaving for protection.
>
> CC: Why do you feel it was necessary to take such a big piece of wood with you?
>
> Thien: These guys, they (were) kind of big and one of them I know was carry(ing) a knife. They were always fighting with us. One time there were about 10 of them and they surround(ed) us. I took this piece of wood and really hit this guy. I think I got him good. Just at that time a teacher was coming out and all of us, (the Burmese) were suspended.
>
> CC: Didn't anything happen to the other group of guys?
>
> Thien: No, nothing. The mother of one of the guys came to school the next day and complained about us but we already were suspended.

The school system chose not to investigate the incident more thoroughly. Rather one incident witnessed by one teacher was evaluated as a solitary event removed from its larger context. I was concerned about this particular narration and was aware that Thien very well may have provided me an especially biased version. However, this particular incident was retold by 2 teachers and 3 resettlement education counselors verifying Thien's version of the incident. As Thien explained, the antagonism between him and his three friends and a group of Latino youths had been on-going since the beginning of the year or for 7 months. Thien later detailed that although he and his Karen friends had remarked on this problem to various school personnel, nothing had been done to alleviate the problem. Since Thien was "caught" being aggressive, it was the Karen group that was punished.

Burmese families living in Nickel City are not exclusively located on the lower west side. A growing community is also established in the city's Littlerock district. In this community poor and working class ethnic whites are the predominant population. When asking several Karen youth who live in this community to share their experiences of living in Nickel City, the responses were somewhat different. Law a 21 year old Karen Youth comments:

> Law: Speaking for myself, I like living here in Littlerock. I like it more than where some of my friends live on the lower west side.
>
> CC: Tell me why if you can.
>
> Law: It's nicer, cleaner, I like the people more. It always seems like there are a lot of problems in the other neighborhood. My friends are always having to get into fights. It seems dangerous or something.
>
> CC: Law, I thought you mentioned earlier that you and some of your friends here in Littlerock were experiencing problems with some of the neighborhood kids?
>
> Law: Yes, yes that's true we are, but it's not as bad as over on the west side. I don't know, I just like it better here.

Ling, a 19 year old Karen asserts similarly.

> CC: How do you feel about living in Nickel City?
>
> Ling: My family is happy to be here because we have friends and family here. My father's mother, my grandmother, is here and I have aunts and uncles from both sides of my family here, cousins too.
>
> CC: That is really great that it was possible to unite families. Do they also live close by in Littlerock?
>
> Ling: No, we have to drive there or take the bus. They live on the west side. I wish they lived here.
>
> CC: So that it would be easier to visit with them and hang out with your cousins?
>
> Ling: Well, yes, and also because I don't really like the lower west side, not as much as here in Littlerock.
>
> CC: Tell me why.
>
> Ling: To be honest, I think it's really dangerous over there. There are so many, you know, black people that live there and they always give all the Burmese lots of problems.

The prevalent inter ethnic tensions on the lower west side are beginning to create identity shifts within Karen youth. On one occasion a Karen mother whom I became familiar stopped me on the street and asked me about numbers her 12 year old son and 13 year old Karen neighbor came home with tattooed on their arms. Initially I stated I did not know what the numbers meant. But over the next few weeks I began to see these numbers spray painted on buildings. I started to ask questions from people in the community and with resettlement counselors, and found this to be a well known youth gang operating on the west side of Nickel City and in other cities across the US. Of particular concern are the ages of the children. Also of concern is the lack of information Karen adults have about such realities and how to prevent their children from being recruited.

Similar to Cambodians, Laotians, and Vietnamese of the 1990s and early 2000s (Centrie 2004; Hein, 1995), the Karen Burmese are experiencing racism and interracial conflict in their quest to become a part of US society. Further complicating an understanding of Southeast Asians is the dual image of model minorities on the one hand and images of low achievers, high school drop outs, and youth gangs on the other (Lee & Ngo, 2007). What appears clear is that the location in which refugees are settled determines various perceptions and outcomes. Southeast Asian immigrants and refugees settled in predominantly middle class white communities frequently experience racism as a result of the black/white binary construction of race historically inherent in the US (Centrie, 2004). However, in Nickel City, with a majority of non-whites and located in a poor diverse neighborhood, an understanding of Karen experiences becomes more complex.

I have come to understand inter ethnic and interracial conflicts, particularly as it pertains to poor and minority communities in the US, to be a product of racial and ethnic hierarchy. As a result of colonization, interracial/inter ethnic conflicts occur within the same nation, sometimes as a strategy of the colonizer and sometimes as a result of economic marginalization as groups search for recognition and parity with the dominant culture (Fanon, 1952). While the Karen are not experiencing anything unique in terms of intergroup politics in Nickel City, the fact they are being targeted by two groups, African Americans and Latinos/a, suggest turf wars of domination in the community and the expectation that everyone find their place in the hierarchy. Despite having similar problems in the predominantly white Littlerock district of Nickel City, several Karen youth who live there prefer it to the lower west side.

Throughout Karen youth's narrations are the uses of the terms "them" and "we." This suggests Karen youth are beginning to formulate a racialized critique of US society. In their work exploring race, Fine and Weis (1998) find groups look to identify the "other" as a means to define themselves. McLure (2003) contends the most common way in which people create a self is through binary constructions of opposition in the form of "us" versus "them." Within this framework there is the understanding that difference of the constructed other is one which hierarchal difference is implied. Within the context of the transnational, the additional "space" created by a transnational experience allows for a dual reference framework based on previous experiences. In the case of the Karen they have a collective memory of interethnic conflict in Burma as well as similar experiences in refugee camps in Thailand.

Stacey Lee commenting on race dynamics in the US (2005) posits "white" as viewed as the normative standard of "good" while Blacks and Latinos/a become the "bad" and undesirable "other." In the narratives presented here, Karen youth have identified white people as a preferred standard to emulate for personal and group success despite experiencing similar ethnic tensions. When discussing the communities in which they live, various Karen youth suggested they would most prefer to live in the northern part of the city among its predominantly white communities. They believe they would not have as difficult of a time there where the "neighborhoods are cleaner and seem safer, and where (they) don't think they would have such big problems." Although there are few differences between the lower west side and the Littlerock district of the city, the Karen youth would also prefer to live there. The major difference is the population composition which is more diverse on the lower west side and primarily poor and working class whites in Littlerock.

A BETTER FUTURE

Nevertheless, a majority of Karen youth comment they believe their futures are brighter living in the US because they have access to education – something that was nearly entirely lacking in the refugee camps. In the interviews, getting an education was always explained as having central importance among Karen youth leaders and parents. Most of the Karen youth I interviewed, 12 of the total 15, remarked going to school was the road to a solid future and a major advantage of coming to the states. All of the Burmese youth I interviewed spent at least 5 years in Thai refugee camps and most spent 10 years or longer as they and their families waited for a host country assignment.

In Burma, children's education was often disrupted by civil war and in the refugee camps education is often spotty at best. In the case of the Karen, education that is available was rudimentary. In addition, camp members are not allowed to manage their own schools, teach their language, nor teach a curriculum of Burmese history that does not conform to the Burmese government sanctioned version. Compared to their Thai peers, refugees are generally disadvantaged in the depth and quality of education (Oh & van der Stouwe, 2008). As all Karen parents and students describe in the interviews, they came to the US with no documentation of any schooling or what they may have learned.

All of the Karen youth I interviewed stated they are or have been enrolled in the Nickel City public school system. Everyone arrived with English language skills that were limited to the necessary phrases they learned in their orientation sessions sponsored by the resettlement agency. The youth who attended school in the US or are still in school have acquired a better command of English. However, English is almost exclusively limited to use when interacting with US institutions such as school while the Karen language is always spoken at home and within the community. Many of the Karen remarked that communication with non-Karen people is almost non-existent.

With no documentation, the school system places children in age appropriate classrooms rather than at skill level. Ms. Rocco, a public school teacher in one of the neighborhood schools that many west side Karen youth attend comments:

> Ms. Rocco: The Karen come with no papers, no documentation, no anything which gives an indication of what kind of education they may have had. Instead of testing, the public schools place them in a classrooms levels they would be in if they had gone through the system.
>
> CC: How is that possible?
>
> Ms. Rocco: On the one hand, what is the school system as it is configured supposed to do? Let's say that a student comes with little or no English has no documentation and is 15 years old. They are placed in 10th grade. And let's say this student has the equivalent of a second grade education. They can't be placed in 3rd grade. Everyone else would be around 8 years old.
>
> CC: How then do they make this work up?
>
> Ms. Rocco: They don't. They have to get up to speed or they don't. Based on their ages, many of them just get passed to the next level.

In an interview with a resettlement education coordinator, Ms. Weinstein states: "The Nickel City school system is simply not prepared to handle the needs of refugee children. As a matter of fact, I would say that the school system sets them up for failure." The perception that the schools are not prepared to accommodate the needs of refugee children was uniform in all of the narrations of school teachers and education coordinators of the resettlement agencies. Because of language problems, their inability to keep up with heavily language based courses (such as English, history, and social studies), many of the older Karen youth simply drop out of school. Helen, a Karen youth from the Karen Baptist community explains:

> Helen: Yes, I am glad to go to school. I want to be a fireman or a police officer when I grow up. I do really good in math and my science classes but I don't do so well in English and history.
>
> CC: I'm glad to hear you like school. Why do you say you don't do so good in English and history?
>
> Helen: I don't understand what the teacher is say most times.
>
> CC: How are your grades?
>
> Helen: I get A's in all my math and science classes but mmmmmm I think I don't do so well in the other things. I get C's and sometimes a D.

Karen youth often commented that language based courses were the most difficult and were discouraging them from continuing their education. However there were differences with younger children and teenagers. All education coordinators agreed that for the younger children, those in grammar school are in a much better position to handle the changes then older teens:

> Ms. Weinstein: Education for refugee children is not in a good state of affairs generally, but it's in a particularly bad state for the older children, the teenagers.
>
> CC: Explain to me why that is?
>
> Ms. Weinstein: the younger grammar school children, they can adjust better. A child in second grade, third grade, they are going to quickly adjust to the language, cultural changes in the school, and just the education system itself. But the older teenagers, they are really getting it bad. There is no room to make the adjustment. They become frustrated. Many of them just drop out. Imagine that you are 21 and all your peers in the neighborhood are going to college, working, or planning to go to college and you are still in high school and you are not really getting it. It's hard; we are losing them.

The community leaders and parents of Karen children agree. The leaders and parents believe they have a lost generation of children. They are concerned they will be losing the cultural values the community believes are important and they are being absorbed into US street culture. The teenagers for the post part are not doing well in school, and many are dropping out. John, a Karen adult often identified as a major leader in the Karen community comments: "We feel we are losing the older Karen children. Many have dropped out of school and they are joining gangs. They are unable to find work and are just going about the neighborhood and getting into trouble. It's a big worry for us." Sharing a similar concern Ms. Rocco explains:

> Remember that group of 4 Karen teens we all talked about last interview; the ones that were suspended for getting into a fight outside of school? The saddest part of the story for me is that after the Karen students were readmitted into school, after they were, in my opinion, unjustly suspended for defending themselves, but also they were placed in different high schools to break them up as a group. They all dropped out after that. It really makes you wonder if administration is thinking at all.

From the perception of both resettlement education coordinators and Karen community leaders, the Nickel City public school system is not prepared to provide the necessary support to Karen refugee children for them succeed in education. What is clear from the narrations is the Karen youth most devastated by ineffective education policies are the older students, especially those in secondary education. The younger grammar school students are described by teachers and education directors as more flexible and are most likely to adapt. The older students however have much less time to catch up and are more likely to become discouraged. While catching up is an important theme in educational rhetoric, it is of particular concern that Title VII of the Elementary and Secondary Education Act of 1968, which recognizes the complex needs of limited English language ability students, is not being enforced. It is the older youth who are most at risk and appear to have fallen through the cracks of the system. One teacher lamented that refugee children are expected to take State English exams that are so difficult she doubts even native speakers can do well on them without intensive practice.

DISCUSSION AND SUMMARY

The members of the Karen community presented here describe backgrounds from small villages and rural areas in their native Burma with the majority of Karen youth and families interviewed claiming family histories of agriculture as their occupations. In Burma, the Karen faced a long history of oppression from the central Burmese government to disenfranchise them from a voice and to prevent Karen cultural and linguistic autonomy and government representation. Subsequently, the central Burmese government unleashed force to silence their voices resulting in thousands fleeing Burma, many finding shelter in Thai refugee camps. While there are exceptions, the majority of Karen refugees spend 2 to over 10 years in refugee camps as they await approval from a host country to accept them. As often as possible, refugees are reunited with family members living abroad.

The US, to its credit, accepts more international refugees than any other country in the world with over 70,000 arriving annually. Since 2005, the Karen Burmese are one of the largest ethnic groups to come to the states. Nickel City has one of the largest Karen communities in the nation, with over 8,000 documented Karen refugees. It has become the state's preferred destination in the last 5 years for newly arriving refugees of all backgrounds, creating a large and visible diversity to the city's once traditionally white and African American populations. Once accepted to the US, Karen and other refugees are sponsored by a number of resettlement agencies which meet them at the airport and settle them in an apartment that can accommodate one individual or an entire family. Over the last 7 years, federal appropriations for refugee individuals has risen from a meager $400 per person to $1,800 making a more comfortable settlement for a family of 2 or more.

Out of necessity, Karen refugees are placed in the lower west side and the Littlerock urban neighborhoods. Both communities are poor and working class but are distinctive in the respect that the west side has historically a diverse community comprised of African American and Latino families and Littlerock has historically been a poor or working class white neighborhood. The decision to place the Karen Burmese in these specific communities is based on a number of practicalities including the cost of housing, the need to create a critical mass, and the extent to which resettlement agencies believe these environs will be more accepting of refugees. In addition, although not in the most accessible parts of the city, refugees in these urban neighborhoods do have access to better public transportation, schools, city and county government, and health services. Not all communities may be as accommodating. As one school administrator from a nearby affluent suburb commented to me in a personal communication, "We certainly don't want all these immigrants and refugees here in Jamesville (upper middle class suburb). They should stay in the city. Besides the city is a mess anyway. Let them stay there. We are already footing the bill for them through County assistance."

No matter where these families are placed there are challenges. Unlike the Vietnamese I researched 10 years ago (Centrie, 2004), the Karen Burmese do not come with middle and upper class backgrounds. In spite of the South Vietnamese also being subject to state sponsored oppression by the previously North Vietnamese, and risking flight to Thai refugee camps, the initial wave of Vietnamese came with a great deal of cultural capital. This served them well in organizing their community and negotiating benefits with the public school system. Such benefits include advocating for special Vietnamese homerooms with an educated Vietnamese teacher and aides to look out for the well being of their young. Later waves of Vietnamese, like the Karen refugees, were also primarily rural with agricultural backgrounds. By the time these groups arrived, the Vietnamese community had long established itself, and despite class background differences of significance in Vietnam, created a common biography of one community with similar experiences of oppression that bound the group together. The Karen Burmese community presented here has far less cultural capital to negotiate with US social institutions. When considering class background as a framework for understanding the refugee experiences of the Karen Burmese, they are placed at a deficit when negotiating US social institutions.

An overwhelming concern of Karen parents is that their youth maintain the Karen language and culture, the very reason why they fought in Burma and ultimately became refugees. The Karen also place a strong emphasis on "family values," defined as the maintenance of strong ties to their families and communities, marriage within the group, children remaining at home until they are married, and respect for parents and family and taking care of the elderly. These values are understood to be challenged generally within US culture but especially so in the lower west side and in Littlerock. They voice concern over the violence their children are exposed to and how limited they are in protecting them. On one visit to a Karen family, I was quickly ushered in the apartment because a man was shot to death outside of the home only hours before. Within minutes the neighbors knew the reason was a drug deal that had gone bad. The Sung family was regretful that their children ranging from 5 to 14 years old saw the entire event.

Some of the Karen youth express fear while some older youth in their late teens and early 20s are prepared to fight back. Children as young as 11 and 12 are being groomed to join youth gangs. Though not pleased with this alternative, some youth interviewed suggest this might be the only way to survive in these communities. Ainsworth (2003); Burton, Price-Spratlen, and Beale Spenser (1997); and Leventhal and Brooks-Gunn (2003) contend the neighborhoods in which children grow up have a significant impact on outcomes. The Karen Burmese communities are part of larger areas with few positive role models to look to for guidance. Like the West Indian neighborhoods explored by Waters (1998) these surroundings may be viewed as toxic areas in the sense they are short on city services, have marginal public transportation, and are challenging to find healthy and affordable food. The social problems associated with poverty exist in abundance and influence Karen youth identity choices.

Though not new to ethnic differences, the Karen are confused by the binary race relations of US society. The youth are developing identities which differentiate the Karen from African Americans and Latinos/a as they create a "we" versus "them" dynamic. Though perhaps not fully developed, Karen youth are beginning to understand the subtle realities of white privilege (Fine & Weis, 1998). They are also understanding the extent to which identifying with African Americans and Latinos/a in their communities has limited social value in US society except as a mechanism to survive the brutalities and realities of street culture. With a scarcity of assets in the lower west side and in Littlerock, youth groups vie for control and dominance, creating a ethnically based pecking order which attempts to place the newly arrived Karen at the bottom and which these youth are fighting. As one African American colleague discussed with me, Black youth become resentful of the perceived special treatment of the refugees and cannot understand how many of them find employment while they (African Americans) struggle to survive after 400 years of building this country.

Ms. Sung, the mother of a family of 6 sees this quite differently. She works like many employed Karen in the service sector industry 7 days a week as part of a housekeeping staff for a local hotel. She has come to realize national chain will not employ her full time to keep from giving her benefits. She now also understands that the service sector which employs the Karen as bus boys, dish washers, and housekeepers prefer them over African Americans and Latinos/a. In the view of Ms. Sung, this is because the Karen are known to work hard, do not complain because they are afraid to lose their jobs, and have limited English ability to make their concerns understood. Ms. Sung's children know how difficult it is for their mother and wish they could help.

Historically, education in the US has been viewed as the great equalizer. Reproductionists such as Bowles and Gintis (2002) have posited through correspondence theory that schools exist merely to maintain the status quo. These researchers continue to defend their position 23 years after their ground breaking piece of the same name. Still others as early as the 1980s (e.g. Willis, 1981) have argued that students are not merely recipients of school culture but are active participants in its production. Sometimes the production of school culture is oppositional. In the case of the Karen, it is too early to tell what their long term relationship will be with the education system. The data presented here suggest a number of things. The Karen have a strong belief in the value of education, perhaps even more so since they were denied the full benefits of schooling in refugee camps and in Burma. Both the Karen youth and parents have narrated that education is viewed as one of the benefits of living in the US.

Education coordinators of resettlement agencies and teachers alike believe the public school system is positioning Karen youth for failure. Teachers and educational coordinators believe the policy of placing students in age appropriate classes without regard to previous educational levels makes it most often too difficult for students to play catch up. The lack of English language ability is also making catching up much more difficult, especially in courses that are heavily based on language ability. This is less of a problem with younger grammar school children, but is especially problematic for older teenagers who have less time to make up lost skills and material and whose courses are more difficult. Further, school administrators appear to be unaware of the ethnic conflicts which occur even within their schools. By not addressing these problems there is additional alienation being experienced by older Karen youth which is contributing to a drop out problem with this age group. There is a keen understanding in the Karen community that education is the key to getting a good job and having a promising future. For the older Karen youth their futures are looking bleak. As many Karen parents and community leaders believe, these young people may be lost.

REFERENCES

Ainesworth, J. W. (2002). Why does it take a village? The mediation of neighborhood effects on educational achievement. *Social Forces, 81*(1), 117-152.

Appaduri, A. (1991). Global ethnoscapes: Notes and queries for a transnational anthropology. In R. G. Fox (Ed.), *Recapturing anthropology: Working in the present* (pp. 191-210). Santa Fe, NM: School of American Research.

Aron-Dine, A., & Shapiro, I. (2006). *New data show extraordinary jump in income concentration in 2004.* Washington, DC: Center on Budget and Policy Priorities. Retrieved from chp.org/7-10-06inc.pdf.

Bourdieu, P. (1977). Cultural reproduction and social reproduction. In J. Karabel & A. Halsey (Eds.), *Power and ideology in education* (pp. 487-511). New York: Oxford University Press.

Bowles, S., & Gintis, H. (2002). Schooling in capitalist America revisited. *Sociology of Education, 75*(1), 1-18.

Brantlinger, E. (2003). *Dividing classes: How the middle class negotiates and rationalizes school advantage.* New York: Routledge.

Burawoy, M., Chang, M. K., Hsieh, M., & Fei-Yu (Eds.). A. Adrews, E. Fidan Elcioglu, & I. K.Nelson (Assoc. Eds.). (2010). Facing an unequal world: Challenges for a global Sociology. *Conference Proceedings (3),* Taipei, Taiwan: Institute of Sociology at Academia Sinica.

Burton, L. M., Price-Spratlen, T., & Beale Spenser, M. (1997). On the ways of thinking about measuring neighborhoods: Implications for studying context and developmental outcomes for children. In J. Brooks-Gunn, G. J. Duncan, & J. K. Aber (Eds.), *Neighborhood poverty: Policy implications in studying neighborhoods* (pp. 132-144). New York: Russel Sage Foundation.

Centrie, C. (2004). *The identity formation of Vietnamese youth in an American high school.* New York: LFB Publications.

Charney, M. W. (2009). *A history of modern Burma.* New York: Cambridge University Press.

Chauduri, M. (2005). Betwixt the state and everyday life: Identity formation among Bengali migrants in a New Delhi slum. In M. Thapan (Ed.), *Transnational migration and the politics of identity* (pp. 284-311). New Delhi, India: Sage Publishers, Inc.

Chauvel, L. (2010). The increasingly dominated fraction of the dominant class: French sociologists facing the challenges of precarity and middle class destabilization. In M. Burawoy, M. K. Chang, M.

& Fei-yu Hsieh (Eds.), *Facing an unequal world: Challenges for a global sociology at Academia Sinica*. Madrid: Council of National Associations of the International Sociological Association.
Crespo-Sancho, C. (2009). *Migration in the age of globalization: Transnationalism, identity, social class, and education of Latino Families*. Retrieved from proquest.com
Creswell, J. (2009). *Research design: Qualitative, quantitative, and mixed methods approaches, 3rd edition*. New York: Sage Publications, Inc.
DiMaggio, P. (1979). On Pierre Bourdieu. *The American Journal of Sociology, 84*(6), 1460-1474.
Fanon, F. (1952). *Black skin, white masks*. Paris: Editions du Seuil.
Fine, M., & Weis, L. (1998). *Unknown city: The lives of poor and working-class young adults*. Boston: Becan Press.
Gilbert, D. (2003). *The American class structure in an age of growing inequality*. Belmont, CA: Wadsworth.
Harvey, G. F. (2000). *The history of Burma*. New Delhi. India: Asian Educational Services.
Hein, J. (1995). *From Vietnam, Laos, and Cambodia: A refugee experience in the United States*. New York: Twayne Pubishers.
Kloby, J. (2004). *Inequality, power, and development*. New York: Humanity Books.
Lareau, A. (2003). *Unequal childhoods: Class, race, and family life*. Berkeley: University of California Press.
Lee, S., & Ngo, B. (2007). Complicating the image of model minority success: A review of Southeast Asian American Experience. *Review of Educational Research, 77*(4), 415-453.
Lee, S. (2005). *Up against whiteness: Race, school and immigrant youth*. New York: Teachers College Press: NY.
Leventhal, T., & Brooks-Gunn, J. (2003). Moving on up: Neighborhood effects on children and families. In M. H. Bornstein & R. H. Bradley (Eds.), *Sociology status, parenting, and child development* (pp. 209-230). New York: Lawrence Erlbaum Associates.
MacLure, M. (2003). *Discourse in educational and social research*. London: Open University Press.
Marshall, A. (11 April, 2011). The slow thaw of the Burmese military junta. *The Times*, U.K. Retrieved 10 Jan. 2012.
Massey, D., & Denton, N. (1993). *American apartheid: Segregation and the making of the under class*. Cambridge, MA: Harvard University Press.
Oh, Su-Ann & van der Stouwe, M. (2008). Education, diversity and inclusion in Burmese refugee camps. *Comparative Education Review, 15*, Retrieved from Google Scholar, June 3. Partnership for the Public Good. (9 June 2009). Retrieved 9 June 2012.
Patillo-McCoy, M. (2000). *Black picket fences: Privilege and peril of the black middle class*. Chicago: University of Chicago Press.
Picketty, T., & Saez, E. (2006). *Income inequality in the United States, 1913-2002*. New York: Oxford University Press.
Reay, D., Crozier, G., & James, D. (2011). *White middle class identities and urban schooling*. New York: Palgrave McMillan.
Rouse, R. (2002). Mexican migration and social space of postmodernism. In J. X. Inda & R. Rosaldo (Eds.), *The anthropology of globalization* (pp. 157-171). Malden, MA: Blackwell.
Sherman, Q., & Aron-Dine, Q. (2007). *New CBO data show income inequality continues to widen after tax for top 1 percent rose by $146,000 in 2004*. Washington DC: Center on Budget and Policy Priorities.
UNESCO. (2005). *Guidelines for inclusion: Ensuring access to education for all*. Paris: UNESCO.
Vincent, C., & Ball, S. (2006). *Childcare, choice and class practices: Middle class parents and their children*. London: Routledge.
Walkerdine, V., Lucey, H., & Melody, J. (2001). *Growing up girl: Psychological explorations of gender and class*. London: Palgrave.
Warner, G. (July, 26, 2009). Burmese refuges find home in Buffalo. *Buffalo News*. Buffalo New York. Retrieved PDF, http://buffalonews. org, January 9, 2012.

Waters, M. (1999). *Black identities: West Indian immigrant dreams and American Realities.* New York: Harvard University Press.
Weis, L., & Dolby, N. (2012). *Social class and education: Global perspectives.* New York: Routledge.

JESSICA NINA LESTER & ALLISON DANIEL ANDERS

CHAPTER 4

Burundi Refugee Students in Rural Southern Appalachia: On the fast track to Special Education

INTRODUCTION

For the last three years, we have been engaged in ethnographic work with commitments to a postcritical perspective (Noblit, Flores, & Murillo, 2004). From 2008 to 2011, we have been learning and teaching with Burundian children and families with refugee status who live in southern Appalachia. We met the children and their families originally as English as second language [ESL] tutors. Each week we joined them to study English, play games, and complete homework at a ministry center or on a front porch or soft couch in the apartments in the public housing project where many of the Burundian families live. Our relationships now are ones still of learning and teaching, but also ones of family advocacy. Further, from 2009 to 2010 we spent time at the two local elementary schools, Red Valley and Riverhill County School,[1] where many of the Burundian children were students. This chapter reflects a part of this long-term ethnographic project, which is still unfolding. As white ethnographers, privileged by race in the US and with the ascribed authority and class of "researcher" and "teacher" at predominantly white universities in predominantly white cities, we commit our attention to our privileges. We commit our attention to emic perspectives as well. Analyzing the ways in which the families navigate economic, social, and cultural practices and institutions in the US, including public education, is one way we engage in the production of understanding their experiences, as well as our own.

This chapter addresses the identities of children with refugee status and explores how those identities were targeted in US public schools, particularly within the practice of tracking that occurred at the intersection of ESL and special education. First we introduce postcritical ethnography and provide an overview of our three-year project with Burundian families. Second, we introduce the issue of targeted identities produced and subjected to the imperialist gaze of the state (Foucault, 1995; Mbembe, 2001; Scott 1998) in relation to the process of tracking – a process we argue is particularly consequential for immigrant children and children with refugee status.

[1] Pseudonyms were used for identifiable institutions and places. Children chose their own pseudonyms.

J. Hall (ed.), Children's Human Rights and Public Schooling in the United States, 71–87.

Next, through the deployment of a performative text based on our narrative analysis (Clandinin & Connelly, 2004; Noblit, 1999) of field notes and observations from 2009 to 2010, we represent the act of targeting and tracking one elementary school-aged child into special education against the wishes of his parents. We focus on one instance of tracking, attending to the particularities and situatedness of this individual case. We aim to produce a rich and layered understanding of the lived experience of this case in order to invite attention to everyday practices of institutionalized power rather than aim to produce an account from which one might generalize. Finally, we argue this tracking makes evident the school's practice of "discriminatory non-fulfillment" of the child's right to education and the child's own right to participate in those decisions that affected him (Convention on the Rights of the Child, 1989, Article 12).

THE CONTEXT

Our work together began in a social justice and education course during which we spent our Thursday afternoons with Burundian children as ESL tutors (Anders & Lester, 2011). Since that time, we have continued to engage in community and ethnographic work with Burundian children and families with refugee status. Primarily, this work has taken place in a predominately white, monolingual, small urban setting within rural, southern Appalachia. Underprepared and under-resourced, Red Valley and Riverhill provided little to no support to the Burundian families transitioning to their new society.

The United Nations High Commissioner for Refugees [UNHCR], the Office of Refugee Resettlement, and faith-based organizations like World Church Services and Episcopal Migrant Ministries, facilitated the resettlement of Burundians with refugee status in communities like this across the country. Initially in the 1970s and 1980s many fled from Burundi to neighboring Congo and Rwanda to escape Hutu extremist violence directed at Tutsi and moderate Hutu. Burundians then again fled in 1994 during the highpoint of the Rwandan genocide, mostly to Tanzania. For the Burundian adults, the US was their third country of settlement. Although the refugee camps were located in rural areas of Tanzania, the rural areas surrounding Red Valley and Riverhill were radically different. There, as well as in public spaces and in public schools, we witnessed xenophobia and ethnocentric policies that reinforced whitestream practices (Grande, 2004).

In our work in the community and the local schools, we encountered classist and anti-immigrant sentiments and white supremacist practices (Anders & Lester, 2011; Mariner, Lester, & Anders, 2012). For example, one district administrator voiced, "We don't want any more [Burundians]," when describing the district's experience with the Burundian children. And one community member asked, "Couldn't they stay in a camp here [in the US] until they're ready to live in Riverhill?" We witnessed also the biopolitics (Foucault, 2004) of distributing bodies to public housing projects and into public school classrooms. Offering the justification that Burundians with refugee status (compared to Iraqi and Burmese individuals with refugee status) would be grateful to have an apartment in a public housing project compared to the camps from which they came, Greenland Refugee Resettlement Agency placed the majority of the Burundian families in two public housing projects in the Red Valley and the Riverhill area. In public school classrooms expectations of emotional capital (Zembylas, 2007) that reflected whitestream practices silenced the voices and restricted the bodies of the Burundian children.

A POSTCRITICAL ORIENTATION

As we research, postcritical ethnography (Noblit, Flores, & Murillo, 2004) resonates with us and offers us a way to frame our relationships and research in ways that address our own power, and issues of power across discourse, practice, and structures. Postcritical ethnography requires us to acknowledge our moral commitments, as we assume we are situated within the "critical discourse that in part makes" us "responsible for the world" that we produce when we "interpret and critique" (p. 24). As such, as we produce this work, we recognize we are always already situated (Habermas, 1988). Further, as we represent our experiences, we engage in recursive reflexivity and interrogate our own power. As we work, we aim to write against ourselves, an endeavor impossible to achieve but pursued nonetheless (Noblit, 1999). We aspire to "multiple perspectives" and include "competing beliefs" (Noblit & Engel, 1999). We position our understandings as always unfolding and partial, as we seek to invite critique and new interpretations. Tantamount to these things, we work to cultivate relationships of reciprocity with the community as we attend to our everyday experiences and actions across community (de Certeau, 1984).

THE TARGET AS "REFUGEE"

This chapter addresses the often embodied-less experience of targets in schools. Such targets include the children for whom policy and categories target race and class, ultimately locating them as *other* (e.g. socioeconomic status, disability label/status, free and reduced lunch eligibility, reading "ability," English proficiency). As in the case of the colony, administrators may justify the targeting and tracking of bodies by deploying a posteriori the progress that has been achieved (Scott, 1999). Here, the UDHR and schools alike name the body as "refugee" and target a child's physical embodiment. As Farmer (2005) noted, "any distinguishing characteristic, whether social or biological, can serve as a pretext for discrimination and thus as a cause of suffering" (p. 46). Readily identifiable among these axes of oppression is the ascription and assignment of "refugee" or immigrant status.

Although Malkki (1996) argues that the aims of contemporary "refugee" studies differ from historical studies of "refugees," both share "the premise that refugees are necessarily 'a problem'" (p. 443). Positioning pathologies on the body produces representations that bound individuals to an assignment. The process contributes to discrimination and oppression, and generates discourses that emphasize individual transition rather than systemic changes in resources, resettlement, and policy. None of the children or their parents with whom we work self-identified as "refugee" – preferring instead "African" or "Burundian." "Refugee studies" however marks these individuals as "an anomaly requiring specialized correctives and therapeutic interventions" rather than "ordinary people" (p. 443). Malkki further contends:

> It is striking how often the abundant literature claiming refugees as its object of study locates 'the problem' not in the political conditions or processes that produce massive territorial displacements of people, but, rather, within the bodies and minds (and even souls) of people categorized as refugees. The internalization of the problem within 'the refugee' is the more contemporary study of refugees now occurs most often along a medicalizing, psychological axis ... The point here is obviously not to deny that displacement can be a shattering experience. It is rather this: our sedentarist assumptions about attachment to place lead us to define displacement not as a fact about sociopolitical context, but rather as an inner, pathological condition of the displaced. (p. 443)

We join the call in education that others have made in anthropology and postcolonial studies to deepen our understandings of the terrain upon which we work. We attend to identity politics and governmentality as we work against the essentialization of identity and monolithic inscriptions upon the body (Ladson-Billings, 2001; Teranishi, 2002).

THE TARGET AND SPECIAL EDUCATION

In the US, Public Law 94-142 (Education for All Handicapped Children Act) was passed in 1975, requiring all public schools provide children with impairments and disability labels access to education. Prior to the passing of this law, public schools provided education for only about one out of every five children with disability labels. Thus, this law was important for creating opportunities for all children to attend school.

Yet, after the Brown vs. Board of Education decision there was a discursive shift within educational settings and policies. The discourses of race were slowly replaced by the discourses of ability (Ferri & Connor, 2006). Some argue this discursive switch allowed for the installation of a new, legalized segregation in the form of ability. In this way, what was positioned as a move toward equality was a structural and discursive move toward a new form of segregation. In 1990, this law was changed and renamed the Individuals with Disabilities Education Act [IDEA]. Revisions surrounding this law clarified that children with disability labels should be prepared for further education, employment, and independent living. In theory, IDEA was constructed with the assumption that meritocracy was already present in some spaces and places or at least a possibility. The myth of meritocracy was not acknowledged, with the dominating assumption being progress inevitably is based on individual merit and hard work.

Within the US, inequality is what some might say is considered justifiable still when dealing with those labeled disabled. From an historical perspective, in the US the concept of disability has frequently been employed to justify discrimination against certain groups. During the nineteenth and early twentieth century, arguments against granting citizenship to women, people of African descent, and immigrants were grounded in the belief that the individuals within these groups were inherently disabled (Baynton, 2001). Despite the heralded "progress" made during the suffrage and civil rights movements, the current educational discourse surrounding children named disabled is often coupled with race. It has been well documented that African American students are overrepresented in special education (Eitle, 2002; Esposito, 1973; Fossey, 1996; Meier, Stewart, & England, 1989). We argue here, like Beratan (2008), that "society's willingness to perceive discrimination against disabled people as being the result of individual deficiencies is [often] used to make racism more palatable" (p. 345).

Historically, the construct of race and disability has continually intersected with that of "normality." In the mid-nineteenth century, nonwhite cultures were frequently imagined with disabilities, often depicted as evolutionarily behind. Regarding "normality," Bayton (2001) stated:

> The natural and the normal both are ways of establishing the universal, unquestionable good and right. Both are also ways of establishing social hierarchies that justify the denial of legitimacy and certain rights to individuals or groups. Both are constituted in large part by being set in opposition to culturally variable notions of disability – just as the natural was meaningful in relation to the monstrous and the deformed, so are the cultural meanings of the normal produced in tandem with disability. (p. 35)

With "normal" standing in contrast to "deformed," a hierarchy of the races was constructed in which a continuum of normality emerged. Whites were situated on the top or superior end of this continuum, while "mulattos" were positioned as slightly more intelligent than "pure" blacks. Here, whites organized and reorganized the terrain of understanding "normalcy" deploying in practice that which maintained white dominance. This classification system fit the need to justify the exploitation of people and resources around the world during the development of capitalism (Bayton, 2001).

One example of how white supremacy/normality constituted and privileged itself in relation to disability may be seen in the original naming of Down Syndrome. In 1866 Down Syndrome was named Mongolism. The doctors who "discovered it" suggested Mongoloism only occurred when whites reverted to the "defective" Mongolian racial type (Kevles, 1985). Embodied differences were quickly named abnormalities, pathologized, and positioned as disorders. The "disabling environments" that produce "disability in bodies" (Siebers, 2008, p. 25) were evaded, as embodied differences were inscribed as pathologies in need of being remedied. This was used to justify colonization and economic imperialism in relation to the institutionalization of slavery in the US and elsewhere. Many slave owners and politicians of the nineteenth century in the US argued those of African descent simply lacked "sufficient intelligence to participate or compete on an equal basis in society with white Americans" (Bayton, 2001, p. 37).

Alongside such rationalizations, during the early part of the 20th century, the ideals of the eugenics movement quickly infiltrated the discourse of the day (Selden, 2000). Wiggam (1922) was a strong supporter of the eugenics movement claiming it is "not the slums which make slum people, but slum people who make slums ... if you want artists, poets, philosophers, skilled workmen and great statesmen, you will have to give nature a chance and breed them" (p. 43). Such ways of thinking were particularly influential in how merit, race, and disability were constructed, tending "to empower the already powerful while disenfranchising those who had the least social purchase" (Selden, 2000, p. 236). Despite many of those of African descent having no access to schooling, the resulting lower literacy rates in comparison to whites was often used as evidence of an inherently ignorant nature of those in this group. The eugenics movement combined with intelligence testing to shape the institutional discourse and educational policies that led to schools becoming the site of sorting children (Fass, 1991; Gould, 1981).

During the 1940s and 1950s, discrimination against African Americans continued through measures such as Jim Crow laws in the south and de facto segregation in the north. Prior to the 1960s, those individuals who were named disabled, regardless of race, were relegated to the margins of the educational system (Bayton, 2001). In many ways, the public school system was the vehicle by which non-white and/or disabled children were systematically targeted (Tyack, 1993).

As the Civil Rights Movement evolved, the issue of race remained central to the discussions of educational access, as well as the construction of special education. After the Brown vs. Board of Education decision in 1954, there was a discursive shift within educational settings and policies. The "talk" of racial deficiencies was subsumed under the "talk" of cognitive deficiencies. As disability law emerged, it was very much constructed as an anti-discrimination law, aligning closely with the discourse of the laws of the Civil Rights movement. Beratan (2008) stated IDEA was "an improvement on the non-educational institutions and asylums it was designed to replace, but being an improvement on institutionalization is hardly a grandiose claim" (p. 341). Through this federal move, the dominant discourse of race was legally replaced by the discourse of ability (Ferri & Connor, 2006). Such a shift functioned to install a new, legalized segregation in the form of ability grouping and special education placements, most notably related to high incidence disabilities.

During the late 1960s and early 1970s, several placements of African American children in special education classes were legally challenged (e.g. Diana v. State Board of Education, 1970; Larry P. v. Riles, 1979). Yet despite this public attention, the reality today remains the same. A disproportionate number of minority students are classified as special education students. Additionally, the classification rates for African Americans and Native Americans are remarkably higher in high incidence categories "that depend on clinical judgment rather than on verifiable biological data" (Harry & Klingner, 2006, p. 2). At present, students of African descent make up about 16.3% of the school-age population, while representing 31% of students labeled with "mild mental retardation" and 23.7% of the students labeled with "emotional disturbance" (Heward & Cavanaugh, 2001). In certain states, an African American child is 2.5 times more likely to be classified having mental retardation compared to their white counterparts (Donovan & Cross, 2002). Some literature suggests this overrepresentation is a result of narrowly interpreting cognitive and affective schemas, drawing from a culturally biased framework (Artiles, Trent, & Kuan, 1997). Cole (1996) highlights how many of the theories of learning that frame much of what is presumably known about human development ignore the ways in which culture shapes and informs individual and collective knowledge acquisition and construction. Further, Kalyanpur and Harry (1999) detail differential cultural interpretations of many disabilities, including learning disabilities, emotional disturbances, and mental retardation.

For years, scholars focused on labeling theories have suggested an individual's official label becomes reified quickly, much like a category like "refugee," acting to wholly define a person (Becker, 1969; Bogdan & Knoll, 1988; Malkki, 1996). Goffman (1963) postulated that a label or classification becomes the "master status" by which one becomes known. Therefore, once the discourse of disability is set into motion, a child's problems become defined as disability, and that disability as fact. Disability, made into that which belongs to a child, is reified, becoming "a thing that would be very difficult to discard" (Harry & Klingner, 2006, p. 7).

The complexity of the special education law and its many disability categories is at once a tool for inclusion and a racially sorting vehicle. Legalized institutional practices, found at the intersection of race and disability, are what we encountered in our everyday work in the schools that the Burundian children attended.

NARRATIVE RETELLINGS

In this section of the chapter, we retrace the process the principal and teachers at Red Valley School took. We argue this path violated, in subtle and not so subtle ways, special education law and *the Right to Dignity and Education for* one young Burundian boy in the third grade. We call this student "Spiderman," as this is his chosen pseudonym. We argue the tracking he experienced made evident the school's practice of "discriminatory non-fulfillment" of the child's rights.

In spring 2010, Spiderman's parents asked us to do what we could to keep him in the "least restrictive environment." After receiving a call requesting their presence at the school, his parents learned their son was being considered for special education placement. Such a meeting is usually structured by safeguards and legalities. The parents however never saw a written prior notice – something required by law. No one ever accessed background material for the parents concerning their child which would help them understand the circumstances.

Below, we represent how we responded to his parents and eventually to the Burundian community. Drawing from our field notes and analytic memos, we share the following performative text, narratively, and at times poetically (Denzin, 2003; Glesne, 2011; Norum, 2000), as we seek to represent the multi-dimensionality of and our positionality in this work.

ONE ACT

It happened quickly.

So quickly it was difficult to follow the storyline, to predict the next move,
to forewarn Spiderman's parents.

All we knew was that Spiderman would soon be placed in special education,
not the inclusive kind.
We knew.
I (Jessica) knew.

I had been a special educator long enough to know, to sense the changing undercurrent that comes along with labeling a body, a black body, ordered or disordered, normal or abnormal. Empire organizing. Reorganizing. It is the kind of undercurrent that is hard to stop, to even slow down, for just one second – impossible. It's the kind of undercurrent that is so surprising you freeze and forget you do know how to swim. It's the quiet kind, the kind that doesn't announce it's coming, but builds up speed secretively. It's the powerful kind – the kind that pulls a child from his classroom and pushes him into a special education classroom long before any qualifying meeting, testing, or conversation with the family about what's best for the family, for the child has been had.

It was coming. Winter 2010. We could feel it. We could hear it. It was picking up speed.

It started with quiet murmurings in the school hallways – "Jessica, you worked in special education, you know. Don't you think Spiderman would benefit?" "Jessica, do you think like Allison? We know she's worried about Spiderman going into special education. It can be good. It doesn't mean he won't get out."

My reply was always the same. "We all want him to get the support he needs, in the least restrictive environment. That's the point of special education. The least restrictive environment."

New country, new language, new family, new home. New school, new teacher, new students, new culture. Brothers and sisters. A home different from the one he shared with his grandmother in Tanzania. A space just he and she had shared. New nights, clock ticking late, listening for his father's return from working. A second shift. Little sleep. New conflict. New behaviors. A psychiatrist who worked tele-medicine miles from Riverhill, miles from Spiderman and his family, named symptoms of depression. Named a need for testing. Testing named Spiderman Oppositional Defiant Disorder.

Medicalization begins. Reorganize, reorder. Prescribe powerful meds for a nine-year-old body, only the label cautions against any prescription for anyone under the age of twelve.

English words tangle his parents' Kirundi fluency and though they cannot enunciate its name, they watch its effects. The new teachers and the new school do, too. Only Spiderman's parents do not know this. We do not know this. Parental signatures obtained under a different rhetoric a season before makes Spiderman's medicalization spectacle for the teachers in the school. The act of medicalizing the body didn't banish Spiderman from the classroom.

It would take an undercurrent to do that – the quiet, strategic, unexpected kind.

Seven months of sleep from 8:00 a.m. to 10:00 a.m., side effects of a medication developed for children over the age of 12, left Spiderman behind in reading and writing. Though math did not require mastery of English, the blustery "so far behind in reading and writing" tossed the undercurrent into a powerful jetstream as the next season broke.

And on a spring morning. A Wednesday. I felt its speed, its power pick up – it was my day to tutor the Burundian children at Red Valley. I was sitting in the back of the classroom, reading with Spiderman, Happy Princess, and Hulk [other Burundi students]. I could hear something coming, but I tried to ignore it. Tried to concentrate on the book the teacher asked me to read with the children– "Jane and Dick go up a hill. Jane, up, up, up." I heard Happy Princess say.

The door suddenly burst open – the children froze. I froze. My stomach sunk – the current was coming. Today was the day. The ESL teacher rushed into the room, motioning for Spiderman's classroom teacher to come to her. We all overheard their whispers. Spiderman, Happy Princess, Hulk, and me. Spiderman's family was nowhere to be found, she said. The special education meeting, the meeting that was going to result in school officials getting the parental signature they needed to give Spiderman an IQ test was happening in 30 minutes. If his parents didn't show, they would, it had been decided, go on without them. Organize. Reorganize.

Quickly I stood up, encouraged the kids to keep reading, and walked to the two teachers. I quietly whispered, "What is happening?" They told me what I already knew. I asked, "Did you give his parents prior written notice?" "Oh, Jessica, of course we did, we called the translator and told her to tell them. We're having the

meeting whether they're here or not. I think someone called the translator." Puzzled, I asked, "Did you call the family? Send them notice? How much time were they given to prepare?" She replied, quickly, "The translator was suppose to tell them."
The current was getting stronger. I could feel it.

"I can find his parents and the translator. I'll be right back," I said.
They were surprised, never having realized that I knew Spiderman and his family well. We were friends. Allison and I had known them for two years, spent afternoons with their children reading, playing, and working on crafts. We had spent weeks talking with them about their rights and sharing special education law with them. We knew it was complicated. But they wanted help for their son, the inclusive kind.

The teachers smiled at me and said, "Do you need their phone number?"
"No. I don't. I'll be back in 30 minutes."
"Thank you," they said in unison, "You saved us."

I ran from the school, called Rukundo, the translator. Called Allison. All I could say was: "It's happening. Someone needs to be here."

I knew we could counter with a lawyer. I'd seen it done before. But the current – it was starting to remind of the kind that defies the law – even the good laws. Imperial power.

Things happened quickly, so quickly it still remains a sickening blur.

Spiderman's mother, Jolene, decided to come to the meeting. His father went ahead to a doctor's appointment that previously had been planned.

We walked into the meeting together – Rukundo, me, and Jolene.
No one questioned my presence. No one even asked who I was.
Five white teachers, a white school psychologist, and the white principal collectively cheered when we walked in, yelling … "You found them. YAY!"

I didn't smile. I was confused, disoriented by the power, the speed. Angry.
I couldn't imagine how Jolene felt. All I knew is that she made me promise to be there.
New terrain.

The meeting unfolded like most special education meetings. They start by sharing the parental rights and responsibilities. And then those who represent a compelling interest in tracking, moved to convince the parent, in technical terms, to agree with their assessment that the child needed more testing. "If we can test him," they said, "we can help him."

They spoke, and spoke, and spoke, as Spiderman's mom rested her head on the table.
As they concluded, they pushed a white piece of paper across the table and said, "Please sign. This is so that we can test your son. We can help him then."

Jolene shot her head up and said, "No."

They gasped, collectively.

For just a moment, I felt the undercurrent shift; ever so slightly it slowed.
Jolene continued, "I have a question."
After a brief pause, she continued, "If my son is tested and you decide he goes to that special room, what will happen in the next school building, when he is in high school, in middle school, will he stay in that room for his whole life? What will happen after high school?"

There was silence.

And then the principal, who had not spoken a word, pushed back his chair, moved his hand to his chin and said with a question in his voice, "I see what she's saying. Hmm. That's a good question. Hmm."

Organize. Reorganize. The school psychologist countered with, "But listen, by signing this paper you are only giving us permission to test him. This doesn't qualify him for special services yet." The wickedness of a justification swept under the door like a draft.

And the current picked up speed again.

The special education teacher added, "Plus at our school we try to get kids out of the resource room eventually. We always do that."

News to me. I'd seen many students land in a special education room. Few ever left. Common knowledge – once qualified, you typically remain qualified. So many new secrets revealed.

Jolene was quiet for a moment. Then she reached for the pen, and just as she was about to sign said, "When my son is tested he needs a translator." The psychologist responded quickly with, "Okay, sure. We can do that."

Jolene signed.

Things moved quickly and silently. We were asked if we knew why Spiderman's family did not want him to get help. On our days in the classroom as volunteers, justifications were offered. Not everyone goes to college.

Long days of testing and secret meetings – we didn't hear anything for weeks. Then, just as suddenly as the first meeting, a secret, second meeting was planned in haste, two days before the end of the school year. The ESL teacher showed up one afternoon at Jolene's door with Rukundo, the translator, and read a letter to his mother:

Dear Mr. and Mrs. Kuyomboka,

The Red Valley Support Team (S-Team) met Thursday … to consider Spiderman's placement for next year. It was recommended by the committee to place Spiderman in fifth grade this fall. He will be skipping 4th grade entirely. The reason for this decision was agreed because of the following:

1. Spiderman's age (He will be 11 this year)
2. Peers – John [a friend] will be in fifth grade with him
3. Social – Spiderman will connect easier with students at his own age level

If you have any questions, please call the ESL Office in Riverhill County Schools …

Sincerely,
Mr. Faith

But he has friends in third grade. Hulk and Happy Princess. Hulk had been retained a year. He caught up. Why not Spiderman?

Quiet strategy now visible. Social promotion. Organize. Reorganize. Spiderman was being promoted to fifth grade – he was going to skip a full grade! Jolene smiled broadly when she told Allison the news. Spiderman was elated. Only brilliant boys skip grades – right?

Then, it came, the rush of the undercurrent – the one that takes what it wants, when it wants.

Before the ESL teacher had left Jolene's home, she told her about a meeting she needed to attend the next morning. I was away. Allison went over early, at 7:00 a.m., and sat with Rukundo, the translator, and Jolene. Jolene was tired. Allison encouraged her to ask questions about anything she did not understand. She offered to go with her. "No." She showed Jolene how to use a recorder. They practiced and laughed at their digitized voices. Jolene tucked it in her pocket. They stopped laughing. They all departed. Jolene and Rukundo to the school. Allison home. Driving north Allison called on all the forces she knew to help Jolene capture the power behind this organizing of her son's body. As she crossed the river, she feared the currents had already carried Jolene down river.

Rukundo contacted Allison at the end of the meeting, and I got the news through Allison.

Bad news.

We never learned all that happened in that second meeting. We just know Spiderman now spends his days in a resource room, joining his peers for PE, lunch, and art.

Fifth grade was the ploy – if he was promoted, he would need extra help; he would qualify for special education, not the inclusive kind. Fail nine weeks of school and you qualify for special education. Placing Spiderman in 5th grade would result in the needed failure.

It was a powerful current – the kind that pulls a child from his classroom and pushes him into a special education classroom long before any qualifying meeting, testing, or open conversation about what's best for the family, for the child. No prior written notice received. No time to prepare. No time to reschedule. The non-fulfillment of these practices that were supposedly in place to protect – left us breathless, confused, surprised.

Dehumanized.

We still hear its roar, feel it coming.

CONCLUDING THOUGHTS: FAILURES AND PRIVILEGED SHARINGS

Categorization of children's bodies may mean access to needed support and resources. In theory, such scaffolding ought to generate something productive and good for the child. In our experience, we witnessed white officials in a system that not only violated the rights of Spiderman and his family, but also reproduced nativist (Higham, 1955; Pérez Huber et al., 2008; Pérez Huber, 2010) and white-stream privilege. While we do not generalize from our experience, and position this retelling as partial and positional (Noblit, 1999), we recognize this nativist, whitestream privileging was at the expense of a nine-year-old boy and his parents. It was at the expense of their agency, their language, and their rights. In this particular knowing, the categorization happened swiftly, as procedures and policies were shifted, "justifiably" adapted, discounted, and evaded. We do not know why the third grade teacher did not want to work with Spiderman another year, as she had with Hulk the year we spent in her classroom. Nor do we know why school leadership turned all communication over to the county office in the form of a written letter.

What we do know is while Spiderman's parents expressed their concerns regarding the placement of their son in a most restrictive of educational environments, white officials managed, organized, reorganized, and swept away their concerns, their voice, their bodies. We know school officials failed on many fronts to inform the family. We know they failed to inform the family the documents they signed that allowed Red Valley Elementary School to access Spiderman's medical records from local health agencies. They failed to inform the family they were communicating with these health agencies, with no such communication being shared with the family. They failed to educate the family about the concept of a Support Team [S-Team]. They failed to inform the family that the S-Team had been having meetings about their son based on their concerns about his progress, test scores, and advancement. We know when a special education qualification meeting was called, they failed to inform Spiderman's parents with adequate notice, let alone assure that a written, translated notice was delivered to the family well in advance. They failed to engage the family directly about Spiderman's social promotion. For though the letter was from Red Valley Elementary School, any questions the family may have had regarding "skipping 4th grade entirely" needed to be addressed to the county English Language Learning office. This office required transportation to get to it and a meeting required a translator to communicate.

These failures, absences, grievances – they demonstrate a flagrant abuse of ethnocentric language dominance and institutional power that functioned to dictate the course, direction, and location of not only Spiderman, but his parents as well. The audacity and disregard for child and parental rights demonstrated by school and county officials by sending the ESL teacher to Spiderman's home 18 hours before his placement meeting, generated confusion and frustration. It also foreclosed all opportunity for a special education family advocate, medical expert, and community advocate to be present at the meeting. The practices of the white teachers and officials organized the terrain, and therefore, the possibilities of resistance. This foreclosure demarcates "discriminatory non-fulfillment" of Spiderman's right to education and his right to participate in decisions that affected him (Convention on the Rights of the Child, 1989, Article 12). Directing through narrow and questionable applications of policy and structure, colonizing through the selective administration of knowledge, and the offering of "salvation," they violated not only parental rights, but also Spiderman's right to education.

Though many of our questions remain unanswered, in the months that followed these events we organized meetings and community forums with Burundi families with the help of Rukundo to discuss "education" in US public schools. In 2011 we met with families and listened to the questions they were asking about tutors, learning English, citizenship tests, the cost of public and private schools, discipline concerns, special education, economic mobility through education, and community college and institutions of higher education. We recorded these conversations and began to answer what questions we could. After we gathered and drafted the information, Rukundo recorded it in Kirundi. We combined the recordings with photographs and English subtitles and created DVDs. We wanted the children and families to have access to that which is tacit and kept hidden. We hope as they confronted the terrains of public education, they might be able to navigate their travel knowing more about whitestream practices and their own legal rights. Rukundo, along with one of the families, named the project "Kanguka." Translated into English, Kanguka means *Wake Up*.

REFERENCES

Anders, A. D., & Lester, J. N. (2011). Living in Riverhill: A postcritical challenge to the production of a neoliberal success story. In B. J. Porfilio & H. Hickman (Eds.), *Critical service-learning as revolutionary pedagogy: A product of student agency in action* (pp. 223-249). Charlotte, NC: Information Age Publishing.

Artiles, A. J., Trent, S. C., & Kuan, L. A. (1997). Learning disabilities research on ethnic minority students: An analysis of 22 years of students published in selected refereed journals. *Learning Disabilities Research and Practice, 12*, 82-91.

Bayton, D. C. (2001). Disability and the justification of inequality in American history. In P. K. Longmore & L. Umansky (Eds.), *The new disability history: American perspectives* (pp. 33-82). New York City, NY: New York University Press.

Becker, H. S. (1969). *Studies in the sociology of deviance*. New York: Free Press.

Beratan, G. D. (2008). The song remains the same: Transposition and the disproportionate representation of minority students in special education. *Race, Ethnicity, and Education, 11*(4), 337-354.

Bogdan, R., & Knoll, J. (1988). The sociology of disability. In E. L. Meyen & T. M. Skrtic (Eds.), *Exceptional children and youth: An introduction* (3rd ed., pp. 449-547). Denver, CO: Love.

Césaire, A. (1994). From discourse on colonialism. In P. Williams & L. Chrismans (Eds.), *Colonial discourse and post-colonial theory: A reader* (pp. 172-180). New York: Columbia University Press.

Clandinin, J. D., & Connelly, F. M. (2004). *Narrative inquiry: Experience and story in qualitative research.* San Francisco: Jossey-Bass.

Cole, M. (1996). *Cultural psychology: A once and future discipline.* Cambridge, MA: Harvard University Press.

de Certau, M. (1984). *The practice of everyday life*. London, England: University of California Press.

Denzin, N. K. (2003). *Performance ethnography: Critical pedagogy and the politics of culture.* Thousand Oaks, CA: Sage.

Diana vs. State Board of Education, CA 70 RFT (N.D. Cal. 1970)

Donovan, S., & Cross, C. (2002). *Minority students in special and gifted education.* Washington, DC: National Academy Press.

Education of All Handicapped Children Act, Pub. L. No. 94-142, 89 Stat. 773 (1975).

Eitle, T. M. (2002). Special education or racial segregation: Understanding variation in the representation of black students in educable mentally handicapped programs. *The Sociological Quarterly, 43*(4), 575-605.

Esposito, D. (1973). Homogeneous and heterogeneous ability grouping: Principal findings and implications for evaluating and designing more effective educational environments. *Review of Educational Research, 43*, 163-179.

Farmer, P. (2005). *Pathologies of power: Health, human rights, and the new war on the poor.* Berkeley, CA: University of California Press.

Fass, P. S. (1991). *Outside-in: Minorities and the transformation of American education.* New York: Oxford University Press.

Ferri, B. A., & Connor, D. J. (2006). *Reading resistance: Discourses of exclusion in desegregation & inclusion debates.* New York, NY: Peter Lang.

Fossey, R. (1996, January). African American students in east Baton Rouge parish: How have they fared in desegregated school? Paper presented at the annual meeting of the Southwest Educational Research Association, New Orleans, LA.

Foucault, M. (1995). *Discipline and punish: the birth of the prison.* New York: Vintage.

Foucault, M. (2004). *The birth of biopolitics: Lectures at the College de France, 1978-1979.* New York, NY: Palgrave Macmillan.

Glesne, C. (2011). *Becoming qualitative researchers: An introduction*, 4th edition. Upper Saddle River, NJ: Prentice Hall.

Grande, S. (2004). *Red pedagogy: Native American social and political thought.* New York: Rowman and Littlefield Publishers.

Goffman, E. (1963). *Stigma: Notes on the management of spoiled identity.* New York: Simon & Schuster.

Gould, S. J. (1981). *The mismeasure of man.* New York: Norton.

Habermas, J. (1988). *Theory and practice.* (J. Viertel, Trans.). Boston, MA: Beacon Press.

Harry, B., & Klingner, J. (2006). *Why are so many minority students in special education?: Understanding race and disability in schools.* New York, NY: Teachers College Press.

Heward, W. L., & Cavanaugh, R. (2001). Educational equity for students with disabilities. In J. Banks & C. A. McGee Banks (Eds.), *Multicultural education: Issues and perspectives.* New York: John Wiley and Sons, Inc.

Higham, J. (1955). *Strangers in the land: Patterns of American nativism.* New Brunswick: Rutgers University Press.

Human rights for human dignity: A primer on economic, social and cultural rights. (2005). Oxford, UK: Alden Press.

Individuals with Disabilities Education Act (IDEA), Pub. L. No. 101-476, 104 Stat. 1103 (1990).

Kalyanpur, M., & Harry, B. (1999). *Culture in special education: Building reciprocal family-professional relationships.* Baltimore: Brookes.

Kevles, D. J. (1985). *In the name of eugenics: Genetics and the uses of human heredity.* Berkley, CA: University of California Press.

Ladson-Billings, G. (2001). New directions in multicultural education: Complexities, boundaries, and critical race theory. In J. A. Banks & C. A. McGee Banks (Eds.), *Handbook of research on multicultural education* (2nd edition, pp. 50-65). San Francisco: Jossey-Bass.

Mariner, N., Lester, J. N., & Anders, A. D. (in press). The politics of nativism in US public education: Critical race theory and Burundian children with refugee status. In T. Kress, C. Malott, & B. Porfilio (Eds.), *Challenging status quo entrenchment: New directions in critical qualitative research.* Charlotte, NC: Information Age Publishing.

Malkki, L. (1996). National geographic: the rooting of peoples and the territorialization of national identity among scholars and refugees. In G. Eley & R. Grigor Suny (Eds.), *Becoming national: A reader* (pp. 434-453). Oxford: Oxford University Press.

Mbembe, A. (2001). *On the postcolony.* Berkeley, CA: University of California Press.

Meier, K., Stewart, J., & England, R. (1989). *Race, class and education: The politics of second-generation discrimination.* Madison: The University of Wisconsin.

Messer, E. (1993). Anthropology and human rights. *Annual Review of Anthropology, 22*, 221-249.

Noblit, G. W. (1999). *Particularities: Collected essays on ethnography and education.* New York: Peter Lang.

Noblit, G., & Engel, J. D. (1999). The holistic injunction: An ideal and a moral imperative for qualitative research, In G. W. Noblit (Ed.), *Particularities: Collected essays on ethnography and education.* New York, NY: Peter Lang.

Noblit, G. W., Flores, S., & Murillo, E. G. (2004). Postcritical ethnography: an Introduction. In G. W. Noblit, S. Y. Flores, & E. G. Murillo, Jr. (Eds.), *Postcritical ethnography: Reinscribing critique* (pp. 1-52). Cresskill, NJ: Hampton.

Norum, K. E. (2000). School patterns: A sextet. *Qualitative Studies in Education, 13*(3), 239-250.

Pérez Huber, L. (2010). Using Latina/o critical race theory and racist nativism to explore intersectionality in the educational experiences of undocumented Chicana college students. *Educational Foundations, 24*(1), 77-96.

Pérez Huber, L., Lopez, C. B., Malagon, M. C., Velez, V., & Solorzano, D. G. (2008). Getting beyond the 'symptom,' acknowledging the disease: Theorizing racist nativism. *Contemporary Justice Review, 11*(1), 39-51.

Said, E. (1994). From orientalism. In P. Williams & L. Chrismans (Eds.), *Colonial discourse and post-colonial theory: A reader* (pp. 132-149). New York: Columbia University Press.

Scott, J. C. (1998). *Seeing like a state: How certain schemes to improve the human condition have failed.* New Haven, Connecticut: Yale University Press.

Scott, D. (1999). *Refashioning futures: Criticism after postcoloniality.* Princeton, NJ: Princeton University Press.

Selden, S. (2000). Eugenics and the social construction of merit, race and disability. *Journal of Curriculum Studies, 32*(2), 235-252.

Siebers, T. (2008). *Disability theory.* Ann Arbor, MI: The University of Michigan Press.

Teranishi, R. T. (2002). Asian Pacific Americans and critical race theory: An examination of school racial climate. *Equity and Excellence in Education, 35*(2), 144-154.

Tyack, D. B. (1993). Constructing difference: Historical reflections on schooling and diversity. *Teachers College Record, 95*(1), 8-34.

UN General Assembly, *Convention on the Rights of the Child*, 20 November 1989, United Nations, Treaty Series, 1577, 3, available at: http://www.unhcr.org/refworld/docid/3ae6b38f0.html [accessed 7 July 2012].

Wiggam, A. E. (1922). *The new decalogue of science*. New York: Bobbs-Merrill.

Young, R. (2001). *Postcolonialism: A historical introduction.* Oxford: Blackwell.

Zembylas, M. (2007). Emotional capital and education: theoretical insights from Bourdieu. *British Journal of Educational Studies, 55*(4), 443-463.

DELORES D. LISTON & REGINA RAHIMI

CHAPTER 5

Taking Toll: The Impact of Sexual and Gender Harassment on the Lives of Middle and High School Students

Middle school and high school are difficult spaces traversed by adolescents. Caught up in the midst of one of the most challenging developmental stages of life, adolescents are simultaneously trying to individuate from others (parents and peers), while trying to fit in with peers and the larger social context. There are many adults who fondly reminisce about their high school days, recalling that time as happy and hope-filled. But, for many young people, those days are anything but care-free. Many students experience sexual and/or gender harassment during their middle and high school years. For some, they are harassed when they go to school, turn on a phone, or go to social networking sites on a computer (Ormerod, Collingsworth, & Perry, 2008). Sexual harassment is experienced by both young females and young males in schools, although it is experienced differently by both groups as this chapter will document. While harassment issues are also prevalent among school personnel, the emphasis here is on students. The Equal Employment Opportunity Commission [EEOC] defines sexual harassment as:

> Unwelcome sexual advances, requests for sexual favors, and other verbal or physical conduct of a sexual nature constitutes sexual harassment when submission to or rejection of this conduct explicitly or implicitly affects an individual's employment, unreasonably interferes with an individual's work performance or creates an intimidating, hostile or offensive work environment. (EEOC, n.d., para. 1)

This is the definition of sexual harassment used in this analysis, although applied to the space of schools and students within them. Recently the term "gender harassment" has been added to the vocabulary in this area to highlight the relationship between harassment and gender norms and expectations. Meyer (2008) provides the following definition of gendered harassment, which is the way the concept is understood in this research:

> Gendered harassment is defined as any behavior, verbal, physical or psychological, the polices the boundaries of traditional heterosexual gender norms and includes (hetero) sexual harassment, homophobic harassment, and harassment for gender non-conformity. (p. 556)

J. Hall (ed.), Children's Human Rights and Public Schooling in the United States, 89–101.

The prevalence of sexual harassment and gender harassment in schools is difficult to measure. Research conducted by the American Association of University Women [AAUW] remains one of the most extensive and thorough studies of harassment in school settings. This study found the percentage of middle and high school students who witness or are victims of sexual harassment to be 90% (2001). More recent work has estimated sexual harassment to be at around 50% (Walsh et al., 2007), still a significantly high number. Many current investigations refrain from statistical percentages, as so much sexual and gender harassment is known to be unreported. Such investigations instead focus on descriptors such as "common" (Ashbaugh & Cornell, 2008) or "almost normative" (Brown & L'Engle, 2009).

Another reason for the wide range in estimates is because it is difficult to define sexual and gender harassment. Both forms of harassment can be perceived as context specific. For example, some students may witness a male student leering at a female student in the cafeteria and consider it just being "friendly" because they believe the male is her boyfriend. Others witnessing this same incident may know the couple broke up last weekend, and the male's leering is intended as intimidation and showing off in front of his peers. Nonetheless, both the students who are harassing and students who are being harassed know it. Often the students being harassed feel the effects of sexual and gender harassment deeply and significantly, reporting a myriad of effects of this behavior on their lives (Rahimi & Liston, 2012). They evidence everything from minor inconveniences such as avoiding certain hallways on campus, to more significant effects such as not being able to sleep or concentrate on school work. Highly negative effects such as dropping out of school, serious health problems, mental health issues, and even suicide have been found to be outcomes (Gillander, 2005; Gruber & Fineran, 2008; Omerod et al., 2008; Yaffe, 1995).

Here we explore sexual harassment and gender harassment among adolescents in public schools through the lens of middle and high school students and teachers. Given the difficulty in working directly with adolescents in schools, we opt to investigate the experiences of 25 college freshman with harassment as they reflect upon their high school experiences. We also sought the narrations of approximately ten current middle and high school teachers aged 25-35, who have been teaching for five-ten years. In order to recruit female and male college freshmen, we set up fliers on campus and solicited participants through word of mouth. We sought students who had direct experience with sexual harassment as well as those who did not, but who were willing to comment on what they saw around them while in high school. The teachers we interviewed were largely found through word of mouth. We did not seek a particular demographic profile regarding any of our participants, but rather simply selected all those who volunteered first. The racial and gender make up of participants ended up as follows: female students – 5 white; 6 African American. Male students – 10 white; 2 African American; 1 Asian; 1 Hispanic. Teachers – 10 white females; 1 African American female.

Investigating sexual and/or gender harassment with students who were enrolled in college meant we missed the population of students who travelled a different path. We do recognize the importance of multiple standpoints in examining social phenomena. In our future work we hope to capture the experiences of students who left high school and/or college to enter the work force, start a family, and so forth. Given the social, psychological, and academic toll harassment can have on its victims, we suspect many persons victimized by harassment may not have been able to continue with their studies.

EXPERIENCES OF SEXUAL HARASSMENT AMONG FEMALE STUDENTS

While males are pressured into a narrow challenge in the development of gender identity (dominate and be a man, or be dominated, and therefore not a man), females navigate a much more disconnected set of expectations. As de Beauvoir demonstrated, women are first and foremost "not men." Nor can they ever become "men." Rather, women are perennially "the other." They are the opposite against which men come to be in the fullness of self. In schools and among the larger culture, traditional feminine norms also remain in place, but these are also tempered with contradictory expectations. Femininity is marked by docility, beauty, purity, softness, dependence, a nurturing demeanor, and a desire to please others, while still all the while being bound up in seductiveness.

Thus, in the conceptualization of hegemonic masculinity, women are there for men to dominate. As part of this patriarchal script, women are a foil against which males demonstrate their sexual and social virility. Thus, while males pursue their status directly, females construct a sense of self through association with males and through demonstrations of purity/seductiveness. These demonstrations are often played out among adolescents in the context of schools.

Media reinforces the mainstream views of masculinity, and contemporary media often perpetuates the sexualization of young women (Durham, 2008; Fausto-Sterling, 2000; Younger, 2009). As Brown and L'Engle (2009) describe "adolescents who used sexually explicit media also had more permissive sexual norms, had less progressive gender role attitudes, and perpetrated more sexual harassment activities compared to their peers at baseline" (Brown & L'Engle, 2009, p. 139). In their study of adult males, Dill, Brown, and Collins also found:

> A significant interaction indicated that men exposed to stereotypical content made judgments that were more tolerant of a real-life instance of sexual harassment compared to controls. Long-term exposure to video game violence was correlated with greater tolerance of sexual harassment and greater rape myth acceptance. (2008, p. 1402)

As mainstream influences press adolescents toward conceptualizations of masculinity and femininity, males who exhibit dominating and bullying traits may experience increased popularity among their peers (Ashbaugh et al., 2008; Pellegrini, 2002). Harassing behaviors among males tend to be encouraged in peer relationships, rather than discouraged during adolescence. Robinson states the case clearly:

> Sexual harassment is integral to the construction of hegemonic heterosexual masculine identities; the importance of popularity, acceptance and young men's fears within male peer group cultures; and the utilization of sexual harassment as a means through which to maintain and regulate hierarchical power relationships, not just in relation to gender, but how it intersects with other sites of power such as race and class. (2005, p. 19)

All females can find themselves vulnerable to sexual harassment nearly anytime and anywhere – within intimate relationships, at parties or social gatherings, when with an authority figure, or when alone with a friend (Livingston, Hequembourg, Testa, & VanZile-Tamsen, 2007). As the female participants in this study narrate, they can be harassed when at home, at school, at work, out shopping, while walking in their neighborhood, practicing sports, attending a party, out on a date, or just hanging out with a friend:

- "He (her step-grandfather) would stare at me while I was doing my homework. He would tell me I was pretty and he kissed my once."
- "guys are allowed to kiss you anywhere, say anything they want to you, but you are supposed to get married and then have sex."
- "there were guys in middle school who made disgusting comments, especially about my breasts because I developed early."
- "boys saying stuff to girls and touching them is common in school."
- "most of the guys on the football team would touch us on the bus."
- "at the mall you know somebody is going to say some kind of thing to you."
- "you can dance and most guys will try to pull up my skirt while I am trying to pull it down. Then I will stop dancing with them and walk off."

Clearly, as illustrated by these examples from our participants, violence, threat of violence, and harassment still remain a part of the female experience. There is not a domain in the social, academic, or vocational experiences of women that is not characterized by at least the possibility of victimization.

As argued, the cultural rules are seemingly set up against girls. They are expected to wear provocative clothing and project sexual allure, yet remain pure and virginal. They are typically accused of being too "uppity," dressing too promiscuously, being too "butch," or "asking for it" through dress or behaviors. Consider how teachers talk about some of their female students:

- "the girls' tops are blatantly sexual, even when they wear uniforms"
- "these little girls are so developed; you can't help but notice their bodies. Tight fitting clothing should be banned in the code of conduct from the district level down"
- "I am just absolutely amazed at how girls are coming to school dressed and they are more and more developed. It's like they are saying 'here it is, come and get it!'"

When girls in general fail to walk this thin line with agility enough to avoid being "too prim and proper" or "too slutty," they may become victimized first through abuse and second through being blamed for the abuse. As told through the teachers we interviewed, girls are often seen to be responsible for their own victimization.

Using an analysis framed by a feminist perspective, we center females, and in particular, girls/women of color in this discussion on sexual harassment. Our findings indicate that teachers (white, middle class teachers in particular) more often ignore the sexual harassment of female students of color. When it comes to the perception of who is sexually harassed, there are culturally specific stereotypes rendering some as "touchable castes." Latina and African American females for example experience the highest instances of sexual harassment in school. Females living in poverty moreover are also more likely to be victims of sexual harassment, yet they are less likely to report it (Miller, 2008). Such realities are largely due to the perceptions of these students by teachers and middle class peers that these females are more promiscuous or therefore more deserving of harassment (Rahimi & Liston, 2012). When asked about sexuality and students today, consider these comments from white, middle class teacher-participants describing African American students:

- "Marriage is a different thing in their culture; sex outside of marriage isn't as taboo as in my culture"
- "I don't think there is any romance with this group whatsoever"
- "I think the bi-sexual thing is definitely more common in the white group, where the black thing is male/female-even the girls are more aggressive than white girls"
- "I don't think the black kids mind anybody knowing that are sexually active"
- "Blacks are more open with (sexuality). They are more apt to have sex and be open with it"
- "I see with that community (Latin, African American) just a global acceptance of open sexuality. You will see it in the way they dress. They are the ones who always wear low cut shirts, they wear tight shirts, you can see their panties – if they have them on"

These examples of comments from teachers indicate racist ideology continues to influence their thoughts regarding sexuality. As we found through our ongoing research, young women of color are often marginalized further by discourse on sexual harassment in schools. The limited conversation regarding sexual harassment has largely been framed from the perspective of white, middle class experience (Richardson & Taylor, 2009). It is therefore imperative to examine sexual harassment as a gendered and raced phenomenon. Again, while all females are "at risk" for violence being perpetrated against them, researchers have shown girls who fit into particular categories, such as females of color, are more vulnerable to sexual harassment, thus making their experiences even more dangerous. As noted in the literature, characteristics of females who are most likely to be targeted include the following:

- Latina or African American girls are more likely to experience sexual harassment than White or Asian girls (Dupper & Meyer Adams 2002; Malay, 2005; Miller, 2008).
- Girls from poor neighborhoods are more likely to experience sexual harassment than girls from middle or upper class neighborhoods (Brandenburg, 1997; Miller, 2008).
- Girls with disabilities are especially vulnerable (Young, Heath, Ashbaker, & Smith, 2008).
- Girls who have already been victims of abuse are especially vulnerable to sexual harassment (Wyatt & Rierdale, 1994). If a girl experiences incest or rape by a relative, neighbor or a peer, her chances of experiencing future incidents of harassment or rape increase exponentially.
- Girls perceived to be lesbian are more likely to experience sexual harassment than girls who are perceived to be heterosexual (AAUW, 2001; Hansen, 2007; Henning-Stout, James, & Mcintosh, 2000).
- Girls whose bodies develop secondary sex characteristics early (Duncan, 1999; Grabe & Hyde, 2007; Lindberg, Grabe, & Hyde, 2007).
- Girls who are labeled as "sluts" become part of a touchable class, fair game for anyone to harass. A variety of factors can contribute to the assignment of this adverse sexual label (Liston & Rahimi, 2005; Tanenbaum, 2000).
- Girls who are timid or shy are more likely to be sexually harassed (Paludi & Kravitz, 2011).

Those females who display multiple of the above characteristics are extremely high risk for targeting. While these factors are not largely within the girl's locus of control, the victim nonetheless, is often blamed for their own harassment.

How a girl responds to harassment may prevent future episodes or set her up for future harassment. Again, there is no clear set of guidelines for the girl to follow, but she must somehow navigate this uncertain terrain in which she may face dire consequences. Girls who find themselves victims of sexual harassment have very limited options in reaction to the harassment (Liston & Rahimi, 2005). From our prior research (Rahimi & Liston, 2012), it is clear girls who feel most vulnerable sometimes attempt to "laugh it off." This response however is often interpreted by teachers, harassers, and other witnesses as enjoyment of the harassment. As they reflect on their high school experiences, the female participants discuss how common harassment occurs and/or how there is no place to go for help in schools:

- "I think guys think they have the right to do things. No one is enforcing it. I mean like me telling them 'no' didn't do much. They were just like OK, and they don't really get in trouble for it."
- "Girls would sometimes go to the teacher and say he is touching me and they (the teachers) would see it and would just turn the other cheek."
- "Most of the time, you keep walking or like you don't hear it unless they come touch you."

- “When we were at (school) events, it would go on there too, like gestures of ‘you look good.’ Most girls wouldn’t think it’s cute.”
- “Some students would run around smacking girls on the butts and the girls would be OK with it, and some teachers wouldn’t mind it. They know they are just having fun.”
- “Sometimes in the halls you would see guys being more aggressive to the girls, ‘let me take you out; you need to go out with me,’ and the girls were kinda trying to get away and they got cornered almost. There was some of that, but nothing real serious.”
- “Teachers never addressed sexual harassment because honestly, they were more focused on shirt tails being tucked in and ridiculous things like cell phones.”

As we have seen from our studies, the wrong place could be home or work or school. Further, it seems no matter what choices a young girl makes, she is vulnerable. As research shows, females who are sexually inexperienced are vulnerable to sexual harassment because of their naiveté. Girls who are sexually active are vulnerable because they find themselves in sexually charged situations where they may not be in control (Young & Furman, 2008). In our ongoing work, girls who were harassed in school grew up to experience more abuse and encountered higher than average difficulties in sustaining intimate relationships. These females experienced dropping out of school, becoming involved with drugs, becoming involved with abusive partners, suffering from depression, struggled with self-concept, and/or harbored suicidal thoughts/attempts (Rahimi & Liston, 2012). In this way, vulnerability leads to future vulnerability and increases risk of heightened physical danger:

> The intersection between [girls’ responses to harassment] and the list of risk factors for sexual harassment is telling. As students experience sexual harassment their self-esteem drops, they feel isolated, nervous and angry. This often leads to feelings of “sensitivity,” “fear of rejection” and “powerlessness” – items on the list of risk factors for sexual harassment. Thus, negative impacts on the girl or boy who experiences sexual harassment generates an exponential increase in risk factors for continued sexual harassment and a cycle is begun that can spin out of control for the victim of this abuse. (Rahimi & Liston, 2012, p. 15)

Females in our present research could speak directly to their instances of harassment in school and the negative impact it had on their lives:

- “I remember the first time I was called a whore … pretty much once you get a reputation around schools, everybody looks at you in a different light. After I got that reputation, it was curtains … time to go. I left school.”
- “For a long time I felt like nobody would accept me just for me because they couldn’t get past the rumors.”

- "I had bad relationships all my life – bad, abusive, especially verbally abusive. The thing is you begin to feel that nobody's every really going to love you. Why should they?"
- "I didn't like myself and I fell into the vicious cycle of dating complete jerks that were going to take advantage of me in some way. I just didn't have the confidence to take myself out of that. I felt like I had to have someone, to be dating someone, to prove that I wasn't that way."

With limited access to critical and constructive discourse regarding sexual behavior and sexuality within the parameters of their formal educational experiences, females are forced to navigate the terrain of harassment on their own. Feelings of shame, isolation, and helplessness often accompany their perceptions of harassment in school (Kiddie, 2009).

EXPERIENCES OF HARASSMENT AMONG MALE STUDENTS

It is important to understand harassment from a variety of perspectives, including those of males. Most often, males are viewed as perpetrators, as sexual harassment is often seen as a binary between females (victims) and males (assailants). This depiction of sexual harassment makes it difficult to discuss openly with males. Indeed, in conducting our research, we had difficulty getting males to participate. Some males informally told us they were reluctant to speak with us for fear of being accused of being perpetrators of sexual harassment. Other males said they did not want to discuss how they were being harassed. As noted earlier, traditional masculinity sets up a "dominate" (and be a man) or "be dominated" scenario. In this sense, the fear of being seen as "unmanly" locates homophobia at the root of much sexual harassment. Our culture is in dire need of discussion on issues related to homophobia, gender, racism, social class, and harassment and how a normative environment has been created where females are targeted and males are defensive and/or afraid to discuss their vulnerabilities (Delgado & Stefancic, 2000; Duncan, 2002).

As we stated above, the pressure to conform to traditional roles of masculinity can encourage young men to perpetuate the practice of sexual harassment (Ormerod, Collinsworth, & Perry, 2008; Timmerman, 2005). In our earlier work with young men, they articulated a social compulsion to behave a certain way towards females (Rahimi & Liston, 2012). Some of the young men in our present study suggest they only behaved in certain ways (like physically touching young girls in the hallways of school) when they were with other males. They noted they would never act in such a way while alone. Some of the participants noted homophobic slurs were also somewhat encouraged, particularly in the male athletic culture.

Just as young women have very few safe responses to harassment, young men are confronted with similar social paralysis. As Young and Furman (2008) assert, young men's responses to sexual harassment run the gamut from thinking it is not a big deal, to being "powerless," and to "becoming a bully" in order to "prove" manhood (Young & Furman, 2008). In a previous study, we found male high school students referred to harassment as "nothing serious," "a joke." Their lack of empathy for victims is illustrative of a larger cultural reality that excludes the experiences of females:

- "We had one male principal … every time a girl would walk by he would ogle them up and down. He was kind of a joke. It was really funny [I thought at the time]."
- "Yeah I heard 'whore,' 'slut,' any form of ethnic slur. Those can be kinda funny actually."

The connections between traditional masculinity, homophobia, and sexual harassment are clear. Traditional masculinity sanctions domination and harassment. Males who fail to live up to this standard may find themselves falling victim to gender harassment. Once again, this highlights the "dominate or be dominated" theme running through traditional conceptions of masculinity. In some ways no different from how females are secondarily victimized by being led to believe they are responsible for their own victimization, male victims are also viewed as responsible for their own abuse (Kenway & Fitzclarence, 1997; Pascoe, 2007; Rahimi & Liston, 2012).

Gendered harassment highlights the push for heteronormativity and restrictive norms of masculinity and femininity. "Bullying" is a representation of this push. We caution when it comes to bullying, discussion largely seems to highlight the experiences of middle class white male students. This discourse further ignores the homophobic, sexist, and gendered nature of bullying and harassment and completely fails to address the daily occurrences of sexual harassment experienced by young females and along lines of sexual orientation. Research indicates male students are very rarely reprimanded for bullying in the form of lewd comments (Miller, 2008; Pascoe, 2007; Rahimi & Liston, 2012). Generally, bullies experience elevated social status, confirming support for bullying behaviors (Duncan, 1999). Clearly this phenomenon reveals the erroneous belief that bullying is gender-neutral and without consequence. We wish to re-center the discussion around the lived experiences of women, and females of color in particular. In so doing, we assert hegemonic ideology regarding race, gender, social class, and sexual orientation are at the core of the harassment encountered by students.

The dominant ideology of sexuality (heterosexual sexuality that is) is used among the broader culture to sell everything from automobiles to deodorant. Familiar in the public eye are images such as scantily clad young women shown draping their bodies suggestively across the hoods of cars, or fawning over the alpha male on his way to work. More than a century and a half has passed since the Seneca Falls Women's Rights Convention (1848) and more than half a century has passed since the Women's Rights Movement of the 1960s. And yet, the same basic gender roles drive our society. Traditional masculine norms remain in place. Males are supposed to be tough, virile, dominating, aloof, independent, strong – and violent. These traits are also ironically associated with being rational, reasonable, and natural leaders. Societal norms suggest there must be opportunities for men to establish their masculinity. Of course, one way in which men can do this is through marginalizing the "other" (de Beauvior, 1971).

In our present research with male students, males who challenged traditional notions of masculinity found themselves victims of gender harassment often in school. As our participants revealed, this presented in the form of homophobic harassment and occurred almost daily in school buildings and school staff often permit or even promote this form of marginalization:

- "… they (other students) just continue to do it over and over again (use homophobic slurs) until they got switched out of class or something. I think teachers get lazy. I think because they hear it so much they aren't going to be like "hey don't say that."
- "In my school, homosexuality was only talked about in a negative context. Teachers never addressed sexual harassment."

As the AAUW reported through their comprehensive examination of harassment, lesbian/gay/bisexual/transgendered youth are three times more likely to experience gender harassment (2001). LGBTQ students are often forced to either hide their sexuality or face a myriad of forms of harassment (Henning-Stout et al., 2000; Meyer, 2008; Rivers, 2011). As we found with our participants who identified themselves as LGBTQ (in our past and current research), harassment was a daily, persistent experience in their lives. Their marginalization was mostly upheld by school personnel and even members of their own communities. They were reminded by ongoing slurs, physical violence, and social ostracism that they were seen as a threat to the existing traditional role of heterosexual masculinity. As one participant shared, "I was bullied all through grade school, called 'faggot' and 'gay boy.' By fifth grade I was sick of it and it had gotten to a point where I didn't want to tell my parents about it. But because I was being bullied so often and nothing was being done about it I had to. I was always afraid of my teachers. I never felt like I was liked by them."

LGBTQ students are most often attacked for their failure to adhere to traditional norms of masculinity and femininity. Traditional gender norms establish the hierarchy with dominating males at the top. Those who range far afield from traditional gender norms may be susceptible to pervasive and virulent forms of gender harassment and bullying. Although society claims to have moved beyond violent enforcement of traditional gender norms, clearly we have not. While males must be held accountable for violence against females, there is also a need for opportunities to challenge a culture that advocates such violence. All students require spaces to discuss issues of sexuality, race, social class, and gender from a critical perspective. Public schools are the ideal forum for this.

CONCLUSION

Most adolescents do not leave their youth unscathed by sexual/gendered harassment. Whether they have witnessed, participated in, experienced directly, or lived with the threat of harassment, students in contemporary school settings continue to be plagued by sexual and gendered harassment. Females from culturally marginalized groups, low income girls, and females with disabilities are especially at risk. LBGTQ youth are also susceptible to forms of harassment, although all youth are potential targets. School faculty and staff are often unprepared or ill-equipped to address these daily occurrences, thus youth are left to maneuver this very complex social system alone. We, as adults, may view this harassment as some rite of passage. However, it is far from absent of consequence to the adolescent who experiences it. As researchers have noted (Klusas, 2003; Larkin, 1994; Polce-Lynch, Myers, Kliewer, & Kilmartin, 2001; Yaffe, 1995), harassment can have dire consequences for students, ranging from academic underperformance, to dropping out of school, to severe psychological repercussions, all which negatively shape future outcomes.

Due to neoliberal education reform, the test-taking focus in schools has created a wider void of trained personnel capable of addressing the affective needs of students. Students in school often have limited access to counselors or other adults who can address issues of harassment on a personal level and as a systemic epidemic. With grossly inadequate education on such issues, there is little space to create institutional change and disrupt the violence directed against students, including those who challenge traditional models of masculinity/femininity. Professional development for teachers should further focus on the ways in which harassment and abuse exist within schools. Sexuality education should also be re-conceptualized to meet much better the needs of students. We advocate for opportunities for youth to discuss issues relating to sexual and gender harassment across curriculum. Teacher preparation programs should focus to a greater degree on critical analysis of these topics. Our students deserve this. To suggest that sexual or gender harassment is not one of the most important issues facing school today would be a massive act of negligence. We argue that the establishment of safe spaces for all students should be a priority in educational discourse and policy.

REFERENCES

American Association of University Women. (2001). *Hostile hallways: bullying, teasing, and sexual harassment in school*. Washington, D.C.

Ashbaugh, C. & Cornell, D. (2008). Sexual harassment and bullying behaviors in sixth graders. *Journal of School Violence*, *7*(1), 21-38.

Bradenburg, J. (1997). *Confronting sexual harassment: What schools and colleges can do*. New York: Teachers College Press.

Brown, J. D., & L'Engle, K. L. (2009). X-rated: Sexual attitudes and behaviors associated with US early adolescents' exposure to sexually explicit media. *Communications Research, 36*(1), 129-151.

deBeauvoir, S. (1971). *The second sex*. New York: Alfred Knopf.

Delgado, R., & Stefancic, J. (Eds.). (2000). *Critical race theory: The cutting edge*. Philadelphia: Temple University Press.

Dill, K. E., Brown, B. P., & Collins, M. A. (2008). Effects of exposure to sex-stereotyped video game characters on tolerance of sexual harassment. *Journal of Experimental Social Psychology*, *44*(5), 1402-1408.

Duncan, G. A. (2002). Beyond love: A critical race ethnography of the schooling of adolescent Black males. *Equity and Excellence in Education*, *35*(2), 131-143.

Duncan, N. (1999). *Sexual bullying: Gender conflict and pupil culture in secondary school*. London: Routledge.

Dupper, D. R., & Meyer-Adams (2002). Low level violence: A neglected aspect of school culture. *Urban Education*, *37*, 350-364.

Durham, M. G. (2008). *The Lolita effect: Media sexualization of young girls and what we can do about it*. New York: Overlook Hardcover.

Equal Employment Opportunity Commission. (n.d.). www.eeoc.gov/facts/fs-sex.html.

Fausto-Sterling, A. (2000). *Sexing the body: Gender politics and the construction of sexuality*. New York: Perseus Books.

Fineran, S., & Bennett, L. (1999). Gender and power issues of peer sexual harassment among teenagers. *Journal of Interpersonal Violence*, *14*(6), 626-641.

Gilander Gadin, K., & Hammarstrom, A. (2005). A possible contributor to the higher degree of girls reporting psychological symptoms compared with boys in grade nine? *European Journal of Public Health*, *15*(4), 380-385.

Gruber, J. E. & Fineran, S. (2008). Comparing the impact of bullying and sexual harassment victimization on the mental and physical health of adolescents. *Sex Roles*, *58*, 13-14.

Hansen, L. (2007). School-based support for GLBT students: A review of three levels of research. *Psychology in the Schools*, *44*(8), 839-848.

Henning-Stout, M., James, S., & Mcintosh, S. (2000). Reducing harassment of lesbian, gay, bisexual, transgender, and questioning youth in schools. *School Psychology Review*, *29*, 180-191.

Keddie, A. (2009). “Some of those girls can be real drama queens:” Issues of gender, sexual harassment, and schooling. *Sex Education: Sexuality, Society and Learning*, *9*(1), 1-16.

Kenway, J., & Fitzclarence, L. (1997). Masculinity, violence, and schooling: Challenging ‘poisonous pedagogies.’ *Gender and Education*, *9*(1), 117-134.

Klusas, J. (2003). Providing students with protection they deserve: Amending the Office of Civil Rights’ Guidance on Title IX to protect students from peer harassment in schools. *Texas Journal of Civil Liberties and Civil Rights*, *8*(1), 91-116.

Larkin, J. (1994). Walking through walls. The sexual harassment of high school girls. *Gender and Education*, *6*(3), 263.

Liston, D., & Rahimi, R. M. (2005). Disputation of a bad reputation: Adverse sexual labels and the lives of twelve southern women. In P. Bettis & N. Adams (Eds.), *Geographies of girlhood: Identities in-between*. New Jersey: Lawrence Earlbaum.

Lindberg, S., Grabe, S., & Hyde, J. (2007). Gender, pubertal development, and peer sexual harassment predict objectified body consciousness in early adolescence. *Journal of Research on Adolescence*, *17*(4), 723-742.

Livingston, J. A., Hequembourg, A., Testa, M., & VanZile-Tamsen, C. (2007). Unique aspects of adolescent sexual victimization experiences. *Psychology of Women Quarterly*, *31*, 331-343.

Malay, J., Laumann, E., & Michaels, S. (2005). Race, gender, class in sexual scripts. In J. K. Davidson & N. Moore (Eds.), *Speaking of sexuality: Interdisciplinary readings* (pp. 155-158). Los Angeles: Roxbury.

Meyer, E. (2008). *Gender, bullying and harassment: Strategies to end sexism and homophobia in schools*. New York: Teachers College Press.

Miller, J. (2008). *Getting played: African American girls, urban inequality, and gendered violence*. New York: New York University Press.

Ormerod, A. J., Colingsworth, L. L., & Perry, L. A. (2008). Critical climate: Relations among sexual harassment, climate, and outcomes for high school girls and boys. *Psychology of Women Quarterly*, *32*(2), 113-125.

Paludi, M., & Kravitz, A. (2011). Sexual harassment of adolescent girls by peers, teachers, employers, and internet predators. In M. Paludi, *The psychology of teen violence and victimization*. ABC-CLIO.

Pascoe, C. J. (2007). *Dude! You're a fag: Masculinity and sexuality in high school*. Berkley: University of California Press.

Pellegrini, A. D. (2001). Bullying, victimization, and sexual harassment during the transition to middle school. *Educational Psychologist, 37*(3), 151-163.

Polche-Lynch, M., Myers, B. J., Kliewer, W., & Kilmartin, C. (2001). Adolescent self-esteem and gender: Exploring relations to sexual harassment, body image, media influence and emotional expression. *Journal of Youth and Adolescence, 30*(2), 225.

Popkin, S. J., Leventhal, T., & Weismann, G. (2010). Girls in the 'hood: How safety affects the life chances of low-income girls. *Urban Affairs Review, 45*(6), 715-744.

Rahimi, R., & Liston, D. (2012). *Pervasive vulnerabilities: Sexual harassment in school*. New York, Peter Lang Publishing.

Richardson, B., & Taylor, J. (2009). Sexual harassment at the intersection of race and gender: A theoretical model of the sexual harassment experiences of women of color. *Western Journal of Communication, 73*(3), 248-272.

Rivers, I. (2011). *Homophobic bullying: Research and theoretical perspectives*. New York: Oxford University Press.

Robinson, K. (2005). Reinforcing hegemonic masculinities through sexual harassment: Issues of identity, power, and popularity in secondary schools. *Gender and Education, 17*(1), 19-37.

Rousso, H. (2000). Girls and women with disabilities: An international overview and summary of research. Oakland, CA: World Institute on Disability/Rehabilitation International. Retrieved January 1, 2005, from http://www2.edc.org/GDI/publications_SR/publications/CRicaPub/RoussoEnglish.pdf

Stratton, S. D., & Backes, J. S. (1997). Sexual harassment in North Dakota schools. A study of eight high schools. *High School Journal, 80*(3), 163.

Tanenbaum, L. (2000). *Growing up female with a bad reputation*. New York: Harper Collins Publishers.

Timmerman, G. (2005). A comparison between girls' and boys' experiences of unwanted sexual behavior in secondary schools. *Educational Research, 47*(3), 291-306.

Walsh, M., Duffy, J., & Gallagher-Duffy, J. (2007). A more accurate approach to measuring the prevalence of sexual harassment among high school students. *Canadian Journal of Behavioral Science, 39*(2), 110-118.

Wing, A. (2008). *Critical race feminism: A reader*, 2nd edition. New York. New York University Press.

Wyatt, G., & Rierdale, M. (1994). Sexual harassment and prior sexual trama among African American and white American women. *Violence and Victims, 9*(3), 233-247.

Yaffe, E. (1995). Expensive, illegal, and wrong: Sexual harassment in our schools. *Phi Delta Kappan, 77*(3), K1.

Young, B., & Furman, W. (2008). Interpersonal factors in the risk for sexual victimization and its recurrence during adolescence. *Journal of Youth and Adolescence, 37*(3), 297-309.

Young, E., Heath, M., Ashbaker, B., & Smith, B. (2008). Sexual harassment among students with educational disabilities: Perspectives of special education. *Special and Remedial Education, 29*(4), 208-221.

Younger, B. (2009). *Learning curves: Body image and female sexuality in young adult literature*. Landham, MD: Scarecrow Press.

VIRGINIA BATCHELOR & ILLANA LANE

CHAPTER 6

Breaking the Code: Domestic Minor Sex Trafficking and School Children

INTRODUCTION

The lived-realities and schooling experiences of children in today's world can prove to be disturbing. As it stands, educators are challenged daily by issues that impact the academic achievement and emotional wellbeing of students who populate their classrooms. Educators however may be completely unaware about the issue of domestic minor sex trafficking [DMST] of school age children in the US. DMST "is the commercial sexual abuse of children through buying, selling, or trading their sexual services. Forms of DMST include: prostitution, pornography, stripping, escort services, and other sexual services" (Kotrla, 2010, p. 182). In some cases, labor trafficking co-exists with sex trafficking. The official Victims of Trafficking and Violence Protection Act of 2000 (the first US federal legislation response) defines forms of trafficking in persons as:

> (A) sex trafficking in which a commercial sex act is induced by force, fraud, or coercion, or in which the person induced to perform such an act has not attained 18 years of age; or
>
> (B) the recruitment, harboring, transportation, provision, or obtaining of a person for labor or services, through the use of force, fraud, or coercion for the purpose of subjection to involuntary servitude, peonage, debt bondage, or slavery. 106th Congress of the United States of America (2000, SEC 103 (8))

Most of the literature regarding DMST is from the field of social work and criminal justice (Hodge, 2008; NASW, 2003; Roby, 2005). The purpose of this chapter therefore is to build awareness of this problem in the discipline of education among teachers, administrators, caregivers, and students. It is vital to help young people avoid victimization by traffickers. The aim is to motivate schools to include curricula that integrates awareness, prevention, and intervention strategies that protect the human rights of children when it comes to human trafficking. It is also crucial to educate the broader public on these issues. This analysis provides basic information on the epidemic of DMST as a way of introducing the problem to educators.

J. Hall (ed.), Children's Human Rights and Public Schooling in the United States, 103–115.

Instances of DMST of children worldwide and in the US are on the rise. DMST is one of the most lucrative businesses in the US following the sale of narcotics and fire arms (Hodge, 2008). DMST is quickly advancing to become the second most profitable business, because while drugs or arms can only be sold once, a human can be resold hundreds and thousands of times. Shockingly, as it stands, the penalty for selling drugs is higher than for selling humans (Fernandes-Alcantra & Siskin, 2011). Children are coerced into DMST in the US in multiple ways. In some instances, the adults in their lives are involved in such acts. According to the US Department of Education (2007), children are targeted through the Internet, telephone chat lines, in the park, on the street, through friends, at the mall, and while waiting for the bus.

According to the Convention on the Rights of the Child [CRC] (1989), specifically Articles 34 and 39, children should be protected from all forms of sexual exploitation and sexual abuse and must be provided an environment that restores health, self-respect, and dignity of the victim. In 2002 the US did ratify an optional protocol to the CRC related to the prohibition on the trafficking of children, child prostitution, and child pornography (Human Rights Watch, 2012). Unfortunately, the US has not ratified the entire CRC, which suggests the absence of a real commitment to protecting the rights of children. As there is no mechanism for enforcing any part of the convention, in many ways the protocol are powerless. In the US there are laws that have been central to the protection of people regarding human sexual trafficking. It is important that these laws are in place to provide protection. Still the laws are often vaguely and inaccurately interpreted. For instance, the Mann Act was enacted by Congress in 1910. It addressed the problem of prostitution and the murky judgment of "immorality." Under this act it is only the transportation for sexual acts that renders the victimization illegal (Mones, 2011). In spite of these laws, DMST is a thriving part of the underground economy.

Domestic minor sex trafficking will continue to grow as an enterprise because buyers and sellers actively engage in increasingly aggressive, abusive, and oppressive behaviors to sustain business. Unfortunately, due to the neoliberal economic climate and the resulting defunding of the public sector, cuts to social services have left many families in disarray. In this climate it is becoming more difficult for schools to provide education and safety measures to prevent and intervene in issues of DMST. Less regulation (in the form of cuts to police, detectives, investigations), also make it easier to exploit along these lines (Clawson & Dutch, 2008; Human Smuggling and Trafficking Center, 2008). Such oppressive economic conditions also result in an increased drive in the underground economy to open up and expand the DMST trade.

METHODOLOGY

As an effort to explain the scope of the issue of DMST in the US, two professionals working in this arena in different urban areas in the Northeast were interviewed. These two women were specifically chosen due to their extensive work with domestic minor sexual trafficking victims and their varied perspectives from different sides of the crisis. One participant works in law enforcement and the other in social work. For the purpose of maintaining anonymity, we refer to the law enforcement professional as "Hope" and the social worker as "Faith." In-depth interviews were conducted to determine how educators can be more informed about this epidemic and the challenges they may encounter in their classrooms. As researchers, we are both African American female academics who became interested in this issue as we increasingly see news stories in the media on this topic yet realized it was seemingly missing from education literature and conversation.

Hope is Latina and bilingual and works in law enforcement. She is a Deputy Sheriff and the director of a human trafficking task force in a large city with 30 years of experience in the field. She has a variety of responsibilities connected to combating sexual trafficking which include following leads/investigating; dismantling human trafficking rings; investigating and working with victims to make sure traffickers get prosecuted in the courts; and education outreach on this issue to constituents entities in the community. Hope is also currently seeking private donations to fund the building of a safe house for female domestic victims of human trafficking. This safe house will include dormitories, counseling and medical services, and job rehabilitation and advocacy.

Faith is an African American social worker at a child advocacy center [CAC]. She is a member of the National Task Force Against Human Trafficking, and is involved with Araminta, a faith based community organization dedicated to the fight against sexual trafficking. She is a lead forensic interviewer with 12 years of experience working with DMST victims. Faith has conducted forensic interviews with victims of sexual abuse, sexual assault, and physical abuse for 17 years. She also assists the director in the operation of the forensic interviewer program and the training of new interviewers. As a lead forensic interviewer, she obtains information on the "who, what, when, where, and how of the sexual act."

Faith works in a CAC that is a grassroots organization funded through private donations. As such it is not restricted by the type of bureaucratic regulations that exist in a law enforcement agency or the Department of Social Services. Thus, those who work with her are not confined by rigid funding stipulations which can limit what they can do for clients. CACs were developed with the premise that traumatic situations (specifically abuse) experienced by children should be attended to in one location that provides a welcoming environment. The multiple professionals in this one environment include detectives, social workers, attorneys, counselors, and medical providers. Faith's position is unique in that her main focus is on children's rights and that her agency can provide what other institutions cannot.

Hope and Faith's fight against human trafficking takes place from two different vantage points. Law enforcement professionals look at the details of the crime while social workers focus primarily on the emotional impact experienced by victims. In Hope's position, a conclusion whether or not an individual is a victim of sexual trafficking is based upon determining if the individual was a victim of force, fraud, or coercion. Minors are always considered victims. According to Faith, the client is identified as a victim at the initial interview. Hope and Faith both talk about individuals involved in human sex trafficking with a sense of care. Both Hope and Faith are providing services that are not currently being met widespread.

DMST WITHIN THE US

Human sex trafficking is both a domestic and an international issue. However many in the US visualize victims as exclusively foreign females who were deceived and coerced into forced labor or commercial sex. The US is on a list of "destination nations" in which these women find themselves being exploited. Many though are unaware that those living in this county – including school age children – fall victim to human sex trafficking at alarming rates (Human Smuggling & Trafficking Center, 2008). Caregivers, teachers, and administrators tend to concern themselves with issues such as drug abuse and bullying. They do not typically see domestic sexual trafficking as an immediate threat to children in their school districts. Yet children who are US citizens are being sold, for example, at truck stops, on the back pages of local circulars, and on the Internet (Smith, 2008).

It is staggering to consider the true number of trafficking cases that exist in the US. Larsen (2011) expresses caution when providing DMST statistics. Her conclusions are based on findings from the 2011 report "Characteristics of Suspected Human Trafficking Incidents 2008-2010" in which federal anti-trafficking task forces opened 2,515 suspected cases of human trafficking between the years 2008 to 2010. Of the number reported, 82% of suspected incidents were classified as sex trafficking; and nearly half of these involved victims under the age of 18. In addition, 83% of victims in confirmed sex-trafficking incidents were identified as US citizens. According to Larsen (2011), the findings represent the government's best estimate. It is difficult to document the number of occurrences of DMST due to unawareness that it is domestic problem, lack of reporting, the tendency to blame the "victim" for "choosing" this lifestyle, and the inability to track children who are being moved from one location to another (Finklea et al., 2011; US Department of State, 2011).

Children are especially sought after by traffickers worldwide because they are thought to have less chance of having an STD. Children therefore can be sold each time at a higher amount that an older victim. Sex sells in the US, including the sexualization of minors. This culture has helped lead to the increased demand for child victims. *Toddlers & Tiaras: TLC* is a reality show that provides an inside view of the "competitive world of child pageants." Parents are involved in coaching and choosing costumes, and little girls (and boys) are dressed and made to look like miniature adults. Such images perpetuate the popularity of child DMST victims. In the US, the sex industry is glamorized through music, television, and gaming that utilizes pimping and prostitution as a ticket to a life of independence, glamour, power, and even happiness. This false image of the sex industry can be appealing to a troubled young person or adult. The character played by actor Julia Roberts in the film *Pretty Woman*, for instance, met the man of her dreams who swept her off her feet and into a world of wealth and love (Shared Hope International, 2009). Conversely, the negative aspects of prostitution and pimping (e.g., disease, abuse, drug addiction, or death) are not reported equally.

CHARACTERISTICS OF YOUNG DMST VICTIMS

Many DMST victims are school age children. A factsheet published by the US Department of Education Office of Safe and Drug-Free Schools in Washington, DC (2007) reports on victims who are as young as twelve. Additionally, just recently a MSNBC television special documents victims who are as young as nine (2011). When the research participants were asked about the average age of the population they work with, Hope, the law enforcement professional says:

> There is no average age in human trafficking. The youngest victim I've had is 12 and the oldest victim I've had is 62. I've had males, young boys, men, women, and older women. I've had every culture. There has not been one culture that has not been affected by human trafficking.

Faith, the social worker, discusses her work experiences with respect to the age of victims during the initial encounter. When asked to describe the population she serves, she explains:

> We do sexual assault and sexual abuse interviews for children as young as three, very rarely two [because they lack the verbal skills]. We try to get out of [interviewing] two [year olds], but occasionally, maybe about 1% [of the time], a two year old is squeezed in just for an attempt [to get information] which is still unsuccessful. We start as early as three years old and we do all children up to age 18 as well as young adults for sexual assaults. We also do [interview] adults who have some form of disability such as an intellectual or cognitive disability.

It has been found child victims of DMST share a number of characteristics (many which are also seen among domestic adults and foreign victims). These include lack of parental figures in the home; turmoil, transience, and drugs in the home; a propensity for depression; having few friends; being a substance abuser; not being aware of technology safety; running away from home or being homeless, and having adults in their lives who are already involved. Poverty as a factor can leave anyone vulnerable to sexual human trafficking. A runaway youth is also a neon sign for the sex trafficker. Gay, lesbian, transgender youth therefore are at high risk. Those already on the streets are more easily coerced into trafficking for their very survival. With few exceptions, most victims of trafficking come from environments where there are high rates of crime and poverty, a lack of family support, and/or a history of physical, emotional, or sex abuse (Clawson & Dutch, 2008).

The promise of legitimate employment lures especially foreign victims to unknowingly walk into various types of sexual exploitation traps. Hope describes how foreign victims are sometimes lured into sexual and labor trafficking:

> 'You only have to do it just once honey. It's only to pay the cell phone bill that we purchased together sweetie.' He talks her into it. Not only does he make her do it once, but he may have a schedule of about 30 different people he's going to take her to that night. That's part of fraud. Telling people you're going to come into the United States of America and we're going to give you a tremendous job and you're going to work eight hours and we're going to give you ten dollars an hour. Then they come to this county and they're working 12 hour days. They don't get any breaks and they only get to eat one meal a day. They don't get to pick where they want to live. They can't talk to people in the community. They don't have any freedom of movement.

Without knowing the language, culture, and having no one they can trust, such victims are at the complete mercy of their trafficker. Hope discusses the notion of "debt bondage" and how it is used by sex traffickers to manipulate both international and domestic victims of all ages:

> Debt bondage is an issue for both US and International victims. For example, you come from Mexico and you want to come into this country and you pay $3,700 to cross the border, which was four years ago. Now it's about $5,000 to cross the border. You will pay out that debt and all the other types of debt he [trafficker] lines up for you. For you to live at the restaurant and sleep on the restaurant floor it's going to cost you $25 a day. They charge you double for food. If they buy a coat they charge triple for it. There are all these costs. Every day you work that's more debt incurred. The person is in the red for a long time and even when they try to get out, he will find something else (other debt) to attach to that. He [trafficker] wants to make sure this person keeps working for him.

Another way traffickers control victims is through getting them chemically dependent on drugs. As long as they are addicted, the trafficker knows their victims will do anything to chase that high – a high which only they supply. Then they are derided by the trafficker for being a drug addict. Although victims suffer abuse from their trafficker, given their destroyed self-esteem, oftentimes they defend their victimizer and internalize the belief that they themselves are at fault for their circumstances.

MISPERCEPTIONS OF DMST VICTIMS PERPETUATED BY LAW ENFORCEMENT

With respect to the commercial sex industry and building awareness of the problem of DMST, it is important to change the perception of the wrongfully accused from "criminals" or "deviant" to "victims" among the larger culture. Amazingly, children who are too young to consent to engage in sexual activity are still often labeled as "prostitutes" and "juvenile delinquents" by US law enforcement, the courts, and the broader public. Sex crimes have a tendency to influence the perception by others that involved minors are deviant and females in particular "choose" prostitution as a lifestyle. They are often perceived as consensual participants especially as they often protect the trafficker due to fear. If they have been forced to recruit they are also often labeled as perpetrators/victimizers (Finklea, Fernandes Alcantatr, & Siskin, 2011; Shared Hope, 2009). In these circumstances, minors are not only victimized by sex traffickers, but also by the system that is in place to protect them. As Hope explains, time and time again she has seen in the courts how traumatized victims are often viewed as criminals:

> [...] Most of these cases when they come into the courts, they just look like prostitution cases. And people think [sex trafficking] – it's the same thing. [And] If you're a judge, and you've been on the bench for 15 years and have never gone for training [although] the law clearly states that at the age 16, 17, 18, you cannot have consent about having sex. We have not started processing the "Johns" that are buying them and that's part of the federal law also.

Domestic children who are victims of sexual trafficking and find themselves in the courts are mostly placed in juvenile detention facilities rather than protective services. Although there are problems with protective services, placement in a detention center reinforces a negative sense of self among that individual and the broader culture. Many of these youth then reenter the commercial sex industry upon reaching the age of 18 with the belief it is all they deserve. Further, it is important to remember those who were sexually abused and become traffickers are still victims. Many feel this may be the only way they can survive (Clawson & Grace, 2007). In order to mitigate the misconceptions among attorneys, police officers, and judges regarding victims, it is essential to provide specific training to these professionals in order to reshape attitudes.

THE SEX TRADE AS A GROWING MARKET

As reported in the documentary "Sex Slaves in the Suburbs," drug dealers are switching from selling drugs to becoming pimps. There are reasons for this. It is more dangerous to deal drugs as interactions involve a deadly combination of arms in the hands of those who are addicted. Argued already is that a person will receive a much harsher penalty for selling drugs than for selling people. The sex industry is also much more lucrative, as mentioned, as opposed to drugs, people are a "renewable commodity." That is "the pimps don't have to buy the product and it is low maintenance" (Kotrla, 2009). Given the high demand for young 'commodities,' child prostitution is very profitable. On the low end, one victim can turn five tricks a night. If a pimp has three victims, they can make $1500 a night or $10,500 a week tax free" (MSNBC, 2008). Hope describes the major problems with state laws:

> According to the victims and the traffickers, it is much easier to sell a person than it is to sell a gun in New York State. Right now, it's a felony if you get caught with a gun and you don't have a license [for the gun] in New York State. If you sell a person, although it's a felony, it's very rare that the judges charge accordingly. I don't think our judges have received the same amount of training as law enforcement. When judges are mandated to take cases and understand what human trafficking is through lessons, I think we will see a turnaround at the local and federal level.

When one does not have to pay for the crime with time spent in prison, sex trafficking will persist. It is also a misconception that human trafficking exists only in low income, urban neighborhoods. It is quite prevalent in upper middle class, suburban areas, as that is where well-paying "customers" live. In many instances wealthy people exclusively are buyers and sellers. Hope explains how the industry is growing due to a willing market among those with privilege:

> Look at the number and stats in [your] own community and read the newspaper. We really need to understand that poverty and what is going on in our own communities is real. Our kids need us to understand that this is happening. It's happening in every community. I went to speak to a wealthy women's group. When I asked them "how many people think human trafficking is in your community." No one raised their hands. Just so everyone is aware last year we had a case of human trafficking in your area. We had a girl who was being bought by many of your husbands or people in your community and they would order her up while they were at work. While you're taking your daughter or son to soccer or basketball practice, these young ladies are being dropped off at your doorstep. These were all professional men that are purchasing these young girls. A lot of times people think this [sex trafficking] is about poor people and we're [other poor people] selling girls in the city. This [sex trafficking] may occur at some of the higher end hotels. Men from other cities order up a young girl and she will come to the hotel; but there are also men in our communities who are very rich and well to do. I'm taking down their massage parlors. I'm not letting these websites continue to go up. I work hard to try to get them prosecuted. It's difficult because it's the wealthy people that are the purchasers. To purchase one of these young ladies is about $200. It's not the guy from the factory or average citizen that can afford it. Part of this whole thing with human trafficking is the power and

> control. In the initial stages of human trafficking, a lot of people really thought it was going to be a bunch of scumbags [read: low income individuals involved in street crime] we were going to arrest. It turns out it is well to do, educated men, who are in powerful positions. It puts a damper on the sex trade. This is what is happening throughout the nation. It's real.

Sex crimes stigmatize and convict victims, but seldom do the same consequences occur for pimps, traffickers, and buyers, including well educated individuals or "upstanding" people in the community. Hope explains "to purchase one of these young is about $200. Wealthy people are the purchaser – that's why it's difficult to get them prosecuted." Judges who are in a position to make a difference must receive the proper training for prosecuting domestic minor sex trafficking cases fairly (Human Smuggling & Trafficking Center, 2008).

Domestic minor sexual trafficking victims can experience a number of negative emotional, physical, psychological, and spiritual impacts. Emotional and psychological impacts include ongoing feelings of anxiety or fear; difficulty trusting others; exhibiting self-destructive behaviors; and profound feelings of shame or guilt. Physical impacts include broken bones and bruising, sexually transmitted diseases, and addiction (Clawson & Grace, 2007). The spiritual impact can include the victim feeling as though God or a higher power had abandoned them. There are obvious ways DMST impacts the learning process of child-victims in school.

EDUCATIONAL IMPLICATIONS OF DMST AND RECOMMENDATIONS

It is little surprise that the academic progress of a student who is being targeted by traffickers will be compromised. Such victims may be nervous and distracted in school, and often end up not attending. In terms of social change, the literature recommends 1) emphasis upon training of people in positions of power to recognize and be of assistance to victims; 2) creating safe houses or CACs for victims; and 3) training for classroom teachers to recognize signs of trauma among youth. People in positions of power must be better trained about the crime of human trafficking, including how to recognize and help victims. Teachers, mental health providers, social service experts, and law enforcement professionals must all receive education on this issue and work together. As previously stated, many such individuals may view human sexual trafficking as an international issue and that the age groups involved are beyond their scope. Many counselors, including school counselors, may not know what questions to ask, how to listen, or how to intervene.

What should school personnel look for in identifying possible DMST victims? Victims may have unexplained absences from school. In addition, they may chronically run away from home; make references to frequent travel to other cities; exhibit bruises or other physical trauma; exhibit withdrawn behavior; and be depressed, fearful, and have lack control over their schedule. Other typical red flags include not having access to identification documents; being hungry or malnourished; being inappropriately dressed for the weather; and showing signs of drug addiction. Further clues may be a change in attire; the acquisition of expensive possessions; having a new cell phone; making age inappropriate references to sexual situations; having a much older boyfriend; and/or using specific sexual terminology related to DMST, e.g. "stable, "buyer," daddy." An appendix with such DMST terminology and definitions is included at the end of this analysis. Ultimately, these children typically stop attending school altogether (US Department of Education, 2007).

Once identified, for the purpose of intervention there is a need for carefully thought-out safe houses or CACs. These facilities should receive public funding and should exist throughout the nation. As stated by Hope: "It takes 17 to 23 months to get a girl back on her feet and to assist her in the right way." A safe house is one way to provide that secure environment for the victims. Basic needs such as food, clothing, shelter, safety, mental health counseling, job training, and medical/dental care are those necessities required to ensure that children remain on the right path. The location of the site must also be kept secret. The child should not feel frightened they will be found by their trafficker. 24 hour surveillance, alarm systems, an undisclosed location, none or limited Internet access and phone use helps in this endeavor. Unfortunately, there are very few such facilities that focus on DMST victims across the US. Those that do exist do so because that community is fortunate to have trained professionals who are politicized and able to fundraise, build, and run such places. However, all communities are in great need of such places, and they should be funded through public revenue streams. They should also be given room to create a set of best practices outside typical restrictions.

Safe house and CAC staff must engage in specialized training in trafficking prevention and intervention. Victims need to be allowed to spend significant time at a site where service providers can help them discern the difference between the dysfunctional familial connections that a trafficker provides with healthy relationships with individuals. This is imperative because traffickers attempt to create familial connections to decrease the chance of a child leaving. Service providers need to create an environment of trust and safety and this must be the first level of defense. Trust takes time to build. If a level of trust is not developed the risk for flight increases. Children can leave due to attachment or fear. This form of trauma can be connected to Stockholm Syndrome (i.e., an extreme form of Post Traumatic Stress Disorder [PTSD] connected to torture victims). Victims of sexual trafficking have a higher rate of PTSD than war veterans. Victims with severe mental issues and suicidal or homicidal thoughts first need intensive treatment in a hospital (Clawson & Grace, 2007).

CONCLUSION

It is important that teachers are trained to recognize possible victims. Spaces in schools need to be created for discussion of this epidemic with students so they can be aware of "smooth-talking" recruiters in shopping malls, in the park, on the Internet, and so forth. This is of crucial importance as DMST is on the rise. As a means of intervention, schools must seek assistance from local agencies such as health and social services, law enforcement, runaway and homeless youth shelters, domestic violence shelters, and child advocacy centers. These partnerships must provide qualified professionals who can help in the restoration of the rights of the child. The larger culture must become aware of the prevalence of DMST. Leniency for traffickers and buyers must be immediately disrupted, and a national plan to assess and combat DMST must be put forth (Shared Hope, 2009). Intervention is also desperately needed for the victims. All victims, including children and adolescents, require a safe space to recover. The ultimate goal is to prevent domestic sexual trafficking from ever occurring (Shared Hope, 2009, p. 26).

Appendix: Select Human Trafficking Terminology

To provide a more in depth understanding of domestic minor sex trafficking practices, the following terms used by sex traffickers and victims are defined. Further understanding the terminology will assist in identifying victims and potential victims. The definitions below were garnered from the following sources: Human Sexual Trafficking, 2008; Faith (personal communication, October 13, 2011); Finklea, Fernandes Alcantatr, & Siskin (2011); Mones (2011).

Boyfriend Pimp: Manipulates the victim over a long period of time solidifying an emotional connection by showering them with gifts and acts of kindness in order eventually to coerce them into selling sex.

Business Pimp: Manipulates the victim by selling them a get rich quick scenario, such as a modeling prospect to get them to an unsafe location to coerce them into selling sex.

Choosing Up: A victim moves from one pimp to another for the purpose of improving their immediate circumstances or status. Even though it appears the victim is self-selecting, it is important to remember they are still a victim and not in a position of power.

Debt Bondage: A loan that becomes inherited with impossibly high interest resulting in continued control.

Grooming: A long term deliberate process used to draw out victims to gain trust and ultimately dependency.

Guerilla Pimp: This pimp kidnaps the victim, threatens their family, and performs acts of violence for the victim to watch or endure.

House Rules: Rules used to control the interaction of the victim with pimps and traffickers, buyers, law enforcement, and other victims.

Buyer: Formerly referred to as a "John." It is an individual who solicits or buys sex.

Stable: A group of victims controlled by a single trafficker.

The "Life:" Refers to the sexual trafficking lifestyle.

Track: The designated area where the victims walk on the street.

Trafficker: A pimp who knowingly manages a human in terms of sexual or work exploitation through use of force, fraud, or coercion.

Trafficking Victim: A person subjected to a form of force, fraud, or coercion to obtain labor, services, or a commercial sex act.

REFERENCES

Clawson, H. J., & Dutch, N. (2008). *Identifying victims of human trafficking: Inherent challenges and promising strategies from the field.* Retrieved December 27, 2011 from http://www.ncjrs.gov/pdffiles1/nij/225759.pdf

Clawson, H. J., & Grace, L. G. (2007). *Finding a path to recovery: Residential facilities for minor victims of domestic sex trafficking.* US Department of Health and Human Services. Retrieved from http://aspe.hhs.gov/hsp/07/HumanTrafficking/ResFac/ib.htm#Residential.

Convention on the Rights of the Child. (1989). *Office of the United Nations High Commissioner for Human Rights.* Retrieved from http://www2.ohchr.org/english/law/crc.htm

Dennett, D. (Writer), & Dennett, D. (Director). (2011). *Our America with Lisa Ling: 3AM.* Ling, L., Smith, D. S., & Henry, G. (Executive Producers).

Fernandes-Alcantara, A., & Siskin, A. (2011). Sex trafficking of children in the United States: Overview and issues for Congress.

Finklea, K., Fernandes-Alcantara, A. & Siskin, A. (2011). Sex trafficking of children in the United States: Overview and issues for Congress. Congressional Research Service, June, 21, 2011), Retrieved October 25, 2011 from http://www.fas.org/sgp/crs/misc/R41878.pdf

Hodge, D. (2008). Sexual trafficking in the United States: A domestic problem with transnational dimensions. *Social Work, 53*(2), 143-152.

Human Smuggling & Trafficking Center. (2008). *Domestic human trafficking – An internal issue.* Retrieved October 23, 2011from http://www.state.gov/documents/organization/113612.pdf

Kotrla, K. (2010). Domestic minor sex trafficking in the United States. *Social Work, 55*(2), 181-187.

Larsen, R. (2011). US Human Trafficking Incidents, 2008-2010. *Journalist's resource: A research portal and curated database.* Retrieved October 26, 2011 from http://journalistsresource.org/studies/government/criminal-justice/human-trafficking

Mones, C. (2011). *Domestic sex trafficking: The struggle to connect girls to services.* In partial fulfillment of the bachelor's thesis, Brown University. Retrieved November 30, 2011 from http://devl1980.files.wordpress.com/2011/09/cara-mones-final-thesis.pdf

MSNBC in association with Santoki Productions. (2008). *Sex slaves in the suburbs*. NBC Universal Media.

MSNBC (2011, October 30). *Sex slaves: Motor City teens*. Retrieved from http://www.msnbc.msn.com/id/3036750/ns/msnbc_tv-documentaries/

MSNBC in association with Satoki Productions. (2009). *Sex slaves: The teen trade*. NBC Universal Media.

NASW. (2003). International policy on human rights. *Social work speaks: National Association of Social Workers policy statements 2003-2006* (6th ed). Washington, DC: NASW Press.

106th Congress of the United States of America (2011, November 11). Victims of Trafficking and Violence Protection Act of 2000 [Description of form] Retrieved from http://www.state.gov/g/tip/laws/61124.htm

Roby, J. L. (2005). Women and children in the global sex trade. *International Social Work, 48*, 136-147.

Shared Hope International. (2009). *Domestic minor sex trafficking: Child sex slavery in Broward and Dade Counties, Florida.* Arlington, VA, 22209. June 2009.

Shared Hope International. (2009). *The National Report on Domestic Minor Sex Trafficking: America's Prostituted Children.* Arlington, VA, 22209. May 2009.

Stanton, E. C. (1898/2007). *The woman's Bible*, Part I & II. Forgotten Books: www.forgottenbooks.org

Stotts Jr., E., & Ramey, L. (2009). Human trafficking: A call for counselor awareness and action. *Journal of Humanistic COUNSELING, Education and Development*, Spring 2009, V48, pp. 36 -47

US Department of Education Office of Safe and Drug-Free Schools in Washington, DC. (2007). *Human trafficking of children in the United States: A fact sheet for schools.* Retrieved October 23, 2011 from http://www2.ed.gov/about/offices/list/osdfs/factsheet.pdf

US Department of State. (2003, June). *Trafficking in persons report.* Retrieved October 23, 2011, from http://www.state.gov/documents/organization/21555.pdf

US Department of State. (2011, June). *Trafficking in persons report.* Retrieved October 23, 2011, from http://www.state.gov/secretary/rm/2011/06/167156.htm

US Department of State. (2011, June). *Trafficking in persons report.* Retrieved October 23, 2011, from http://www.state.gov/documents/organization/164458.pdf, pp. 372-379.

The Human Smuggling and Trafficking Center Fact Sheet: Distinctions between Human Smuggling and Human Trafficking (January 2005). Retrieved October 26, 2011 http://www.defense.gov/home/features/2008/0608_ctip/docs/Smuggling%20vs%20Trafficking%20Guide%20Paper%20Final%202005-01.pdf

- the buyers - not discussed well in this chapt. b/c w/o a market sex trafficking wouldn't be as lucrative. Also, this speaks to the male dominance b/c they're the ones buying the service. Boys R also pimped out.

Toxic masculinity = certain norms of masculine behav. in western world that R associated w/ harm to society + men themselves

masculinity = tied to domination

femininity = tied to docility + submission

BRIAN W. LAGOTTE

CHAPTER 7

Selling the Services: Military Recruiting and Education Policy

Entering with the stated purpose of counseling students about future opportunities, military recruiters treat the school space as a targeted market 'to penetrate'[1] with a variety of sales strategies.[2] Section 9528 of the large omnibus education bill No Child Left Behind [NCLB] codifies recruiter access to students and their private directory data. Recruiters then use their privileged access to set up individual or classroom sales presentations for an armed forces career. This chapter shows that the structure of NCLB section 9528 enables a sophisticated direct marketing campaign, rather than the commonly understood narrative of a career counselor introducing students to the military as "just one option out of many." Recruiting frames schools as markets, students as sales calls, and recruiters as sales representatives. The distortion of the school space perpetuated through military recruiting – and commercialism in general (e.g. Molnar, 1996, 2005) – detrimentally influences a child's fundamental right to education. Therefore, when policy provides the recruiters an avenue to public high schools, the military enters as a well-funded sales force focused on quota.

The most specific task of this chapter establishes the claim *military recruiting is cold-call contract sales, not vocational guidance*. My larger normative argument is we ought to reform the policies within NCLB that enable current military recruiting practices in high schools. When practices do not represent vocational guidance but sales quota concerns, the military's pitch that an armed forces career is but one option contradicts making it *the* option out of many. It appears the neoliberal expression of military recruiting is not vocational guidance completely in the interest of youth.

Neoliberalism can be a slippery signifier, so in this chapter the term refers to the general frame of "the market" as the best model for social interactions, not simply economic relations. For example, a broader critique of the neoliberal expression of NCLB involves curriculum design and teaching. Teachers provide education services to consumers who shop in a competitive education market as selfish, rational individuals. To rank schools in the market, designers create a standard

---

[1] Although outside the scope of this chapter, the sexist nuance of the language in the recruiting manual points to a longer deliberation on the gendered slant of military recruiting in high schools.
[2] An initial sketch of this argument appears in Lagotte and Apple (2010).

J. Hall (ed.), Children's Human Rights and Public Schooling in the United States, 117–135.

curriculum, which highlights schools making adequate yearly progress and shames those who do not. Some savvy consumers can use coupons (vouchers) to make private schools more affordable or tap into the growing market of charter schools. Inside schools, teachers labor to increase student test scores. Federal law connects funding to test scores, holding schools accountable. District officials can also use scores to hold individual teachers accountable (see Turque, 2010). Middle management (principals and vice-principals) sort through test data to shape employee focus for the following month. Students, parents, teachers, and administrators all interact in the education field as consumers behaving in their own best interest.

For one to consider the market model as the common sense understanding of educational relations, policy should habitually show neoliberal tendencies in related fields. I use "common sense" specifically to mark understandings about the world to which individuals consent but which may motivate harmful practices (Gramsci, 1971). Therefore, the more practices follow the market metaphor, the stronger it is normalized as "the" mode of social relations. So, school as marketplace dominates: curriculum politics and textbook sales (Apple, 2006); Race to the Top reforms including expanded charter schools and teacher merit pay (Obama, 2009); data management regarding test scores and achievement (Au, 2009; Clarke & Newman, 1997); and, more explicit projects from soda machines to Channel One advertising (Apple, 2000; Molnar, 2005). In these school policies, efficient schools provide education to youth who are positioned as consumers for aggressive marketing, as future workers, and increasingly, as future soldiers who will provide muscle to the invisible hand. As this chapter shows, the neoliberal logic also dominates military recruiting in high schools.

The overarching ethnographic work from which this chapter partially draws examines the two components of NCLB section 9528 – access to high school campuses and student data collection. The research involves representatives from two different states, three different school districts, and four different high schools. Moreover, interviewees include parents, teachers, guidance counselors, principals, district representatives, recently returned veterans, and a Navy recruiter. The sample is gathered opportunistically. The project began focusing only on parents in one high school district. Observing the variety of actors affected by section 9528, however, motivated the inclusion of a greater breadth in sampling. A forced move in the middle of the field season added a second state and more school districts for comparison. To the interviews, I add documentation from mainstream media sources and three key documents covering section 9528 in NCLB: A Government Accountability Office report on recruiting irregularities (Government Accountability Office, 2006); an American Civil Liberties Union report on recruiting in New York high schools (American Civil Liberties Union, 2008); and, a Rutgers Law School report on New Jersey high schools (Venetis, 2008). Therefore, the "field" focuses on the relations between actors with different access to power in executing the high school policies related to military recruiting.

I structure the chapter mainly around the two NCLB provisions. First, I provide an abbreviated bird's-eye view of military advertising to show the scope of resources available to recruiters. Second, I describe the military's perspective on school visits since the first provision deals with access to high school campuses. Third, I unpack the data collection project inside and outside of schools to highlight the second provision regarding student privacy. I conclude by summarizing how the neoliberal frame of "recruiting is marketing" creates problematic policy areas indicating potential research.

ADVERTISING TOOLS

The slew of high powered marketing companies the DoD contracts for recruiting belies the notion that a recruiter's main role is career counseling. These Public Relations [PR] firms host a range of marketing tools to get product in front of customers. For example, the Army invested $180 million a year for the "Army of One Campaign," which included a mix of media advertising and an original computer game (America's Army) (Davenport, 2004). The video game serves two purposes. First, it distributes information about the military, including activities replicating boot camp training.[3] Second, the game collects information through the registration process. Individuals play on-line via a personal computer. Users therefore must register a game name by entering contact information into the system. The PR firm then collects demographic data to cycle into the database projects.

The Army also invested in a real-world gaming center to attract youth. The Army Experience Center occupied a storefront in the Franklin Mills Mall in Philadelphia, Pennsylvania. The Army contracted the "marketing innovations" firm IgnitedUSA to create the $12 million structure – with an operating cost of $5 million a year (DiMascio, 2009). Although the location included a career navigation center, a warfare simulation room, a video gaming center, a global base locator, and a tactical operations center, officials did not describe the location as part of the recruiting mission. An IgnitedUSA spokeswoman said the army only signed-up youth who already decided to join, which happened 141 times in their first year alone (DiMascio, 2009). Considering the investment in a storefront location and the high-tech entertainment value, framing the resource as simply providing information about an armed forces career falls flat. Even though the center closed on July 31st, 2010, much of the technology from the project may continue to serve recruiting purposes (Colimore & Lockley, 2010). According to the spokeswoman, the touch screen computers and hands-on simulators proved the biggest success of the project. It makes sense then that they will likely integrate into the network of local recruiting vehicles.

Military recruitment advertising is both nimble and well-funded. Recruiters recognize the adults in a student's life exert a powerful influence on the decision to serve. The Pentagon therefore targets resources towards parents. In 2005, the

---

[3] In comparison to the immediate action of first-person shooting games on the various commercial gaming platforms, Veteran Thomas confirmed that "You don't just go out shooting" (personal communication, January 11th, 2010).

military started a campaign with the international advertising group McCann Erickson Worldwide (McCarthy, 2005). The armed services launched a $10 million multimedia program persuading parents and other "influencers" to allow young people to consider the military (Hardy, 2005). Through focus groups, surveys, and interviews, marketing firms can increase the efficiency of the Pentagon's substantial advertising budget. Once the military recognized the power of the parent, PR firms quickly adjusted their messaging to the new demographic.

The military spends hundreds of millions of dollars on public relations. This, in itself, does not necessarily surprise. An extended analysis of shaping the general "common sense" about a military career through advertising, games, and movies extends beyond the scope of this chapter. Here, I focus on what happens when education policy converts high schools and students into the "target market." Returning to the policy anchor of NCLB section 9528, I ask how the twin policy requirements of *mandatory campus access* and *directory information collection* express a broader neoliberal strategy.

"PENETRATING" THE SCHOOL MARKET

To see the market-based metaphor most clearly, I use direct language from the School Recruiting Program Handbook [SRPH] to describe the school as a market (Morris, 2004).[4] The purpose of the manual – produced by the United States Recruiting Command [USRC] – is "to assist in the training of new recruiters and serve as a reference guide," and "is applicable to all elements of the USRC." The handbook shapes recruiters' practices in schools with specific advice on how to approach the task. Besides the advice itself, the language the Recruiting Command chooses also frames the task. Instead of using military jargon throughout, such as making mission, invading the school space, or capturing strategic territory, the manual reads like an employee handbook for a new addition to a sales force.

From the first day on the job, the manual provides steps towards the ultimate goal: quota. To achieve quota, the new recruiter should create an individualized School Recruiting Program [SRP]:

> … to assist recruiters in penetrating their school market and channeling their efforts through the specific task and goals to obtain the maximum number of quality enlistments. The SRP is also an important part of an integrated recruiting prospect lead generation program that ensures total market penetration. (p. 2)

The "lead generation program" begins with the recruiter establishing cordial relations with staff. "This is a basic step in the sales process … To effectively work the school market, recruiters must maintain rapport throughout the SY [school year] and develop good working relationship with key influencers." For this,

[4] A PDF version is available at: http://www.usarec.army.mil/im/formpub/REC_PUBS/p35013.pdf.

recruiters often offer a "pen, calendar, or cup" and they always "remember secretary's week with a card or flowers." During interviews, Guidance Counselor Livingston[5] looked around her desk and found three different pens from the armed services. "They come in and say 'hi' and offer us a pen or stuff like that. Very little as far as recruitment goes" (personal communication, March 24th, 2010). The first steps are crucial because, as the manual repeatedly reminds the new recruiters, "first to contact is first to contract."

Recruiters and school officials report small promotional items in interviews, media stories, and research reports. Guidance Counselor Bradford confirms recruiters bring "pencils like that all the time" (personal communication, March 22, 2010), and in a different school Guidance Counselor Davenport describes how recruiters set up a climbing wall in the parking lot for youth to try (personal communication, June 23rd, 2009). The Boston Globe reported a school graciously allowed a recruiter "to bring a rock-climbing wall to a recent physical education class for potential recruits to try" (Schwom, 2006). Other research found:

> In more than half of the schools surveyed, recruiters give out gifts to the students, such as key chains, t-shirts, calendars, school supplies, and computer accessories. Summit High School reported that the recruiters bought lunch for the guidance counselors. (Venetis, 2008, p. 23)

The prescriptions in the recruiting handbook appear directly to connect to observations from a variety of sources. Two concerns arise: if these practices are merely career counseling, is this the scope of armed forces career counseling with which parents, principals, and youth are comfortable? If this reaches above and beyond career counseling, are gifts appropriate vocational guidance practices in the school space?

Once recruiters enter the school, market share depends upon the amount of time that can be spent attracting the attention of students. Other actors in the "market" vie for their share. Morning announcements, teachers, friends, guidance counselors, and lunch all demand some portion of time. If military recruiters see their goal as dominating that market, then they will have to crowd out other education activities.

> Recruiter presence and visibility in the high schools polled is generally strong. In eleven out of forty-eight (23%) reporting high schools, recruiters from at least one branch of the military are present at least once a week. Recruiters visit thirty-six of forty-eight high schools surveyed (75%) at least once a month. In contrast, recruiters from higher educational institutions and postsecondary employment opportunities visit most high schools solely during their annual career fair. In most cases, the military is also present at those career fairs. (Venetis, 2008, p. 22)

---

[5] I identify all interviewees with pseudonyms.

The handbook advises to "be so helpful and so much a part of the school scene that you are in constant demand." A helpful monthly schedule suggests: leading calisthenics for the football team; providing government class presentations on "the electoral process and how the Army serves a vital role in the security of our nation"; asking for a basketball game between faculty and recruiters; escorting the court on homecoming; and, presenting awards at graduation ceremonies. If the school is a market, this plan is saturation.

Often, to maintain their competitiveness, recruiters can bring props on a scale larger than pens and desk calendars. Recruiters may "obtain a tactical vehicle from a local USAR troop program unit and drive it in" a local parade or onto a high school campus. Recruiters can drive any number of vehicles, including Humvees, helicopters, or race cars. Adults get toys too. After the recruiter identifies the key adult influencers in the school, he may organize an Educator/Centers of Influence [E/COI] tour.[6] The program organizes "tours of Army installations to educators and other COIs," and in return, these adults will "improve access to schools, obtain directory information … and, refer potential prospects to the local Army recruiter." The recommended itinerary ranges from a guided tour of the military museum and attending graduation ceremonies to Weaponeer and Simulation activities – these last two offer "hands-on" experiences. During these events, adults potentially see the benefits of the armed forces for future educative and vocational opportunities.

Ethnographic evidence supports the use of these elaborate "toys" on school campuses. Although I use the word toys in quotes above, at least one administrator sees the larger military machines in this perspective. Principal Newcomb explains:

> Toys are like Humvees and helicopters. They land on the football practice field. Maybe once a year. We have it every year. Occasionally it's just part of recruitment efforts. (Personal communication, March 10th, 2010)

In a different school district, Guidance Counselor Livingston explains "there have been times like during lunch that they might bring a race car … and I guess a military-type vehicle thing" (personal communication March 24th, 2010). The military vehicles can also adapt to the appropriate demographic of a school district.

> In New York, the Army supplied recruiters at high schools with specially equipped Humvees, one known as the "African-American Humvee," and the other as "Yo Soy El Army Humvee" (I am the Army Humvee), outfitted with plasma television screens and blasting rock music and meant to appeal to black and Latino students. (American Civil Liberties Union, 2008, p. 30)

In addition to small items like flowers and pencils for school staff and students, these (quite expensive) larger props begin to stretch the concept of "vocational

---

[6] The following information comes from United States Army Recruiting Command Regulation 601-81, available for download at http://www.usarec.army.mil/im/formpub/REC_PUBS/r601_81.pdf.

counseling" a bit. Furthermore, since the provision in NCLB calls for "equal access" among college, career, and military recruiters, one wonders if the amount of financial resources by just one type of recruiter begins to skew the concept of "equal" campus visits.

All of this investment constructs the "integrated recruiting prospect lead generation program," specially designed to gain recruits from particular schools. Moreover, even if the recruiter can get a general "appointment for a sales presentation … [he] will probably need to tailor [his] sales message to meet the stage of the [school year]." In the school, the terms "sales presentation" and "sales message" refer to those one-one-one sessions in the common narrative when recruiters can provide information about the armed forces being one option of many. According to the US recruiting manual, the military representative does not provide objective information to help students decide between the armed services, entering the civilian workplace, or attending college. The recruiters function as high-powered sales personnel moving used cars off the lot (McCarthy, 2005). And, salespeople want hot leads, not a program that just offers random contact information to cold call. Therefore, prescreening applicants to determine the quality prospects would increase efficiency.

Actors connected to the military recruiting practices quickly identify the marketing aspects of contact in schools – including a military recruiter. First, when asked directly where military presentations sit on a hypothetical continuum between sales and counseling, Guidance Counselor Henderson says "definitely it is closer to the sales end rather than the counselor end" (personal communication, March 15th, 2010). Principal Anderson explains "I think they are more sales, but that is just because the career counseling they are doing is a sales pitch … To me, there is a career counseling component, but it is also a sales pitch" (personal communication, march 12th, 2009). One parent complained, it "is very offensive and inappropriate to promote a military career with a marketing campaign, like selling soft drinks" (Schwom, 2006). Navy Recruiter Anderson explains the best time to incorporate the pitch:

> To be effective, do your job and do it well, there are certain aspects of the job where it is important to know good sales tactics. It is important to rely on your training to be able to talk to a person and figure out what they want, and be able to blue print them, and make sure that they are qualified. When [recruiters] are doing the salesman thing, they are probably in high school and they realize they are going to see someone for 30-45 seconds, and they are going to try to do the "Gee Whiz" presentation. (Personal communication, November 19th, 2010)

By "Gee Whiz," I assume Recruiter Anderson is speaking about free gifts, climbing walls, NASCAR, Humvees, and Blackhawk helicopters on the football field while recruiters do "the salesman thing." Recruiters normally prequalify individuals through "blueprinting" (a common set of introductory questions).

Prequalifying successful leads en masse, however, requires a longer standardized questionnaire.

For the military recruiter, prescreening a group of applicants occurs during the Armed Service Vocational Aptitude Battery (ASVAB) testing process. According to the website, the ASVAB measures arithmetic reasoning, math knowledge, word knowledge, paragraph comprehension, and vocational elements through a multiple-choice test (see http://www.military.com/ASVAB). The scores on the exam "help" students make military, vocational, or academic decisions. When one digs a bit further, however, the ASVAB is also named the AFQT – the Armed Forces Qualification Test. The scores on the AFQT (i.e., the ASVAB) qualify an applicant for positions in various branches and can rank these positions. Therefore, to give prescreening a nuance of counseling, inside the school recruiters describe the test with a more subtle name of "aptitude" rather than explicitly acknowledging the "qualification."

Although recruiting offices make the test available, high schools often administer the exam in the junior year of high school. The level of transparency about the purpose of the test and the option not to take the test varies from school to school. Arranging the exam in the high school, in the language of the School Recruiting Program Handbook, "is called 'Marketing the ASVAB.'" The military clearly benefits:

> First, from the recruiter's perspective, the ASVAB is not only a valuable tool used to maintain and improve school relations, it is also specifically designed to provide recruiters with a source of qualified leads. The ASVAB prequalifies potential applicants academically before more expensive and time-consuming medical and moral qualifications are done.

The Pentagon conducts the test, as one DoD official has claimed, as a "public service," but the test is also "well known as an aptitude screen for military recruitment" (Hardy & Purcell, 2008). The directive to the recruiter is clear: prequalify potential leads. But, like other information gathering projects through NCLB, parents often do not know how to opt their children out of the test nor do they always know when the school conducts the exam.

The ASVAB/AFQT exam, therefore, serves both needs of military recruiters: data collection and qualifying sales leads. The test begins the data-collection process by gaining student contact information with their individual strengths and weaknesses. The SRPH promises "a printout provides the recruiter with concrete and personal information about the student." The initial survey assists recruiters in shaping sales messages accordingly. Second, the test "prequalifies applicants" since the branches of (and jobs in) the armed services require a certain score on the test. The exam helps recruiters categorize contacts and streamline their market base for targeting.

The USRC sees the duty of recruiters in schools as a sales mission for representatives in markets to interact with prequalified leads. So far, focused on the NCLB requirement of equal access to recruiters on school grounds, positing that the military is a commodity marketed to students seems like neither an editorial nor a normative claim. The SRPH, serving as the guide for beginning recruiters, speaks plainly to the armed forces idea of schools. So, when evaluating the effectiveness of Section 9528, mandating equal campus access to military recruiters (holding school funding contingent), one can reflect on the everyday practice of military recruiters in high schools. Does the public find adult sales representatives pressuring children an appropriate activity granted to recruiters – whether they come from colleges, companies, or the corps? Whatever the answer, at least the question can focus on what recruiters are actually doing on school grounds.

STUDENT PROFILE DATABASE

In this section, I untangle confusion around student privacy and database management. Two items relating to "opting out" blend together – at the school level regarding call lists and at the national level regarding a much larger privately-contracted project. Thus, discussion around the collection of student information remains unclear. While schools notify parents and students with varying efficiency, many do not know the extent to which private vendors profile individuals. This section highlights how the management of information on multiple levels influences the ability of individuals comprehensively to grasp policy implications.

For now, I use the phrase "management of information" to describe these processes, specifically avoiding terms such as rationing and manipulating. While the latter two terms imply a known purposeful motive, management just indicates a process wherein data is collected, analyzed, and disseminated. Implementation and transparency of the management process help determine the purpose as an increase in efficiency, a consequence of heightened bureaucracy, or intentional subterfuge. For example, having two separate databases operating simultaneously but only requiring parental notification for one, masks the more controversial of the two. Was this the intention of policy design? Whether we can answer with a definitive yes or no is less of a concern at this point. However, if policy obscures the awareness of those affected, perhaps it requires reform.

NCLB mandates schools to distribute directory information about each student to military recruiters upon request. These directories normally contain name, address, and telephone numbers; but may also include gender, date of birth, and parental contact information. Parent and students, under NCLB, have the right to opt out of this distribution process in writing. Initially, the obscurity of the policy created the main problem because the language provided no specific feedback on how to process the mandates. A school district-level communications director stressed the need for "schools, especially principals, to stay on top of making sure parents understand what it is" (personal communication, communications director Jenkins, March 16th, 2010). Unfortunately, as evidenced by the ACLU and other reports, with no overarching direction, variability in practice prevails:

> … while the law provides for an opt-out procedure, many school districts do not have a clear process in place by which to do this. The safeguard

> rests entirely on the efforts of local school officials: the opt-out procedure only works if school districts inform parents in a timely manner and effectively instruct parents on how to opt out, and federal and state governments provide no meaningful enforcement mechanism. (American Civil Liberties Union, 2008, p. 24)

> The Rutgers School of Law study found that in New Jersey there is no uniform policy to ensure that the opt-out requirements are being enforced. Parental notification of the right to opt their child out of military recruitment varies from school to school or does not exist at all. As stated elsewhere in this report, officials in only four of the forty-eight schools visited (10%) were aware of their opt-out obligations. Some school officials did not even know what an opt-out was. (Venetis, 2008, p. 26)

Few people – including school staff and district administrators – know how to implement the directory data collection policy nor how best to inform parents of their opt-out opportunities. Therefore, when the media finally highlighted the data collection process and issues with student privacy in the mid-2000s, the school-level opt-out process gained the majority of the attention.

When focus is only on the school-level policy, however, less light shines on the much larger data-mining/target marketing project for military recruitment. In 2005, the larger project grew until it required a notification into the Federal Register, which drew the attention of the press. Due to the *Washington Post*, a different picture of student data collection emerged (Krim, 2005a, 2005b, 2005c, 2005d). Instead of merely a directory database, the Pentagon also collects individual profiles of students through BeNow, a firm designed to buy data sets from a constellation of sources, cross-check and compile the data into categories, and finally, design marketing plans targeted to those categories. David Chu, then Undersecretary of Defense for Personnel and Readiness, attempted to minimize the scope of the project at a hastily arranged press conference the afternoon Krim's first article broke in the *Post*.[7] Comparing his answers at the 2005 press conference with other reports and policy data speaks to the level of Pentagon forthrightness regarding the DoD and student privacy.

The Federal Register, linked to the Privacy Act, promotes transparency when the government gathers private information about American citizens. From its passage in 1974, the Privacy Act "requires public notification when a system of records is being compiled by a federal, state, or government agency" (Peng, 2005, p. 1). According to Chu, "Under the Privacy act if you maintain a system of records – if a government agency maintains a system of records, both through a private organization, you have to give public notice if you're doing so." The regulations prevent government agencies from secretly gathering information on

[7] Chu's quotes here, unless otherwise noted, are from a 2005 DoD transcript of the mentioned media event ("Media Roundtable with Deputy Under Secretary of Defense for Personnel and Readiness David Chu," 2005).

individuals and creating dossiers on citizens. Therefore, by noting the recruiting program in the Register, the Pentagon notified the public that they, or a private contractor, would be collecting private information and keeping records on individuals.

The Pentagon sub-contracted BeNow for the database in 2002. Thus, the entry in the Federal register three years later on May 23, 2005 raised questions (Kolben, 2006; Peng, 2005; S. Rosenberg, 2005). When called to answer, Chu explained – but did not defend – the delay. The confusion occurred because when the Pentagon hired BeNow, officials assumed an earlier entry in the Federal Register covered the arrangement. Chu reported, "First, it was only triggered by a review of where we stood on all these matters that we realized we should be filing a new notice. And, these notices do take a while to prepare." Chu deemed the pushback on the Federal Register delay "a fair complaint."

The line of questions regarding the Federal Register implied the Pentagon delayed purposefully. Several reasons could support this. In 2002, privacy concerns grew in the public after the passage of the PATRIOT act, and although citizens may be willing to give up a degree of liberty for security, parents are probably less inclined to be so forthcoming with their children's data. Furthermore, war began. For the Pentagon to be constructing a database on all 16-25 year-old citizens pointed towards the draft. Finally, the newly minted NCLB narrative promised "closing the achievement gap," not "target marketing your children."

Thus far motivation remains conjecture. Included here is the Pentagon's position as represented by Chu:

> So it's the new notice that gained people's attention, and I think created this impression that somehow we were doing something new and different. The short answer is generically this is something we've done for a couple of decades or more.

If the practice was decades-old, one wonders about the need for a new Federal Register entry. Indeed, the Privacy Act review of the new practices of recruiting students (and other young adults) determined the Privacy Act demanded a new notice. The debate is not merely *an impression* the Pentagon began recording private information differently, the new notice is *evidence of* a new process. Rather than educating the press on the complexity of the new project, Chu's approach basically assured everyone there was nothing to see here, and they could just move along. He held that line of reason throughout the press conference.

Chu framed the purpose of hiring BeNow as a consolidation of data from a variety of lists the Pentagon had been collecting for years. Although he did not mention them, opportunities to collect individual data could come from standardized testing (Krim, 2005c), ASVAB testing, school directories, signing up for merchandise at a recruiting event (Teicher, 2005), the selective service, and credit reports. The power of the last technique increased because Equifax, one of the three main credit rating agencies in the country, purchased BeNow to consolidate data management potential ("Equifax Acquires," 2005). In 2002,

BeNow began sorting the information into one comprehensive database. Chu firmly explained the private sub-contractors could not use the data in any fashion. They merely organized it with a specific task to create non-duplicate lists. According to Chu, consolidating data increased efficiency and avoided badgering individuals whose name appeared on more than one of the lists:

> One of the last things you want to do when you're sending people material is to send the same person five copies of the same thing. That's a quick turnoff, that I couldn't even take the trouble to make sure I only sent it to you once. So their job is to put together a single file, give it back to us, we give it to the military departments to use. We try to take advantage of all the information about who doesn't want to be contacted.

By "take advantage" of those "who do not want to be contacted," Chu referred to the individual data stored in "suppression lists" even if one opts out of receiving any information from the military. To avoid double contacting individuals, the database still tracks those individuals who opt out of the tracking process.

Concern revolved around the amount of discreet information in a database that a private company controlled. Beyond the actual content of the database, which proved problematic for both higher-education officials (Lipka, 2005) and members of the US Congress (Peng, 2005), critics questioned the legal ambiguity of the move. Although the Federal Register required announcing the relationship, hiring a private sub-contractor may circumvent other federal privacy laws (Mulvihill, 2005), specifically those "to prevent the federal government from collecting information on its citizens who are not suspected of any wrongdoing" (Proctor, 2005, p. 1). The private firm was specifically a direct-target-marketing company tasked with collecting private data. Contracting or sub-contracting sensitive directives should not bypass laws.

The DoD avoids accountability of the direct marketing mechanic since they contract with Mullen Advertising, who then contracts with BeNow. When asked why the Pentagon picked a target marketing outfit to run the database, Chu explained that Mullen chose BeNow, and the choice had nothing to do with their targeting skills (Krim, 2005b). However, when one examines the processes BeNow offers the Pentagon, the narrative that Chu proposed at the initial media event in 2005 weakens. Hiring a direct marketing firm to construct profiles on millions of individuals aged 16-25 "had [not] been done for decades," or a new Register notice would not have been required. BeNow was not merely consolidating lists to avoid double contacting individuals. As a corporation, the design accomplishes substantially more.

BeNow uses a variety of tools to manage data and design marketing narratives targeted to specific demographics. Beyond the service provided to the military, BeNow also represents General Motors, Four Seasons Hotels and Resorts, Hammacher Schlemmer, Tower Records, MetLife, Saab, and Smart Bargains, and – joined with Equifax – it now "provides faster and easier ways to find, approve and market to the appropriate customers" ("BeNOW Caps," 2005; "BeNOW

Multi-Channel," 2005, p. 1). Another issue centers on what happens to the data after consolidation. The Chief Technology Officer at BeNow, Tom McGinley, claimed "the company's software is the best in the business at consolidating disparate data sources into a centralized customer view" ("DataMentors and," 2002, p. 1). Under direction from the Pentagon, BeNow used this technology to create the Joint Advertising Market Research and Studies Program [JAMRS], the specific database project BeNow uses to create targets for marketing. JAMRS triggered both privacy and direct marketing concerns at Chu's press conference.

Once the PR firms have this amount of student data accumulated, they also add new soldier demographics to form identities to focus future marketing. Software systems collect and disaggregate the data on all new recruits. Writing in the trade journal *Advertising Age*, James Arndorfer (2005a, p. 4) reports on the variety of labels:

> The groups – given labels … such as Beltway Boomers, Big Sky Families, Sunset City Blues (blue collars) and Shotguns & Pickups – represent a diverse range of households … For instance, the "down-in-the-city" segment consists of urban black and Hispanic households of low socioeconomic status, who tend to rent and whose parents have elementary and high-school educations. They tend to read Jet and Vibe, watch SoapNet and eat burgers at White Castle, Rally's and Checkers. The "out-of-downtown" segment consists of white and Asian households of upper economic status that are mostly rural and suburban, tend to own their own homes and whose parents attended or graduated from college. They read Golf Digest and Discover, watch "Movie and a Makeover" and "Movie Break" on TBS and eat at Golden Corral and Chick-Fil-A.

With the groups defined, the work now turns to a marketing message ("for those who have no other option") and various advertising campaigns located in the access points (*Jet* magazine), which the software tools identify. Contemporary corporate public relations polish the messages with sophisticated marketing methods. Thus, the messages are rarely a comprehensive presentation of all the complex consequences of choosing the armed forces as a career opportunity: the information is carefully managed.

At the press conference, Chu downplayed the wealth of material kept in the database. Again, he argued the database had been maintained for decades by referring to the 1982 Defense Act, which ordered the Pentagon to collect directory information about military eligible individuals:

> For many years we simply acquired various lists. Some of them were purchased, commercial lists, some of them were government lists. The services did it for a period of time on a decentralized basis. In the last decade or so we've tried to give this a more organized supervision … We're only using it to mail stuff to people … My wife has received this stuff. It's very well done. It's actually very interesting.

Due to the restrictions on data collection under the 1982 Privacy Act, however, Chu had to maintain the simplicity of the government files versus the database BeNow maintained. The government could only store directory information, but JAMRS contained: Social Security numbers, birthdates, grade-point averages, ethnicity, e-mail addresses, subjects students are studying, telephone numbers, high school name, graduation date, and college intent, not to mention consumption habits (Doughty, 2005; Kolben, 2006; Liptak, 2007; Proctor, 2005; M. Rosenberg, 2005). Chu acknowledged "there are occasions where the commercial list contains some other fields," but

> it's not from government lists. That's from commercial lists … We're not, this is not a government file. This is off a commercial file … Well, I'm not sure I see the big issue there, quite candidly.

Since the Pentagon contracted Mullen for recruiting PR work, and Mullen contracted BeNow for the direct-marketing database JAMRS, Chu claimed the Pentagon was not accountable for management of the larger database.

The database is indeed large. At the roundtable event, media directly asked how many individuals the database contained. First, citing the high school master file, Chu claimed 4.5 million names. But, the question came again, asking for the total number. Chu's assistant clarified the database contained a total of 12 million names. That number grew as well. The reporter asked his question a third time, citing data from the website. The 12 million names just consisted of "keeping a maintenance of names on an annual basis, based on the target audience range, on the prospects that we're trying to recruit," and the total number of names in the database, collected over the years, reached 30 million (Peng, 2005, p. 7).[8] Thirty million comprises nearly 10% of the entire population of the United States. JAMRS is, according to the Pentagon, perhaps the largest collection of data on 16-25 year-olds in the country (S. Rosenberg, 2005). So, the claim this database activity resembled the same thing that had been done "for decades" (i.e. collecting directory information as per the 1982 Privacy Act), rings hollow. Since 2002, BeNow, a sub-contractor of the Pentagon, has been consolidating information from government files and lists bought from an amalgam of commercial outlets to form profiles on individuals aged 16-25 for military recruiting. The activity is not, as Chu claims, very straightforward and simple.

Direct marketing requires utmost complexity. Shifting through a huge amount of information, consolidating it into usable demographic categories, and constructing marketable identities from those categories demands technique. Chu remained resolute in his characterization of the program,

> We're not trying to create very fancy files here. So this is not high end, this is not like the magazines targeting different advertising inserts for

[8] Another report had the number at 16 million names (Rhen, 2005).

> every city in the country. We're not – maybe we'd like to be at that level of sophistication, but that's not what we are.

Again, the semantic hair being split reads: the Pentagon *runs* a program that lacks sophistication; however, the Pentagon *buys* a program for hundreds of millions of dollars that is very sophisticated. The Pentagon knows this. At a subsequent DoD press conference, Lt. Col. Ellen Krenke of the Office of the Assistant Secretary of Defense for Public Affairs explained how the direct marketing approach can help profile teens; for example, Hispanic audiences are targeted with messages about strong family values (Mulvihill, 2005).[9] The Pentagon further claims the program "enables the services to better target qualified candidates for particular mission needs" (Cooper, 2005, p. 1c), and assists the military in its "direct marketing recruiting efforts" (Doughty, 2005, p. 4a). So, contrary to Chu's claims, the program does appear like a high-end operation targeting youth with advanced marketing tools. As stated above, files of this detail represent individuals as young as sixteen years of age. Parents can shield their children from this database by opting out in writing, which brings us full circle to the NCLB regulations regarding a similar process.

Individuals can opt out of the JAMRS database by submitting a letter to the program or filling out the official opt-out form on the JAMRS website. Although opting-out limits the contact individuals have with military marketing, the program still actively collects information under "suppression files" designed to "ensure that those who declined to be included were not contacted" (Proctor, 2005). Very few parents know about this opt-out process and believe the NCLB opt-out provision includes this notice. To clarify, filling out a district opt-out form according to NCLB orders the school to remove the student's directory information from the list sent to the local military recruiter. Filling out the JAMRS opt-out form – not distributed in schools – keeps the military from contacting individuals from the database, but the file remains active and continues to gather data (Peng, 2005). But, neither form does both. Even if parents know of the school level opt-out process, no equivalent notification of the JAMRS program exists.

The database and opt-out procedures function explicitly and implicitly. First, NCLB regulations require high schools provide the contact information of all students to local military recruiters. These directories serve as comprehensive call lists of all students in the district. Then recruiters contact students through cold calls. During the calls the recruiters can access information on the students by consulting the JAMRS database or equivalent software. Having the district and JAMRS opt-out as separate procedures masks the larger program. As illustrated by Undersecretary of Defense David Chu's testimony, the emphasis was the "simple" procedure to keep "government files." Many critical parents, educators, and students may focus on the school-level information sharing at the expense of

[9] In reference to the previous paragraph about database size, in this interview Krenke placed the number of individuals at the highest level reported: 36 million names (Turay, 2005).

questioning the larger marketing project. Introducing both NCLB and JAMRS at roughly the same time, including both opt-out issues, confuses the two processes.

CONCLUSION

A neoliberal strategy of market-based solutions to social issues employed for military recruiting does not belong in high schools. First, viewing a school as a target market skews the relationship between military recruiters and youth – as well as parents, educators, and school administrators. The common narrative about recruiting highlights other options open to students after graduation. For some students, the occupational, educational, and training benefits may suit their long-term purposes better than entering the workforce or university immediately after high school. Recruiters represent the branches of the armed services, describing the different opportunities. They describe the education benefits and potential career paths of a military career. Then, the student can weigh various future options such as college or the military.

That story does not, however, portray what the training manual instructs recruiters to do. A recruiter's mission is first to contact, because first to contact is first to sign. To complete this task, recruiters tempt key school influencers with pens, desk calendars, doughnuts, and flowers on Secretaries' Day. They bring "toys" like Humvees and Blackhawk helicopters to the students and take teachers to military installations so they can also partake in "simulations." Recruiters tailor their sales approach to the school schedule and occupy school space in foyers, lunchrooms, and classrooms. They use ASVAB test results to target key students so they can acquire signing bonuses for recruiting highly talented youth. These practices are much more invasive than the stated goals. The aggressive techniques recruiters use to get into the schools and sign recruits are bound to affect parents and administrators – not to mention the recruiters themselves. The question is *how* this neoliberal mode of policy execution influences those it contacts, not *if* it is modeled on the market.

Furthermore, the collection of data on US youth requires transparency. Even if individuals 18 and over are eliminated, the JAMRS data collection affects millions of children. Parents, with the proper knowledge, could restrict the dissemination of the directory information to local recruiters and limit the contact from Pentagon marketing, but ultimately cannot stop data collection under suppression files. The question remains about how knowledgeable parents are about recruiting programs. Furthermore, from a policy perspective, we can evaluate how the structure of the policy works to increase or decrease opportunities in which parents can critically reflect on the options. The confusion between NCLB and JAMRS may leave both processes unclear to those affected.

The legality of a private marketing firm, contracted by the Pentagon for data collection, is also opaque. The Privacy Act, oft-cited by David Chu, limits the amount of data the Pentagon can collect to directory information of prospective recruits. But, the mass of private data BeNow collects stretches the definition of what the Pentagon actually authorizes and may motivate the reason to hire the contractor in the first place (Boule, 2006). Chu's evasiveness on this exact issue during his media roundtable does not help dispel these concerns. At first, the explanation cited "normal procedure." Although the Pentagon hired Mullen for their PR work, "Mullen chooses a subcontractor. That's standard contracting procedure … prime contractors typically subcontract tasks that are the province of a high quality provider to the best quality, best cost source." But, contracting in general missed the point. The controversy revolved around the decision about the marketing firm, the amount of data the company collected, and the Pentagon's access. Although Chu tried to deny BeNow collected commercial data, the reporter clarified the notice in the Federal Register stated the vendor could collect commercial information. Chu's definitive response: "I'm not the lawyer here. I'll defer to the legal staff as to why this is worded the way it is."

The charge "recruiting is marketing and should therefore be reformed" does not merely hinge on the statement "it's marketing, so it's bad." The crux of the critique argues the marketing mode of recruiting distorts the pedagogical principle of education. Most superficially, recruiting simply pulls children out of the classroom towards individual sales presentations or events like NASCAR visits. Military recruiting in schools trims the time needed for educating children. Also, the sales presentations skew the communicative event between recruiter and child because the recruiter may not explain all the consequences of an armed forces career, nor does the recruiter have the child's long term interests as the prime directive. As the recruiting manual indicates, the prime concern is "first to contact is first to contract," thus, making quota. The public school space is supposed to promote critical thinking with evidence from all sides of issues. Thus, policy should promote those practices around children and suppress practices that dull the critical capacity in students.

REFERENCES

American Civil Liberties Union. (2008). Soldiers of Misfortune.

Apple, M. W. (2000). *Official knowledge: Democratic education in a conservative age*. New York: Routledge.

Apple, M. W. (2006). *Educating the "right" way: Markets, standards, God, and inequality*. New York: Routledge.

Arndorfer, J. B. (2005a, July 11). Army looking for a direct jit. *Advertising Age, 4.*

Arndorfer, J. B. (2005b, November 28). Target practice. *Advertising Age, 1.*

Au, W. (2009). *Unequal by design: High-stakes testing and the standardization of inequality*. New York: Routledge.

BeNOW Caps Fiscal 2005 with 22% Growth. (2005, June 6). *Business Wire*.

BeNOW Multi-Channel Marketing Clients Up. (2005, April 11). *Business Wire*.

Boule, M. (2006, May 18). Pentagon launches invasion of privacy, Boy Scout says. *The Oregonian*, p. E1.

Clarke, J., & Newman, J. (1997). *The managerial state: Power, politics and ideology in the remaking of social welfare*. London: Sage Publications.

Colimore, E., & Lockley (2010). Army experience center in Northeast will close. *The Philadelphia Inquirer*, June 10th.

Cooper, W. (2005, August 7). Activists target recruiters' efforts. *Palm Beach Post*, p. 1C.

DataMentors And BeNOW Join Forces. (2002, January 30). *PR Newswire*.

Davenport, C. (2004, August 8). ThemMission. *The Washington Post,* p. W12.

DiMascio. (2009). Activists protest war simulator. *Common Dreams*. Retrieved from http://www.commondreams.org/headline/2009/09/18-4

Doughty, M. (2005, June 28). Pentagon criticized. *The Capital Times,* p. 4A.

Equifax Acquires BeNow. (2005, August 29). *PR Newswire US*.

Government Accountability Office. (2006). *DoD and Services need better data to enhance visibility over recruiter irregularities*. Washington D.C.: Government Accountability Office.

Gramsci, A. (1971). *Selections from the prison notebooks of Antonio Gramsci*. New York: International Publishers.

Hardy, D. (2005, October 9). Military access, parental protests. *Philadelphia Inquirer,* p. B1.

Hardy, D., & Purcell, D. (2008, August 6). Growing hesitancy over a military test. *The Philadelphia Inquirer,* p. B1.

Kolben, D. (2006, April 25). Students at Top City Schools Suing Rumsfeld for Violating Privacy. *The New York Sun,* p. 2.

Krim, J. (2005a, June 23). Pentagon creates student database to identify recruits. *The New York Sun,* p. 5.

Krim, J. (2005b, June 23). Pentagon creating student database. *Washington Post*.

Krim, J. (2005c, June 24). Pentagon says it wants accurate student data. *The Washington Post,* p. D1.

Krim, J. (2005d, October 18). Recruitment tool targeted. *The Washington Post,* p. D5.

Lagotte, B. W., & Apple, M. W. (2010). Neoliberalism, militarization, and education reform. In P. Trifonas & B. Wright (Eds.), *Critical issues in peace and education*. London: Routledge.

Lipka, S. (2005, July 8). Pentagon system to gather student data raises privacy fears. *The Chronicle of Higher Education,* p. 30.

Liptak, A. (2007, January 10). Defense Dept. settles suit on database for recruiting. *The New York Times,* p. 19.

McCarthy, S. (2005, December 10). "Making mission" in a tough market. *The Globe and Mail,* p. A23.

Media Roundtable with Deputy Under Secretary of Defense for Personnel and Readiness David Chu. (2005, June 23). *US Department of Defense Information*.

Molnar, A. (1996). *Giving kids the business: The commercialization of America's schools*. Boulder, CO: Westview Press.

Molnar, A. (2005). *School commercialism: From democratic ideal to market commodity*. New York: Routledge.

Morris, B. D. (2004). *School recruiting program handbook* (350-13). Department of Defense, retrieved from http://www.usarec.army.mil/im/formpub/Pubs.htm#pamphlets.

Mulvihill. (2005, June 24). Pentagon database: Be now afraid. *The Boston Herald*.

Obama, B. (2009). Remarks of President Barack Obama: A complete and competitive American education US Hispanic Chamber of Commerce. Retrieved March 11, 2009, from http://www.whitehouse.gov

Peng, C. (2005). Military reveals recruitment database. *Daily Californian*. (1). Retrieved from http://archive.dailycal.org/article/18913/military_reveals_recruitment_

Proctor, C. (2005, June 27). UCLA unlikely to release data for military recruitment. *Daily Bruin*. Retrieved from http://www.dailybruin.com/article/2005/06/ucla-unlikely-to-release-data

Rhen, K. T. (2005, June 24). Potential recruits list critical to "all-recruited" force. *US Department of Defense Information*.

Rosenberg, M. (2005, February 13). Latest military front. *The New York Times,* p. 2.

Rosenberg, S. (2005, June 30). Military taps firm for data, *The Boston Globe,* p. 11.

Schwom, P. (2006, October 29). You could be in the Army now, *The Boston Globe,* p. 1.

Teicher, S. A. (2005, August 18). No-fly zones for military recruiters, *Christian Science Monitor,* p. 11.

Turque, B. (2010). Rhee dismisses 241 D.C. teachers. *The Washington Post*, July 24th.

Venetis, P. (2008). Targeting youth: What everyone should know about military recruiting in public high schools. Retrieved from http://law.newark.rutgers.edu/files/u/ MilitaryRecruitingReportConLitFinal.pdf.

KEITH M. STURGES

CHAPTER 8

Representing Failure: The Depiction of Low-Income, Mexican-American Students in School-Based Program Evaluation

EVALUATION AS OFFICIAL RECORD AND GOVERNANCE APPARATUS

In conjunction with its anti-poverty campaign, the Elementary and Secondary Education Act [ESEA] of 1965 mandated the use of an adapted form of social scientific research to report on the effects of Title I-funded reforms. Social science, framers of the Act argued, would contribute to social change. The evaluation mandate had three explicit aims: 1) to identify efficient approaches to educating disadvantaged students; 2) to arm parents of disadvantaged children with facts to enable them to participate in open debate; and 3) to stimulate competition among educators through standards and achievement according to those standards (Abert, 1979). Satisfaction of these expectations has leaned disproportionately in favor of increased competition while families have been dissociated from reform dialogue.

Emblematic of increased privatization, evaluation as an apparatus of education reform has, since the 1980s, become an instrument of neoliberal policy; it functions to certify and sanction "what works," thereby enabling model developers and contract service providers to encounter wider markets under the auspices of and support from federal and state governments (Sturges, 2011). Neoliberalism offers a set of refinements to the neoclassical liberal economic thought that dominated the US economy during the 1970s. Among these is support for a largely unregulated capitalist system that emphasizes free individual choice and strives for economic efficiency and growth, as well as technical progress (Apple, 2001; Harvey, 2007). In this context, the state's role is to define and defend rights, enforce contracts, and oversee spending. ESEA reauthorizations paved the way for networks of interest groups and service providers to carry their messages directly into the reform sphere whereas government agencies are repurposed to serve as brokers and orchestrators (Slaughter & Rhoades, 2004). Although privatized reform serves multiple, sometimes competing, interests that are rallied around the agenda of improving schools, it seldom includes representation from reform target communities.

To illustrate the interplay between the reform agenda that draws together those multiple interests and a target community, I explore how one Southwestern state's

J. Hall (ed.), Children's Human Rights and Public Schooling in the United States, 137–157.

installation of a college-readiness reform, College Preparation Now,[1] intended to increase the number of underrepresented students in higher education, fell short of its objectives. At the state education agency level, the US border city of Parrita and its largest public high school, Lawrence, represented a stronghold of the cultural "other" (that is, a group of people whose culture and political beliefs are represented as radically different from those of the dominant, and represent-*ing*, group). Explanations of Lawrence High School's high dropout rates, low performance on state tests, and low college attendance[2] fell on a continuum that, at one extreme, expressed sympathy for the community's ignorance about education and, at the other, disdain for what appeared to be active resistance to educational reform. This deficit orientation manifested itself in the reform's conceptualization, support systems, and evaluation. School and community interpretations were absent.

I became interested in Lawrence's Advanced Placement expansion while producing an oral and archival history of the school's curriculum from 1904 through the 1960s. As advanced history high school students assisted me in reviewing yearbooks for that period, we talked about the school's context, how their parents and grandparents had gone to the same school, and the school's recent curricular diversification. Later, while interviewing a 96-year-old former teacher and her students, many of whom were first-generation college-goers, discussions about how the state regarded locals pervaded our conversations. After I completed my historical analysis, curious about the rivalry between the state and local levels, I explored the recent curricular changes, the state department's involvement in those changes, and how they manifested themselves at the school. I accessed an evaluation report from the state department's website and was struck by the ambitious reforms scheduled for the school. Moreover, I was struck by the language evaluators chose to describe teachers and students. I wondered what unwritten purposes the evaluation might serve.

I write not as a representative of the target population, but through the eyes of a white, middle-class researcher who has ample experience both as an evaluator and as an educator who has worked in partnership with external evaluators. Part of the story I offer is what van Maanan (1988) refers to as the confessional tale, a critical self-exploration. Ethnographic research can be challenging not only for its partiality, but also for the way researchers position themselves and, through their writing, position participants. Throughout the study, I assumed that people are conscious, reflexive actors who make use of and adapt a variety of cultural tools, even if seemingly contradictory to positive gains models, in a world they recognize as structured (Foley, 1995). While I believe most teachers, administrators, evaluators, and state employees wanted students to learn and succeed, much of what I observed and heard reflected vaster enterprises of inequity. As I attempted to note how my preconceived notions influenced my writing (Davies, 1999), I

---

[1] *College Preparation Now* and all other names in this chapter are pseudonyms.

[2] Based on measures of college application and acceptance during the senior year of high school.

struggled to represent people across social positional levels and geographic locations.

The ethnographic context extends across sites. It includes the Parrita school district central office, Lawrence High School (the site of implementation), the state department of education, and the offices of the program evaluators. Across these domains, over a two-year period I conducted interviews with seven Advanced Placement teachers who participated in the College Preparation Now [CPN] reform and the school's principal and assistant principal. I also collected information in classrooms through participant-observation. In addition, I interviewed three contracted program evaluators and the two Southwest Department of Education [SWDE] officers. Informal and unstructured interviews provided insights into how each group of stakeholders made sense of the tenets foregrounding CPN and how their interests were (or were not) served by the reform. Since this chapter concentrates on representation, I also collected and analyzed evaluation reports and data collection instruments.

Like many schools relegated to the "low-performing" list, Lawrence High School was eligible for and had been awarded multiple state, federal, and private funding sources in addition to CPN. Principal Ramirez, who was close to retirement at the time of my data collection, had grown accustomed to the "comings and goings of a lot of reforms over the years." He went on to say, "They offer us important resources, funding streams, ways to survive." Lawrence's teaching force of 127, with an average of 16 years of experience, had also gotten used to the ebb and flow of curricular reforms (less than 1% of the teaching force was new). Furthermore, 91% of the teachers were Mexican-American and most had graduated from Lawrence.

Lawrence High School was one of several local sites of the post WWII Chicano civil rights movement. Returning veterans, many of whom had dropped out of Lawrence to join the war effort, relied on the GI Bill to access the christening of Parrita's community college. During the 1950s and 1960s, many veterans completed undergraduate and graduate degrees, thereby creating a middle class consisting of professionals in law, business, and education (including the father of Principal Ramirez). This set of events created an educated populace that became accustomed to confrontations with the state, and may also have given rise to a local norm of postponing higher education until after entering the workforce. While a smallish percentage of contemporary Lawrence students ultimately elected to go to college, those who did tended to postpone their application and entry.

Lawrence, comprised almost entirely of Mexican descent students, is situated less than a mile from the US-Mexico border. With 95% of the nearly 2000 students receiving free or reduced-price lunch, Lawrence was not representative of Parrita's overall population, since wealthier youth attended one of Parrita's private schools. One scandal at the time of data collection involved a runner-up for Parrita's superintendency whose children attended a private school. This class distinction was multi-generational, since most of Lawrence's teachers and parents, and many grandparents of current students, had also attended Lawrence. Ethnicity is also key to understanding the context, since students and adults distinguished themselves from the less affluent, phenotypic analogues just a mile away. "They are Mexican. We are Hispanic," one Lawrence senior told me. At the same time, they stood in stark contrast to College Preparation Now's developers and evaluators, all of whom were white, middle-class and many of whom had teaching experience in predominantly white, middle-class schools. Not surprisingly, the sociocultural distance between the state department and Parrita impacted the reform's im-plementtation, as did the evaluation.

The evaluation, which is a kind of "official knowledge" (Apple, 1993; Bourdieu, 1977),[3] provided purportedly-neutral and objective substance to the sociocultural distance. I demonstrate how representation of Lawrence High School students supported curricular decisions that diminished educational opportunities. While I do not indict all evaluation as disparaging representations, I hope to problematize common practices of state sanctioned knowledge work that may perpetuate deficit perceptions of student subgroups. In doing so, I do not hastily conclude that all pernicious reform activities stem from the neoliberalism. School reform has long served a wide variety of interests (e.g., early 20th century Americanization). Yet, a strong body of evidence (e.g. Apple, 2004; Popkewitz & Brennan, 1998) illustrates how the current dominant way of thinking helps normalize the ideologies of powerful interest groups (Apple, 1993) while appropriating the language of equitable access to education in the service of profit from servicing the "other." Evaluation's fashionable veil of neutrality is part of a set of institutional practices that normalize white, middle-class views on college preparation. In practice, such normalizations "assess" the extent of "other-ness," which, given its service to reform, suggests that is has the potential to authorize or to exclude.

CONCEPTUAL ORIENTATION

Evaluation is promoted by its own industry and by reform program developers as an imperative, non-partisan voice in the national conversation about school reform (Datta, 2000). It is also a vehicle of power. The Education Reform Discourse[4] is put into action through legislative, economic, and symbolic exchange. When Popkewitz (2000) tells us, in his cogent history of education reform, that the nation-state is the locus of modern power, he overlooks the non-profits, trade associations, and corporate entities that affect distribution of fungible and symbolic resources. A collection of national standards and economic inducements (e.g., ESEA's No Child Left Behind reauthorization) does not represent the totality of

---

[3] Initially contrasted with *practical knowledge* (Bourdieu, 1977) to exemplify reproduction of inequalities through the creation and distribution of *official knowledge*, I refer to the tactics wherein dominant groups optimize control over the production of *official knowledge* (Apple, 1993).

[4] The Education Reform Discourse (Sturges, 2011) is a set of repeated messages that permeate public spaces, making the drive to improve education through program theory a moral imperative that benefits the community's civic and the state's economic well-being.

power. Instead, power is distributed throughout the reform industry's networks, partnerships, and collaboratives.

Such networks, representing a wealth of organizations that consists of private sector model developers, federally contracted technical assistants, and regional non-profits, share a rationality to solve common education-focused problems (Slaughter & Rhoades, 2004). They also encourage some interest convergence of their constituent organizations. In particular, these networks provide "the educational conditions believed necessary both for increasing international competitiveness, profit, and discipline and for returning us to a romanticized past of the 'ideal' home, family, and school" (Apple, 1999). Power, in this context, is exercised through a collective form that Deem, Hillyard, and Reed (2007) refer to as "organizational hybrids." These hybrids possess mechanisms of institutional governance that legitimate the actions required to address common problems through a complex of "entrepreneurship, evangelism, and mimicry" (Suchman, 2003). Thus, reform service providers operate as "loosely linked dynamic and efficient businesses set-free from the restraints of centralized political administration and control" (Deem et al., 2007). A more accurate depiction, therefore, places the seemingly marginal organizations into influential positions while the nation-state operates as regulator. The configurations are ambiguous and unstable, making them amenable to rapid redirection of material and human resources to suit changing conditions.

The shared rationality to "fix" education both draws from and solidifies the Education Reform Discourse. Meanwhile, program evaluators produce records of reforms' theories of action (i.e., inputs, outputs, outcomes) by focusing solely on the local sites of reform deployment. They do this with the intent of measuring implementation fidelity and the reform's impact. Evaluators, who make sense of and depict actualized theories of action, also depict localized characters, the targets of reform – poor, minority students and their teachers. These depictions of education reform generally are sparse on holistic analyses that reflect how reforms intersect with local communities. Evaluation's calculated gaze on the generalizable effect of curricular models renders particularistic perspectives and wishes unsuitable for the official record. Furthermore, this gaze filters out complicated and critical analysis of interests, beliefs, and potential benefits among model developers and clients from its characterizations of the programs and the people depicted. Supported by the state and encouraged by market interests, the gaze is directed econometrically – the modernist project of making the messy social world legible to state representatives for the purposes of management, production, and taxation.

I situated this critique of the reform and its evaluation in Trouillot's (1995) analysis of the relationship between power and the production of social scientific knowledge to interpret evaluation's influence in widening the gulf between program developers and intended reform recipients. While perhaps unintentional, official evaluation reports generated an image of recalcitrant, poor academic performance. Service providers,' state employees,' and evaluators' assumptions about economic and cultural others not only persisted without question, but were supported by a "culture of poverty" argument (Harrington, 1962). This lattermost notion has resurfaced in the past decade in popular education, not as a critique, but as a well-intended diagnosis of voiceless lurkers in the shadows of ignorance (Gorski, 2008). Its core deficit orientation, which was manifested in evaluation reports, supported a shift in the reform's emphasis from college readiness to workforce development.

COLLEGE PREPARATION NOW FROM CONCEPT TO DEPICTION

Since 1999, the US Department of Education Office of Postsecondary Education has offered six-year discretionary grants that are intended to increase low-income student entry and success in college through its program Gaining Early Awareness and Readiness for Undergraduate Programs [GEAR UP]. Accordingly, GEAR UP state grants support "both an early intervention component designed to increase college attendance and success and raise the expectations of low-income students and a scholarship component" (US Department of Education, ND). Stakeholders representing the state department of education and Lawrence High School made somewhat different sense of this vague purpose. The next section overviews the reform, its oversight, implementation and the people who helped drive its operations. Working between what I refer to as the "sites of conceptualization" and the "site of implementation" required moving between two worldviews.

SITES OF CONCEPTUALIZATION, MONITORING, AND OVERSIGHT

This section illustrates how dynamics at the state were influenced by increased privatization. Reductions in authority and expertise at the state level, co-occurring with temporary, tactically-oriented contract relationships, corresponded to the need for enhanced compliance monitoring and the prevalence of the temporary nature of the reform. State department staff selected four high schools (from among its lowest scoring on state tests) and their feeder middle schools (representing three districts) to participate. Among these, Lawrence was selected both because of test scores and its high percentage of Latino students. According to the grant's plan and written as the preface to the first year's evaluation report, College Preparation Now would "educate parents and students about the importance of higher education" by opening a college access center at Lawrence that organized college visits, prepared information packets for parents, provided training sessions for parents, and handled the state's incentive program that paid for students to take the advanced placement examination. Most centrally, the school would have expanded advanced course offerings, support for teachers through the College Board, and permit all students access to advanced classes.

State department staff and three partner purveyors assembled the pieces of CPN's framework. Replicating a neighboring state's framework for its GEAR UP award, the reform partners refined the model according to areas of expertise and interest. Whereas the neighboring state's framework emphasized parent involvement in gradually expanding the advanced placement curriculum, CPN took a more streamlined approach to college awareness and teacher professional development. Specifically, the first partner, a fee-for-service non-profit organization, created the central structure and provided background research on college access. Experts from the organization visited Lawrence once each year to refine the college access center's offering and activities. It also provided feedback on the advanced program's curricula. Another partner organization consulted with school and district leadership, as well as with state department staff, on professional learning needs for the reform. Its staff worked with the implementation team to organize on-site teacher training content and selection of teachers, and also recommended training providers (themselves included). The third organization, a university-based center, oversaw the community outreach component of the framework. In particular, its staff wrote press releases for local papers, produced media materials such as brochures, and helped organize parent classes that were intended to promote higher education. Beyond this thin description, little information is available about the contract partners, since none of the planning was included in the evaluation or other public records.

Two Southwest Department of Education program officers, Jenny and Sarah, shared monitoring duties, approved expenditures, and coordinated efforts on behalf of partners. Since news of the GEAR UP award coincided with the department's reduction in force by nearly 50%, Jenny and Sarah balanced an array of responsibilities. Sarah recalled:

> Those of us who made it went into survival mode to outlast the next rounds of cuts. We had to do everything we could to keep doing our multiple jobs, and to do what the cut staff did. I mean we also had to make sure our programs impacted student learning and that we could show that to the public and our bosses.

Those who "went into survival mode" competed for large reform awards. An important demand of survival mode was balancing competition with what Jenny called "laying low." She recalled, "We had to avoid any kind of strife in the department, which might have forced us to amp up the compliance side." Knowledge that someone would be held responsible for accountability measures undergirded Sarah and Jenny's involvement in technical assistance provision. In other words, the reform had to work.

School reform literature offers idealized, prescribed roles for state department of education personnel as educational reformers (Hamman & Lane, 2004; Lusi, 1997). Sarah and Jenny helped me get a sense for what their jobs entailed and why they chose to do those jobs. Neither had ever taught. Sarah briefly served as an assistant principal before returning to school to pursue a Ph.D. in educational administration. While working on her degree, she made important networking connections in the research center and contract service provider world. These connections helped her "farm out the work to think tanks and university faculty who were more familiar with the content."

Both white, middle-class staff members came to the department as self-appointed "missionaries." Jenny commented, "You'd be appalled if you knew how little people here get paid." When I asked Jenny why she stayed, she said, "It's addictive. I'm accomplishing something and I get a lot of respect. Not that I know everything, but I also have a unique knowledge of [our state's] educational needs." While neither had visited Parrita before the program's implementation, both shared worries about communication (since neither spoke Spanish) and about the extent to which they would feel the need to be directly involved in order to ensure the reform would be successful.

The mixed-method evaluation (based on achievement data, program participation rates, exam participation and performance, application to institutes of higher education, surveys of participating teachers and students, 680 classroom observations, and 460 student and teacher interviews) was conceptualized by a "non-partisan" contract research organization with Sarah's input. After three bids, the state department selected Southwest Research Center [SRC] because of its price and, as Sarah said, "We have a good working relationship with Sally. She is easy to work with and gets it done on time." SRC's board of directors, comprised of former state department of education commissioners, business leaders, and non-profit service provider representatives, hired Sally to direct the evaluation team. Sally had spent much of her career as a teacher and, after completing her doctorate in research methods, as an internal researcher for an urban school district. As the director of SRC, she managed a small staff, with advanced degrees in psychology, anthropology, economics, and sociology. The team typically worked on five to six contracts and was dedicated full-time to evaluation contracts. For larger evaluations, Sally called on colleagues to subcontract as data collectors.

In one of our interviews, Sally commented that, "Hispanics and other poor minorities seem to be stuck. If we can help them value education and help them help their children, we can improve the education system." According to Sally, the problems of poor teaching and family disengagement could be addressed through the knowledge provided through evaluation with the input and guidance of SWDE and its partners. Her evaluation team held varying viewpoints on reform's function, but held a common belief that evaluation could improve programs and, therefore, increase equity. One member of Sally's team, a psychologist who had worked for the same school district previously, said, "I feel like I am helping to give a voice to the little guy, whereas before I was doing a lot of analysis of test scores and that wasn't really a service." Next, I explore ways in which evaluation as a service and an apparatus of governance took shape at the site of implementation.

SITE OF IMPLEMENTATION (AND CENTER OF DEPICTION)

Typically, Advanced Placement programs are established through a gradual development of internal supports. A successful outlay consists of administrative support (for leveraging funds, orchestrating key events, and providing moral support), establishment of a teacher mentoring system, counseling support (for appropriate student placement), support within academic departments to develop vertical teams,[5] and collaborations with feeder schools (The College Board, 2006). This development may take several years. Lawrence's expansion would bypass early implementation; from four to 21 Advanced Placement courses during the first year. Before full implementation, 16 teachers participated in summer College Board training. Those teachers also participated in vertical teaming training, which would allow them to plan the scope and sequence of the advanced courses. By Year Three, 43 teachers had completed College Board Certification. Access to advanced courses also increased. While fewer than 2% of the school's students participated in the existing Advanced Placement program, 63% of Lawrence's students enrolled in at least one CPN-sponsored advanced course.

A leadership team, consisting of the assistant principal, a counselor who directed the college access center (converted classroom with local college application and other materials), and the district's curriculum specialist, put Lawrence's curriculum expansion into operation. The team participated in monthly conference calls with Sarah to discuss the budget, activities, and next steps. Sometimes the external purveyors joined the calls. In turn, the implementation team met periodically with Lawrence's core content department heads to discuss progress. According to plan, content department heads would work with their teams to develop the scope and sequence of courses. Additionally, the leadership team hosted whole-faculty professional development sessions, and with considerable input from Sarah, determined the content for training provided by external providers. Thus, the reform's management was responsible for curricular decisions that both affected implementation steps and tidbits of ideology embedded in those steps.

A strong body of evidence illustrates how learning opportunities for minority and poor students are often dictated by dominant cultural beliefs (Apple, 1990; Hurd, 2008; Oakes, 1985). For example, ethnographic literature examines school-level reproduction of class and ethnic struggles, showing differences in teacher and student ethnicity affect expectations, and therefore, learning experiences among students (Gandara, 1999); power differentials between school administration and communities lead to the silencing of struggling students (Fine, 1991); and/or institutional practices of dominant groups can impede school involvement (Hurd, 2008; Sturges, Cramer, Harry, & Klingner, 2005). These studies have helped understand how prevailing beliefs influence learning opportunities among marginalized students through sometimes subtle interactions. Yet, because of their focus on the microcosm, they seldom help us understand the relationship between disparities in educational opportunity and institutions outside the school.

Valenzuela (2005) provides an illuminative example of the relationship between educational disparities in schools and external pressures in their ethnographic accounts detailing the ways in which Mexican-American students are "pushed out" of high school through state testing regimes. Similarly, nearly 52% of Parrita

---

[5] Vertical teams are comprised of educators from across grade levels whom collaborate to develop, refine, and implement curricula that align across those levels (Kowal, 2002).

students drop out of high school. Sarah and Jenny speculated the dropout rate was indicative of the community's devaluation of schooling. Sarah, for instance, commented, "They think, 'Why should I be in school when I can make money now?' They don't really think about the consequences of dropping out." The complexity of the relationship between dropout and testing was not included in evaluation reports. In fact, the reports contained little localized information outside the immediate scope of the CPN model. Aside from a demographic description, analysis of the class and ethnicity of students and any differentials in outcome by group were omitted from the evaluation reports.[6] For instance, the localized norm of postponing college did not appear in any of the thousands of report pages. Thus, even though the reform involved institutional strategies such as increased access to advanced classes, participation in Advanced Placement exams, and counseling access, interpretation of the school's limited success in altering patterns of student nonparticipation in higher education reverted to faults with the local population.

EVALUATION NARRATIVE AND THE POWER OF DEPICTION

Over the past 40 years, the intention and practice of much program evaluation has drifted. With its origins in the School Survey movement of the early part of the 20th century, earlier evaluations were used to guide local improvement (Lagemann, 2000). A glance at contemporary publicly-available evaluation reports, however, reveals a concentration on proprietary feedback for generalizable models. This is particularly in relation to teacher accountability and academic outcomes of failing low-income, minority students (Sturges, 2011). The scramble for universal models perpetuates a market demand for technical certification while the "at risk" discourse makes that demand an ethical, state-managed service. Evaluations contribute to decisions about the distribution of funding and symbolic assets (e.g. discourses about underserved student abilities and white, middle-class views on how best to help *these* students). Together, they call for a standardized market-based approach to education, facilitated by external service providers. This call accentuates evaluation's detachment from public service, diminishes its potential for civic engagement, and hinders its capacity to attend to local perspectives. The distancing also denies entry of narratives that counter evaluation characterizations. Circumvention of local voice in favor of paternalistic attempts at assimilating marginalized students co-occurs as the "state shifts the blame for the evident inequalities in access and outcome it has promised to reduce, from itself on to schools, parents and children" (Apple, 2001).

The exclusive right among evaluators to depict a brand of neoliberal empowerment defines the privileged status of the evaluation while excluding contributions to educational goals and measures of success among subjects. This representational hegemony is especially problematic when it entails a substantial

[6] Since reforms are meant to be scaled up to universally-implementable models, local knowledge, class differences, and program micropolitics are seldom recorded as relevant program features.

distance between the "knower and the known" (Fabian, 1990). Evaluations are conducted with pre-determined normative rules and dispositions of the ideal student, which fosters a "norm" that is both a construction of and means of reproducing the dominance of the groups responsible for curricular reforms (Apple, 2004). Representation of "at risk" reform targets (an extreme divergence from the norm) and the concomitant use of replicable measures of their success and failure serve as proxies for degree of assimilation. Consequently, evaluation reporting conventions that denote what is knowable, what is important to know, and how it will be known (Foucault, 1977) imply amplification of some specified voices over others. In his analysis of the ways power shapes the production of historical knowledge, Trouillot (1995) examines how silencing pervades the space between actual events and the record of those events. Although events leave traces in the form of records and texts, which are used to create the narratives, no narrator has complete access to social data and each filters through the myriad potential sources. Evaluation knowledge is particularly exposed to exercises of power through representation of the "other" during its conceptualization, data collection, analysis, writing, and editing.

Researchers may intend to tell accurate stories from available data. Nonetheless, naturalized discourse, or what Bourdieu (1977) refers to as *practical knowledge*, that which "goes without saying because it comes without saying," conveys lived commonsensicalities that draw on epistemological convention and micropolitics to inform the substance of those stories. Such discourse makes certain assumptions *invisible* even to evaluators who may think of themselves as informed and progressive. Evaluators often recognize themselves as "soft activists" who contribute to program improvement by influencing institutional decisions and brokering differing perspectives (Sturges, 2011). In doing so, evaluators, as SRC's sociologist noted, "give voice to students and teachers." Nevertheless, that voice is framed by the structured questions that seek to gauge program impact and that are posed according to what the researchers and state staff deem to be normal and expectable from the program. For instance, the evaluation team spent months nurturing a relationship with the state's higher education board to access data on the number of students entering college just after high school.

This is not simply an epistemological foible. When only a small number of students "succeeded" according to the evaluation, explanations for program failure were directed at the school and its community. Although the evaluation team might have intended to give voice to Lawrence students and staff, it also provided information that helped solidify state staff's perceptions of a set of pervasive and seemingly-irrational resistances to planned educational change. In this case, the evaluation not only wrote about, but wrote *at* the target populations (Fabian, 1990). In the following section, after describing the evaluation reporting process, I explore how particular normative evaluation practices and perspectives enabled the deficit interpretations about Lawrence students and community members, and how conventional evaluation practices led to the omission of certain interpretations and pieces of information.

EVALUATION REPORTING, READING, AND OBJECTIVES

Throughout the reform, evaluators submitted five annual reports and one final, summative report to SWDE. Each report was between 263 and 337 pages plus appendices and had the same structure: description of the evaluation, findings arranged by data collection mode and role groups (e.g., teacher survey, student focus groups, Advanced Placement exam scores), and formative recommendations (except the final report which contained a longitudinal analysis of College Preparation Now's impact). The evaluation team also offered easily-digestible executive summaries of 8-12 pages. As Sally noted:

> The full report takes about three months to prepare. We do the analyses, write a draft and then meet with [SWDE] for their feedback. Then, we have a careful editing process. We know that no one will probably ever read the full report, but we never know, so there's no room for error. We *do* expect a lot of people to read executive summaries, though.

In executive summaries, the evaluation team distilled what they deemed to be the most salient findings and recommendations from full reports. The team emphasized content that had been pre-determined by convention, the constraints of time, and in accordance with client input.

In the service of large-scale reform developers, policy and funding streams pressure evaluators to focus on generalizable, outcome-oriented knowledge over situation-specific findings (Patton, 2011). Concurrently, the contract stipulates the scope of work, questions to be answered, methods, a description of deliverables, and the focus of the inquiry. One evaluator, Fred, noted, "You don't have permission to ask questions the client doesn't want you to ask; there's no money or time to do additional analyses either. It's focused on particular questions," as he recalled the initial planning meeting with Jenny and Sarah. Being aware of these constraints helps shape specific project reports and, as importantly, general processes for reporting. Mary described the method she used to analyze teacher surveys, for instance:

> Data analysis is pretty standard. They complete surveys online and I transfer the data right into SPSS. Then, I do basic statistics, frequency and standard deviations and so forth. I usually take out the open-endeds and put those altogether and look for commonalities. Then, I write those findings and insert in the part of the report dealing with that objective, describe the evaluation methods, all the basic kind of things that you would put in to kind of tell the difference between the years.

In brief, the evaluation reports showed that CPN-sponsored training enabled Lawrence to build a "cadre of teachers trained in AP methods that emphasized content-specific knowledge and innovative instructional strategies that enhance students' ability to learn on their own." The reports also showed Lawrence's advanced course offerings had been expanded and student access to those courses had been opened. The evaluation reports also suggested although SWDE sponsored and supported these structures, the combination of teacher resistance, lack of parental support, and student failure undermined the reform's potential for success. For instance, the observation section from the Year Four report revealed sparse use of advanced strategies. In over 90% of Advanced Placement classroom observations, evaluators reported that teachers lectured to students most of the time and used questioning strategies that seldom involved more than one-word answers. Project-based learning and guided discussions were not observed.

Outcome data illustrated the effects of teacher and parent reluctance to participate in CPN. During the fifth and sixth years (which coincided with my data collection), while 57% and 59% (respectively) of students took at least one Advanced Placement exam, only two students each year scored at or above criteria. The evaluation reports linked student growth shortcomings to entrenched cultural norms that maintain among students and families the "failure to understand the importance of preparation for higher education." For instance, the recommendations from the Year Three report indicated that while the state can support advanced test-taking, "responsibility for participation and interest rest, ultimately, with the community." This finding diverges from the local Parrita interpretation – namely, that the cultural norms may have less to do with devaluation of higher education and more to do with acceptance of the delay of entry into college.

Evaluation reports and, more widely in terms of readership, executive summaries, revealed additional tentative explanations for the reform's shortfall in expected impact. The first of these was the ineffectiveness of professional development. In the Year Five report, several teachers said they did not recall any of the College Board training they received. One recalled, "I think we had something three years ago." Teachers also indicated they did not perceive the professional development to be particularly useful. One example, drawn from the Year Four report, characterized the training as follows:

> The first 36 hours is a series of mandated fluff about learning styles, nature and needs of the gifted child, and a bunch of goofy make-and-takes with something about Bloom's Taxonomy. The 18 annual maintenance hours can be earned doing a variety of stuff.

Taken out of context, comments among teachers seemed to be indicative of a staunch resistance to change and issue with the College Board. The next section of the same evaluation report offers snippets of student descriptions of their Advanced Placement classroom experiences:

> Students described AP as 'practically the same thing as the regular classes, except that they're more strict.' A senior said, 'My AP history teacher doesn't really teach AP. She just makes you do another paper.'

While these sections illustrated a lack of "implementation fidelity" among teachers, the reports did not connect the apparent lack of enthusiasm among teachers with other facets of the reform's deployment, such as mandatory teacher participation in CPN's advanced courses, unavailability of leadership support, and perhaps most importantly, major shifts in professional development offerings.

The above referenced "variety of stuff," which might have seemed both incongruent with the reform and a tad petulant, may hint at a broader pattern. Each evaluation report listed professional development topics and the number of teachers that participated. For instance, in Years One and Two, district-selected teachers were required to participate in Advanced Placement Summer Institutes and follow-up training on vertical teaming. The district's curriculum specialist and the school's advanced coordinator worked with department teams monthly after school to develop the curricular materials and assessments for the new courses. The Year Four report noted "that teachers ceased participation in vertical alignment and curricular planning." In interviews I conducted, teachers said vertical teams met three times after the initial training and were provided neither oversight nor technical assistance afterwards. One teacher said, "What do they expect from us? We didn't have a common time to get together, no planning period. We didn't have support. And, most of us had no idea how to proceed."

The Professional Development Story

Drawing from the six annual reports, I explored the shift in College Preparation Now's training focus. While the decrease in Advanced Placement institute and vertical team training might be explained logically, in great part, by the fact that fewer teachers remained untrained, Lawrence retained 54% of Advanced Placement-certified teachers (compared to 72% who were not required to participate). Table 1 illustrates the gradual shift in professional development emphasis.

Table 1. Number of Teachers Participating in College Preparation Now Training

Event	*Year 1*	*Year 2*	*Year 3*	*Year 4*	*Year 5*	*Year 6*
Advanced Placement summer institute	16	27	21	9	0	0
Active research	12	18	14	22	0	0
Curriculum writing	8	16	4	2	0	0
Test-taking strategies	0	0	0	2	26	16
Thinking maps	5	14	3	31	9	0
Vertical teaming	33	20	44	0	0	0
Ruby Payne's *Aha! Process*	0	0	0	16	38	43

The Year Three full evaluation report noted "Interviewed teachers complained about some colleagues' lack of implementation (e.g. following the vertical team plan) that made a seamless alignment of curriculum difficult." It also reported that:

> Teachers cited a lack of guidance and accountability as another challenge to vertical plan implementation. Teachers viewed inadequate leadership as contributing to organizational problems with the campus vertical team, which also resulted in implementation difficulties: "Two years ago we put together a vertical team plan with the teachers at [Lawrence] and ... somebody lost all the material. We've never had access to it.

In the Year Three executive summary, the evaluation team wrote, "While teachers recognize the value of vertical teaming and report positive impacts, greater campus level leadership is needed to reduce implementation difficulties. [CPN] leaders should address leadership difficulties that impede progress in curricular alignment." When the school year ended, Sally met with district leadership to make sense of the findings and make sure the reform could reach its federally-funded objectives. The team agreed the district curriculum specialist would work with Jenny to map the curricula and have materials ready by the time the new semester began. Since teachers would no longer be responsible for vertical teaming or curriculum planning, the district removed these from mandatory training, and before the school year began, also removed them from the buffet of voluntary training selections. In their place came the "variety of stuff." As Table 1 shows, one event dominated Lawrence attendance. Drawing from the same year's evaluation finding that the Parrita community did not value education and was unfamiliar with college, Jenny was excited she was able to secure Ruby Payne to work with the school directly.

Payne Comes to Town

Payne, (a fee-for-service training provider), offers seminars many observers suggest essentialize differences between students who come from poor, middle class, and wealthy backgrounds. From her "analysis," Payne makes recommendations about how teachers can better educate poor students (Gorski, 2006). According to Bomer, Dworin, May, and Semington (2008), federal reporting requirements that emphasize poor children's academic performance have "fueled the demand for professional development programs such as that offered by Ruby Payne and her Aha! Process, Inc." In this training, Payne characterizes people living in poverty as leading chaotic lives, unable to discern cause-effect relationships, and incapable of long-term planning. Payne claims because of these shortcomings, poor students are deficient in cognitive strategies and judgment. Payne's deficit characterizations suggest to teachers a need to lower expectations for "at risk" students, expectations which often land them "in lower tracks or lower ability groups and their educational experience more often dominated by rote drill and practice" (Bomer et al., 2008).

Payne visited Lawrence High School four times. Principal Ramirez recalled a telephone conversation with Sarah in which she asked that at least two teachers from each core content area participate in Payne's workshop. During the first visit, Payne trained 16 teachers in an all-day session. The sessions began with an overview of the fundamental cultural differences between the poor, the middle class, and the affluent. At one point, Payne demonstrated even affection or love was regarded differently by each of these class culture ideal types. She then explored the innate differences in learning styles and structures between these groups and implications for teaching. At the core of her argument was what she refers to as cognitive strategies, a kind of hardwire "infrastructure" of the mind. Children living in poverty, according to Payne, lack the development of abstract thinking, and therefore, have random/episodic memory, are unable to plan or predict, and fail to make cause-effect relationships. She then spent the afternoon working with teachers on particular scenarios.

By the final year of CPN, more than 70% of the teaching force at Lawrence had attended the Aha! Process. Many teachers who participated shared concerns about their students' abilities and felt they needed to "dumb down" the curriculum so students could pass. After attending Payne's seminars, an Advanced Placement history teacher said, for instance, "We worry about putting too much pressure on students and having them drop out of school. Many of these students are at-risk." An English literature teacher commented, "So many kids are involved that sometimes the class gets a little watered down. Instead of it being challenging where you have to selectively throw things at them, you have to water things down." The at-risk designation spoke for itself since teachers came to perceive a cap to what students could learn. One teacher said, "I try to ensure all students succeed and understand the material but unfortunately because of lack of interest or because of not caring, it is hard to have a success." The assistant principal proclaimed, "Teachers work in a challenging setting. We often squeeze water from rocks here."

It is important to note teachers did not "squeeze water from rocks" at Lawrence High School at the outset of the reform. The water from rocks comment indexes a bifurcation of the local discourse. Some school personnel showed signs of Payne's "scientific" analysis of poverty. These teachers came to see CPN as a method to resist inequity, while local external challenges, such as poverty, competed with the program. Delaying college was reinterpreted as a signifier of lower class culture. This was a contrast from earlier interpretations in which teachers and SWDE staff insisted on a college preparatory curriculum for all Lawrence students that would provide a means of resisting the inequalities of institutionalized tracking of Parrita students (Sassen, 2006). There was an acknowledgement that the process would be gradual and that it would make *access* easier. But, as the reform's planners came to see in evaluation reports, CPN left a minimal *effect* on state test scores and advanced exams. This was translated into a prevailing conviction that these students and their families do not value education, an orientation that reinforced Jenny and Sarah's felt need to intervene on the behalf of students and their families.

Building Classes

Evaluation reports excluded pertinent reform mechanics about student participation. In particular, two processes were set into motion early on in the reform that affected how students participated. First, CPN's Federal reporting required the state department reveal the number of teachers trained, students participating, and courses created. Sarah recalled being worried that few students would willingly participate in advanced courses, and therefore, suggested to Parrita's Central Office a very active recruitment of students.

In the interviews I conducted, teachers linked placement decisions to CPN's funding. One said, "Administrators looked at how many advanced courses we could have. So, we paid a course.[7] Then, we had to stick students in there." Teachers and students commented that some students did not want to be in advanced classes, but "the administrators and counselor talked them into it." A Literature teacher said, "If the students want to get out, they go to the counselor. And, then they come back and they say that the counselor said 'no.'" Some students were resentful about being "forced" into advanced classes. Some speculated they were selected for Advanced Placement because there were no other classes available or the counselor "just wanted us in the class." An 11th grader who helped me with my historical study said she thought she had been placed in advanced History because some boys were "messing with me and [the counselor] put me with a better batch of kids." The same day, the counselor explained she tries to get all the students who are "nice, friendly, and good people," especially the "good girls" into Advanced Placement classes.

Teachers and students also described two, separate advanced tracks. One of CPN's history teachers commented, "We have two AP programs. One is open to all students and the other, the real AP, is more selective, more like the Advanced Placement we had a few years ago," a point that failed to appear in evaluation reports. Over the reform's implementation, those students who were most likely to have taken advanced coursework regardless of open enrollment policies took slightly different paths from the "at risk" students. The "real AP" offered small class sizes, possessed numerous resources (e.g., computer simulators for biology classes), and were much more involved in project-based learning. Furthermore, its teachers were those who had been teaching the same courses since before CPN was initiated. Conversely, CPN's advanced classrooms had an average of 30 students, relied primarily on textbooks and worksheets, and had the Advanced Placement-certified teaching staff that turned over the most.

Although the state department and the district took active steps to improve access to advanced classes, little was done to address quality of advanced coursework and even less to provide students a sense of distinction through their

---

[7] College Preparation Now course creation was contingent upon sufficient numbers of students. When enough students were enrolled in a class, the class would, in essence, "be paid."

participation. Such accessibility and distinction would require an environment in which Parrita students could feel welcome to participate under conditions of mutual respect (Fine, Jaffe, Pedraza, Stoudt, & Futch, 1997) and in an educational system designed for their success rather than to placate perceived deficits.

Summarizing Representation

While evaluators had little sway over how reports would be used, they had tremendous influence over how data depicted reform participants and the context. For instance, evaluation reports were devoid of attempts to understand the cultural ecology, exchanges of power, and project politics that might undergird "failure to understand the importance of preparation for higher education" among families (Year Six report). By ignoring these differences, the evaluation helped normalize white "normalcy" as official record. Furthermore, unreflective conventions such as assembling data hierarchically for analysis and structuring reports are the spaces in which the *practical* is the ontological basis for the *official*. For example, training and personal sense of data value among evaluators, which emphasized the general over the specific, provided the reporting structure. The evaluation reports presented outcome data (e.g., the number and scores of students taking advanced examinations) as the most important findings, evidenced by the amount of attention in recommendations and that they were included in the executive summary. At a lower value, classroom observations offered indications of classroom implementation quality. Next in the hierarchy, surveys were generalizable and passed technical quality tests. Finally, while evaluation reports contained illustrative snippets of qualitative information, executive summaries were devoid of interviews.

Evaluators are trained to use the tools of social science, but are often rewarded to use them in a technocratic manner that aligns with the prevailing econometric view of education (Sturges, 2011). Concurrently, pressures to please clients limit the extent to which evaluators critique programs. For example, Helen, SRC's qualitative researcher recalled a Year Two planning meeting in which Sarah demanded removal of an analysis of Parrita community members:

> She called it minutiae. I felt like we were compromising the perspective the interviewees had shared with us, that we were holding fast to some idealized reporting. Mostly, I felt the hold. It signaled for me that this kind of work has constraints related to who pays you and what authority they have over you.

"The hold" meant removing the entire section, a simplified version of Bourdieu's analysis of social capital (1977) articulated in relation to CPN's approach to educating parents about the importance of higher education. Helen's analysis offered program staff an opportunity to access perspectives among parents on the program and their ideas for improving it.

CONCLUDING THOUGHTS

Nowhere in the evaluation was there mention of two extremes: 1) the perspectives of CPN developers and their assumptions about Mexican-American students and 2) a cultural ecological analysis of students and teachers, their aspirations, and how they made sense of the reform. Through these omissions, the evaluation bypassed deliberation of the ways in which inequity was embedded in the ideological fabric of the reform's multiple positionalities. This omission helped mask the enactment of power directed at the *at risk* through professional development (e.g. Culture of Poverty), CPN's marketing language (e.g. "enhancing teaching competence"), and in expectations that teachers would be able to implement Advanced Placement strategies effectively without coaching or support (Joyce & Showers, 2002). The evaluation was not equipped (or intended) to scrutinize the reform's production, funding, or negotiations between influential groups that decided how Advanced Placement might be used to address socioeconomic disparities in college attendance.

As noted earlier, the reform was developed and refined according to program theories that were constructed with assumptions about categories of subjects. Decisions based on evaluation information helped repurpose CPN from an emphasis on equity and college preparation to an emphasis on efficiency and workforce development. Both discourses – the discourse of educational equity which claims to move past class-based and ethnic consciousness to offering standards-based programs and the discourse of workforce development – work together with a common focus on the needs of the student (e.g., as the oft-heard notion goes, *putting children first*). Thus, the evaluation represented a dual framing of accountability and "knowing what's best for *these* kids."

Cross-cultural and cross-class implications are paramount in educational reforms such as CPN, particularly since dominant educational processes that engender curricular tracking accept both inequities and minority school failure as natural. The logic for this is congealed through a distancing – or othering – and, subsequently, the production of a general category, a global "culture of poverty," thereby moving reform farther from the specific and uniqueness of place, people, and local history. Student stories about their aspirations, class experiences, and ethnicity are seldom central aspects of evaluations (much less reforms). Expanding the notion of evaluable "program" to include planning stages with an intention to question purposes of reform and the assumptions planners have about reform targets, involves re-scoping beyond technical measures. Such a project alters the basis of evaluation. Social scientists who work in the contract industry have great ethical responsibilities. With the distribution of resources and the right to depict students and teachers in an official capacity at the center of their work, evaluators must be cognizant not only of compliance and practical requirements of their evaluations, but must also be attuned to the ways power enters their work and the ways in which their work has the potential to maintain existing power structures. If evaluation is truly a democratizing enterprise, the official story tropes must be rethought.

REFERENCES

Abert, J. G. (1979). *Program evaluation at HEW: Research versus reality.* New York: Marcel Dekker Inc.

Agar, M. (1996). *The professional stranger: An informal introduction to ethnography.* Berkeley: Academic Press.

Apple, M. (1990). *Ideology and curriculum.* New York: Routledge.

Apple, M. (1993). The politics of official knowledge: Does a national curriculum make sense? *Teachers College Record, 95*, 222–241.

Apple, M. (1999). *Official knowledge: Democratic education in a conservative age* (2nd ed.). New York, NY: Routledge.

Apple, M. (2001). Comparing neo-liberal projects and inequality in education. *Comparative Education, 37*, 409-423.

Apple, M. (2004). Creating difference: Neo-liberalism, neo-conservatism and the politics of educational reform. *Educational Policy, 18*, 12-44.

Bomer, R., Dworin, J. E., May, L., & Semington, P. (2008). Miseducating teachers about the poor: A critical analysis of Ruby Payne's claims about poverty. *Teachers College Record, 110*, 2497-2531.

Bourdieu, P. (1977). *Outline of a theory of practice.* Cambridge: Cambridge University Press.

The College Board. (2006). *A Report on the Design and Development of the College Board Leadership Institute for Principals.* New York: The College Board.

The College Board. http://professionals.collegeboard.com/k-12/assessment/ap/plan

Davies, C. A. (1999). *Reflexive ethnography: A guide to researching selves and others.* New York: Routledge.

Deem, R., Hillyard, S., & Reed, M. (2007). *Knowledge, higher education, and the new managerialism: The changing management of UK universities.* Oxford: Oxford University Press.

Datta, L-E. (2000). Seriously seeking fairness: Strategies for crafting non-partisan evaluations in a partisan world. *The American Journal of Evaluation, 21*, 1-14.

Fabian, J. (1990). Presence and representation: The other and anthropological writing. *Critical Inquiry, 16*, 753-772.

Fine, M, Jaffe, R., Pedraza, P., Stoudt, B., & Futch, V. (2007). Swimming: On oxygen, resistance, and possibility for immigrant youth under siege. *Anthropology and Education Quarterly, 38*, 76-96.

Fine, M. (1991). *Framing dropouts: Notes on the politics of an urban public high school.* Albany, NY: State University of New York Press.

Foley, D. (1995). *The heartland chronicles.* Philadelphia: U Penn Press.

Foucault, M. (1977). *Discipline and punish.* New York: Random House.

Gandara, P. (1999). *Paving the way to higher education: K-12 intervention programs for under-represented youth.* Washington, DC: National Postsecondary Education Cooperative.

Gorski, P. (2008). The myth of the "culture of poverty." *Educational Leadership, 65*, 32-36.

Hamman, E., & Lane, B., (2004). The roles of state departments of education as policy intermediaries: Two cases. *Educational Policy, 18*, 426-455.

Harrington, M. (1962). *The other America: Poverty in the United States.* Simon & Schuster.

Hurd, C. (2008). Cinco de mayo, normative whiteness, and the marginalization of Mexican-descent students. *Anthropology & Education Quarterly, 39*, 293-313.

Joyce, B., & Showers, B. (2002). *Student achievement through staff development* (3rd ed.). Alexandria, VA: Association for Supervision and Curriculum Development.

Kowal, P. (2002). Vertical teaming: Making connections across levels. *Middle Ground, 6*, 20-22.

Lagemann, E. C. (2000). *An elusive science: The troubling history of education research.* Chicago: University of Chicago Press.

Lusi, S. F. (1997). *The role of state departments of education in complex school reform.* New York: Teachers College Press.

McNeil, L. (2005). Faking equity: High-stakes testing and the education of Latino youth. In A. Valenzuela (Ed.), *Leaving children behind: How "Texas-style" accountability fails latino youth*. Albany: SUNY Press.

Oakes, J. (1985). *Keeping track: How schools structure inequality*. New Haven, CT: Yale University Press.

Patton, M. Q. (2011). *Developmental evaluation: Applying complexity concepts to enhance innovation and use*. New York: Guilford Press.

Popkewitz, T. (2000). The denial of change in educational change: Systems of ideas in the construction of national policy and evaluation. *Educational Researcher*, 17-29.

Popkewitz, T., & Brennan, M. (1998). *Foucault's challenge: Discourse, knowledge and power in education*. New York: Teachers College Press.

Sassen, S. (2006). *The global city*. Princeton: Princeton University Press.

Slaughter, S., & Rhoades, G. (2004). *Academic capitalism and the new economy: Markets, state, and higher education*. Baltimore: Johns Hopkins.

Sturges, K. (2011). The making of program evaluators in education: Agentic response and neoliberal prefiguring. Presented at the American Educational Studies Association Annual Meeting in November. St. Louis, Missouri.

Sturges, K., Cramer, E., Harry, B., & Klingner, J. (2005). Desegregated but unequal: Some paradoxes of parent involvement at Bromden Elementary. *International Journal of Educational Policy, Research, and Practice*, *6*, 79-104.

Suchman, M. (2003). The contract as social artifact. *Law & Society Review*, *37*, 91-142

Trouillot, H. (1995). *Silencing the past: Power and the production of history*. Boston: Beacon.

US Department of Education (n.d.). http://www2.ed.gov/programs/gearup/index.html. Accessed on April 12, 2012.

Valenzuela, A. (2005). *Leaving children behind: How "Texas-style" accountability fails Latino youth*. Albany: SUNY Press.

van Maanen, J. (1988). *Tales of the field*. Chicago: University of Chicago Press.

CARL E. JAMES WITH SAM TECLE & DESMOND MILLER

CHAPTER 9

The Game Plan: How the Promise of US Athletic Scholarships Shapes the Education of Black Canadian Youth

A recent (April 7, 2012) CNN Program, "CNN Presents: The real march madness," reported on the failure of some National Collegiate Athletic Association (NCAA) postsecondary institutions to graduate their basketball players. It explored the NBA dreams and ambitions of NCAA players, providing an in-depth account of how one player understood his failure to graduate from university. With reference to the graduation record of Senior Men's basketball players at the University of Connecticut [UCONN],[1] the program host, Drew Griffin, pointed out that "UCONN may have the best basketball team in the land, but in the classroom, they were darn near the worst. Just 25 percent of UCONN's men's basketball players graduate within six years. And if you break it down racially, a Black player's chances of graduating from UCONN is just 14 percent" – excluding players who leave school early for the NBA draft (Cable News Network [CNN], 2012).

Presented as "one of the statistics," was a former UCONN basketball player, Jonathan Mandeldove. He had to leave school early for failing to maintain an adequate GPA and just three classes short of what he needed to graduate. A basketball player since age 14 years and a coveted seven-foot center, Mandeldove admitted to "struggling" in his classes; and at the age of 24 years with no degree, his future seemed unclear. Nevertheless, he remained optimistic about potentially making it to the pros, "I think I can [make it to the NBA]. I'm still young …. Sky's the limit. I don't think there's an age limit where they stop, you know, taking guys to the NBA. So I'm going to continue to push forward and continue to work and do whatever I need to get there" (Cable News Network, 2012). It is understandable that Mandeldove would remain optimistic, for he understands it is up to him – his abilities, skills and efforts – to determine his educational and career attainment. As he put it, "I fault myself for my downfalls in class. I don't fault anyone else. I don't fault the institution. Because they offered the help. You know, it's just there for us to take. We have to take it. If we don't, then that's a problem for us" (Cable News Network, 2012).

[1] UCONN was banned from for the 2013 season due to its poor academic track record.

J. Hall (ed.), Children's Human Rights and Public Schooling in the United States, 159–174.

Aquille Carr, a five-foot-seven high school basketball player was also featured on the show. According to reporter, Chris Lawrence, Carr "isn't just keeping up with his much taller opponents. He's passing them." Lawrence goes on to say that Carr lives in East Baltimore which is "a tough place to grow up. Constant violence and the fifth highest murder rate in America. A lot of kids his age have already ended up in jail" (Cable News Network, 2012). Noting that Carr's "success is a credit to his teammates, coaches, and above all, his family," Lawrence tells of his parents' expectations that he gets an athletic scholarship and eventually makes the NBA. Indeed, as Carr said, "I know. I have to work 10 times harder than the next person ... Failure is not an option" (Cable News Network, 2012). UCONN was among the colleges that recruited Carr, but as the program host indicated, he elected to play at "a smaller school where he hopes to get the playing time and exposure to vault him to the next level, the NBA" (Cable News Network, 2012).

Clearly, both Mandeldove and Carr believe their educational achievements, and eventually, the chance to play in the NBA are solely of their own making – it is up to them to work hard and take advantage of the opportunities offered to them. So, despite the evidence that the institutions bear some responsibility for the failure of basketball players to graduate, these two players, like many others (Eitzen, 2009; James, 2005; The Institute for Diversity and Ethics in Sport, 2012; Wells, 2009), remained convinced their academic and career trajectories are all within their control. The logic of these two basketball players is fueled by a neoliberal ethos of individualism which holds that meritocracy, competition, choice, resilience, individual responsibility and agency, and freedom to pursue whatever one needs, are the bases of success (Saunders, 2010; Spaaij, 2009; Sukarieh & Tannock, 2008).

In this chapter, we discuss how young Canadian male students, like their US counterparts, similarly aspire to US athletic scholarships with the dream of eventually making it to the NBA. What is interesting is how these Canadian youth, residents of a foreign country and miles away from the eyes of US scouts and coaches, believe that they can beat their US counterparts for coveted athletic scholarships and NBA places. In fact, for the majority of high school basketball players, the US athletic scholarship is considered to be the golden prize or expected trajectory of an athletic career. Pursuing postsecondary education in Canada tends not to be an option, for to hold such aspiration would be admitting that "you're not good enough" (see James, 2005). Would this be the reason why we see so few high school basketball players attending Canadian universities? Or is it that the students are so invested in the sport they spend most of their time on the basketball court and less time in the classroom, thereby failing to attain the necessary academic requirements to enter postsecondary institutions without an athletic scholarship?

We bring to this discussion our experiences as observers, teachers, researchers and athletes. Carl James has been conducting research on the schooling experiences and outcomes of Black students, and Black male athletes in particular, for over twenty years (James, 2005, 2011). He recalls teaching in the Faculty of Physical and Health Education at one Toronto University and in classes of about eighty having less than ten Black students while high school basketball, track and field and football teams, were dominated by Black players. Sam Tecle was a multisport athlete in high school who aspired to go South on a basketball athletic scholarship. Though he did not realize this aspiration, he did keep sport in his athletic and educational life by enrolling in Kinesiology and Health Sciences in university. A qualified teacher who grew up in one of Toronto's marginalized communities, Sam is currently in a graduate program in sociology pursuing scholarship in the aspirations of Black Canadian youth and the deterrents to them accessing postsecondary education. Desmond Miller grew up in the east end of Toronto playing basketball and, like Sam and many of his contemporaries, pursued the dream of winning a US athletic scholarship. Unsuccessful in attaining this goal, he decided to pursue an undergraduate degree in Physical and Health Education and is now completing his graduate studies in education. For his thesis work, he is exploring the experiences, drive, and aspirations of Black Canadian youth who have gone to the US on an athletic scholarship but returned to Canada without completing their degrees.

Our examination of the educational participation and achievement of Black male high school athletes[2] is influenced by social reproduction theory operating in a context of neoliberalism which holds that the social, cultural, educational, economic and political obstacles of the past have either been eliminated or can be overcome through individual efforts, hard work, and determination (Walcott, 2009, p. 76). Within the hegemony of neoliberalism, writes Walcott, Black masculinity is always constructed as deficient, and "set up for repair within an ideological and political frame of neoliberal capitalism that assumes a narrative of progressivism from a dreadful past to a victorious present that can be individually driven" (p. 77). In the Canadian context, neoliberalism is sustained by the multicultural discourse of cultural freedom, color-blindness, and equality of opportunity which mask the fact that race matters, and as in other societies, racism operates to limit individuals participation in the society and their outcomes.

The commonsense logic of neoliberalism has wide appeal through its reasoning that individuals' abilities and skills, and the rational choices they make, can lead to self-actualization in the competitive labor and consumer markets (Luxton, 2010). Luxton also writes:

> The widespread acceptance of personal responsibility lends credibility to neoliberal demands. At the same time, the experiences of living under a neoliberal regime encourage people to narrow their vision of what is possible and to accept responsibility for their own circumstances. This

---

[2] We avoid using the term "student athlete" because we maintain that essentially the youth to which we are referring are students; and the fact that they are athletes, or that that they play sports, must be considered additional to their student role – similar to other student roles like artist and musician (see Eitzen, 2009; Staurowsky & Sack 2005).

> perverse individualism easily immobilizes people, making it hard for them to envision alternatives and rendering them politically inactive. The sense of individual agency is reduced to a notion of choice … and they are inclined to assume that their circumstances are a result of poor choices they have made, rather than that the choices available were problematic or wrong. The net effect is to obscure or even deny the class, gender, and racialized relations that are fundamental to contemporary society. (p. 180)

Social reproduction theory points to the ways in which the inequities of society, and correspondingly its institutions, are reproduced in the opportunities, access, and outcomes of members of the society. The theory is concerned with, as Singer and Buford May (2011) state: "the ways in which the educational or schooling process, in particular, has helped to perpetuate or reproduce the social relationships and attitudes needed to sustain existing dominant economic and class relations of the larger society" (p. 301). Scholars assert the values, behaviors, preferences, credentials, aspirations, and competences of upper and middle class individuals – typically White Europeans – tend to be privileged and form the basis on which institutions operate, thereby guaranteeing the success or upward mobility of individuals (Braddock, 2005; Singer & Buford May, 2011; Yosso, 2005). But while as Yosso (2005) argues, racialized youth can benefit from "community cultural wealth" – "an array of knowledge, skills, abilities and contacts possessed and utilized by Communities of Color to survive and resist macro and micro-forms of oppression" (p. 77) – the fact remains their educational outcome, life chances, and/or social mobility are highly influenced, not only by their own efforts, but by the interlocking structures of social class, race, ethnicity, gender, area of residence, birthplace, and other demographic factors.

Black male high school athletes, often with the encouragement of teachers, coaches, school administrators, and even parents, tend to perceive sports to be a way to engage with their schooling, mitigate the deficit approach to their learning, and ensure their educational success. But this perception often turns out to be limited. For in the face of the competition in a credential-based inequitable society, lacking academic credentials would mean they have few or none of the valued resources on which to rely in their bid to attain economic, social, and occupational success. So in a neoliberal context Black male high school athletes might concur with the notion that, on the basis of merit and fairness, their athletic abilities, skills, hard work, keen interest, physicality and coachability will win them their educational scholarships and career aspirations (James, 2005; Spaaij, 2009). In time they will however realize their outcome is never purely an individual endeavor.

In what follows, we reference the educational, athletic and schooling experiences and achievements of Sam (Samuel) and Desmond, noting what accounts for their academic achievement. How, unlike some of their peers, were they able to reconcile their unrealized US scholarship ambitions and settle for the more reachable goal of university education in Toronto? How did they use their notoriety, encouragement, supports, agency, and confidence in themselves to enhance their learning, expand their horizons, and construct possibilities outside of sports? But first, we briefly review the educational and schooling experiences of Black students, and Black male athletes in particular.

THE EDUCATIONAL SITUATION OF AFRICAN CANADIAN STUDENTS WITH A FOCUS ON TORONTO

Research has long shown the Canadian education system has been failing to meet the needs, interests, expectations, and aspirations of Black youth, often schooling them in a manner based on constructions of them as socially, culturally, and academically deficient – and in some cases delinquent (Codjoe, 2007; Dei et al., 1997; James, 2012; Solomon & Palmer, 2004). In their examination of Black Canadian high school students' beliefs about their schooling and academic achievements, Smith, Schneider, and Ruck (2005) found like their US counterparts, Canadian students had a disproportionately high level of poor academic performance and failure rates, and males were more likely than females "to be at risk academically" (p. 356). The study conducted in two Canadian cities, Toronto and Halifax, also found that regardless of gender and city, most of their research participants "were quite positive about education, had high aspirations and expectations, and highly valued success ... [and] appeared to be quite optimistic about their chances for success later on in life when armed with an education" (p. 355). The authors go on to point out:

> The fact that Black Canadian students underachieve despite the beliefs by many that achievement is possible serves to document the 'paradox of underachievement' .... Perhaps their beliefs are not to be translated into the daily behaviors that lead to academic success, or perhaps their attempts to achieve are thwarted by closed doors or other social inequalities. (p. 355)

A recent (2010) Toronto District School Board report on the "achievement gap" among students identified that for many years, Black students have been dropping out of Toronto schools at a rate of about 40% – one of the highest rate among its student population.[3] (The rates of Aboriginal, Latin American, and Portuguese students were similarly high.) An even more recent report (May, 2012) of the 2006-2011 grade 9 cohort of students, indicates only 65% of Black students graduated within the four year span. 13% were still in school past the normal four years, and 23% were reported as having dropped out.[4] In the case of English speaking Caribbean-born students, the data show in the four years only 51% of

[3] It is important to caution that this 40% figure which has become a component of the popular discourse used to represent how Black students are doing in Toronto schools must be read like any all other figures on dropout, they are never accurate or truthful because of the difficult in knowing for sure if students have indeed dropped out, stopped out or were pushed out.

[4] It should be noted that the "drop out" figure included having "no information" about the students.

them graduated, 20% of them were still attending school, and 30% of them dropped out. The graduation rates for Somali students, who are among the more recent immigrant group of students to enter the Toronto school system, are somewhat similar to that of the Black student population. And while there was a 2% higher dropout rate among Somali students, they were less likely to stay in school beyond their four years – it was indicated only 9% did.

Not reported in these Toronto District School Board studies is the gender breakdown of Black students. But if we go by the overall rates of graduation (83% females, 75% males), continuing school (6% females, 9% males), and dropouts (12% females, 17% males), we can conclude that Black males tend to have lower rates of graduation and higher rates of dropping out. They are the students for whom athletic activities, both co-curricularly and extracurricularly, help to keep them in school and, for some, help to foster dreams of postsecondary educational and career opportunities and possibilities. But notwithstanding the problems with the statistics related to drop-outs – hence their undependability – in the absence of other reliable data this disproportionately high rate of dropping out seems, understandable, if not logical, given Black students' – especially males – reported experiences with alienation, disengagement, detentions, suspensions, and discrimination (James & Taylor, 2010; Solomon & Palmer, 2004). These students' disengagement from their schooling seems logical when they have been promised they will be treated in an equitable and meritorious manner in an education system that will reward them for their hard work, self-regulation (or disciplined behavior), and career goal-orientation. Furthermore, when the needs, interests, and aspirations of Black students are not addressed, or the social and cultural capital they bring to their schooling situation is not acknowledged or taken into account in the curriculum, pedagogy, assessment, and "teacherly ethos,"[5] it is understandable they would disengage and eventually leave school.

Elsewhere, I (James, 2012) have written that Black youth, and males in particular, "are counted among the most 'at risk' students because of their continued disengagement from school, poor academic performance, and high rates of absenteeism, suspension, expulsion, and dropout, due in part to the school's 'progressive' disciplinary policies and practices" (p. 466; see also Bhattacharjee, 2003; Henry & Tator, 2010; Raby 2012). This "at risk" label "tends to be less about the probable learning needs of the youth," and more about what is perceived as "their deficits that make learning and their educational engagement and outcomes problematic" (p. 465; see also Wotherspoon & Schissel, 2001). Five factors – immigrant, fatherless, troublemaker, athlete, and underachiever – come

[5] We borrow this term from Gregory (2001) who, in referencing Socrates, writes that "good teaching" involves "befriending" students. He suggests that students and teachers need each other "to become the best version of themselves, and in this reciprocity of mutual assistance all of us, students and teachers alike, may learn, if we are careful, how to tend better through education the fragile relations of personal development, human community, and civilized conduct" (p. 87).

together in the construction of Black youth as "at risk" which, as a "web of stereotypes" (Howard, 2008), operates within the hegemony of neoliberal schooling policies, programs, and practices to regulate the learning process, educational opportunities, life chances, and academic outcomes of students (James, 2012).

The athlete stereotype is one of the most prominent for Black males. On the basis of this stereotype or essentialist notion, coaches recruit, train, and "father" Black male athletes, and teachers and administrators collaborate or oblige by encouraging Black males (even rewarding poor academic performance) to put their energies and hopes into sport, for it holds educational and career possibilities for them (James, 2012; see also Harrison et al., 2011). For their part, as unwitting parties to this manufactured educational allegory – indeed a process of racialization – many parents dutifully cooperate with educators believing participating in sport is in the best interest of their children (it is for their children's good). In addition, peers, especially those similarly sold on sport, through their affiliation – facilitated by their "basketball culture" – help to keep alive the optimism, the deceptive power of sport, and the idea of the educational, social, and economic opportunities and possibilities it offers. But it is possible for young Black males to incorporate and use sports to access educational and career opportunities in Canadian postsecondary institutions – how Sam and Desmond did so is discussed in the following section.

SPORT, SCHOOLING, AND EDUCATIONAL ACHIEVEMENT: THE CASE OF TWO FORMER HIGH SCHOOL ATHLETES

Sam Tecle

As a former high school athlete, and like many of my basketball playing peers – as many still do today – I held aspirations to go south to a US college or university on athletic scholarship. Though I participated in sport in primary school, it was in my low-income marginalized community where I was initially introduced to sport learning of the role it could play in my schooling and in my life generally. There were many subsidized sport-based programs that ran either out of my apartment complex or the local community center. My apartment building also had a basketball court on the grounds where many of us boys played. We constantly spoke of, dreamt of, and aspired to play in the NBA (or professionally), and we knew the first step to realizing these sporting goals, was to be the best in the building, the best in the neighborhood, then the best at school, and finally get profiled in at least one of Toronto's newspapers as one of the best in the city. So with these aspirations, much of our time was spent practicing, competing, and working on our skills on the outside court, sometimes for more than twelve hours a day.

In spite of the marginalized northwest Toronto community where I grew up with my working class Eritrean-born mother and father, I managed to display academic promise – something which was noted by my grade three teachers and principal who recommended I attend an enrichment program in a middle school outside of the community which, as they advised my parents, 'offered more opportunities.' The middle school, located in a middle class predominantly White neighborhood, promoted academics over athletes. So rather than participating in interschool athletic competition, I participated in school house leagues and academic competitions such as Science Olympics and local, provincial, and national math contests. It was also in that middle school that the principal would open the gym for a few hours after school on Fridays while he did his paperwork for us – Black male students – to play basketball. The eight of us who would play were never enough for a full game since we needed 10 players. I always wondered: Why didn't anyone else come and play? I wondered if this was to support our inclusion into the school, or a mechanism designed to make us feel comfortable and committed to the school.

The high school I attended, which was located in the same community as my middle school, encouraged (quite strongly) participation in inter-school athletic competition. I participated in soccer, swimming, track and field, making it to city finals in basketball and provincial competition in cross country. Though I was very active and engaged in sport throughout my schooling, I was constantly and forcefully reminded and encouraged by my refugee parents to make academics my central concern (Harris, 1994). And being the oldest of four children, I was expected to set a "positive example" for my siblings. Notwithstanding this expectation, it was in high school that I was able to realize my ambition of playing and competing in school sports. In fact, in most of my time in high school, I was very much committed to sport. A typical day would be: getting up at 5am to train for 2-3 hours – either at home or at school. Practice and more training in the afternoon supplemented the morning training. This level of intense training was maintained throughout my five years of high school. While this routine was encouraged by coaches, teachers, and peers, the same dedication, time, and commitment to excellence was not encouraged for our academic work. I recall in a huddle of a basketball game, the coach saying to a student who had a mid-term failing grade in English: "We are all here; we are a family and that 55 you got in English was more like a 35." We surmised from this statement the coach had spoken to the player's teacher and the teacher had raised his grade. I remember we collectively shared a laugh over the incident and the teammate who had received this 'favour' was very appreciative of coach's 'advocacy.' As I now reflect on this incident, I ask, how did this help the academic performance of our teammate? What were the lessons being given, encouraged, and supported by the coach and teacher's practices? Was this a way of keeping our teammate on the team and prevent him from becoming ineligible to play because of failing a mandatory course?

After five years of unwavering commitment, intense training, unrelenting sport competition, and a plethora of sport achievements (in the name of the school) certain realizations began to set in. One of which was despite these athletic achievements I was amassing the stark reality was I was not getting much interest from US basketball scouts – no recruiting letters. It became increasingly clear my long-held dream of playing basketball at a US college/university was not going to materialize. As devastating as this was, it was not the most important realization that occurred that final year of high school. This was a year of high school when grades mattered significantly in order to gain admission into university. So being heavily involved in sports and the added pressure of performing academically had ramifications for me, making my final year of high school quite stressful.

I recall an incident in which I had a big test in finite mathematics and the afternoon before the morning of the test, I participated in the district finals cross-country competition in which our team did exceptionally well – the best the school had ever done. We won medals. I gained a ranking of fourth in the city, and our team gained entry to the provincial finals – all of which gained the school media publicity. I received many congratulatory comments from the principal, fellow students, and teachers. But amid it all, I was feeling ill-prepared for my test because of the many hours I had dedicated to training for the competition. For this reason, I asked my teacher for a pass on the test or a week's extension to prepare. He refused saying there were strict regulations regarding when these tests were to be written; and to make it "equal" for all students, all such tests were to be written in class during the prescribed time. No exceptions were to be made unless it was an emergency, and even then, those situations were to be considered on a case-by-case basis. Doing well on the test was important to me since there was no athletic scholarship coming, and I needed to do well in all my courses to gain admission to university. I remember feeling quite dejected, thinking that after running with the name of the school on my jersey, attaining fourth place in the city, and receiving handshakes from the principal proved not to be enough for me to get a week's extension on an important test. I learnt that while the school was prepared to make accommodations (e.g. missing classes) for us to compete in the cross-country provincial finals, no such accommodation was possible for me to do an important test.

This experience opened my eyes to the limitations of this total commitment to sport. Finite was one of the math courses required for me to be gain admission to medical school where I planned to specialize in sports medicine as my then backup plan. This interest was inspired by an amazing course, Bio-Scientific Perspectives (essentially a Physical Education course), I took in my final year of high school. This interest in sports medicine also came from having been to see the Leafs' hockey doctor for an injury I had sustained to my iliotibial band while running cross-country. I was impressed with the doctor's work having seen him on television on the ice attending to injured hockey players. I remember thinking at the time that I could see myself having a career in medicine, perhaps as a team doctor for the Toronto Raptors. For this reason, I applied to the Kinesiology and Health Sciences Program at the university near my community, intending to eventually go on to do medicine. After completing my undergraduate degree I was accepted into the physiotherapy program at a US college, and the teacher education program at the university from which I had just graduated. Given my experience working as a youth worker in my community during my undergraduate years, I elected to attend the teacher education program with the hopes of eventually contributing positively to my community.

So my injury, the realization that the system *can be* bent but not for me – no matter how well I did athletically, and receiving no scholarship offers, both forced and compelled me to seek alternative routes to postsecondary education. Furthermore, I had parents who strongly believed hard work would lead to success, and for this reason they were not going to tolerate failure. This neoliberal ethos my parents instilled in me seemed at the time to be well-founded, for there were no alternative pathways possible. Besides they saw me as having all the necessary opportunities to succeed in school and in the society generally – after all, my academic achievement throughout school seemed to demonstrate that it was the case. However, things were definitely not as easy as my parents believed. Yes, I did well in school, and I had many supportive teachers, but ultimately I had to take agency: commit to my academic program and study in order to ensure I gained access to postsecondary education. For unlike my basketball teammates – most of whom were Black and were fully immersed in the game – I became disheartened at the machinery of schooling, and critical of how sport in school was often used (even today) to position me and many of my Black peers as mere athletes (James, 2011).

In essence, I did well in school but I did not construct my school experience or identity completely around athletics – even though it was in athletics that my peers and me were pushed, encouraged, and appropriately rewarded with many accolades. My trajectory might have been otherwise if I did not have other avenues by which to pursue my educational and career ambitions. My experience with caring teachers, an enriched educational program in middle school, and a marginalized community for which I was fast becoming an "example" of what was possible (Tecle, 2012), allowed me to develop the educational, social, aspirational, navigational, and resistant capital (Yosso, 2005) on which I could call upon when constructing my own pathway to postsecondary education. Another constant was parental encouragement and my forcefulness and steadfast dedication to education which enabled me to resist my high school's positioning of athletics over academics particularly for Black male students. These, combined with the experience of taking the Bio-Scientific Perspectives course, and my parents' wishes (they never even attended any of my games) to have me attend university helped to set me on a path to where I am today. Today I am a graduate student who, in my teaching and activities – seeks to contribute to my community in ways that enhance and improve outcomes and the well-being of its young people.

Desmond Miller

Sport was a more recreational than competitive activity at the elementary (K-8) school I attended in the Catholic School Board. So most of my competitive participation in basketball took place outside of school. For instance, toward the end of my elementary school years, I attended a basketball camp run by the Toronto Raptors where I successfully completed a challenging drill in front of the entire camp – including then Raptors head coach Butch Carter. This was a big confidence boost and I was noticed by one of the coaches at the camp who offered to take me, along with some other youth from Toronto, to a similar basketball camp at the University of Kentucky. This was a pivotal experience for me and the beginning of my thoughts toward winning a US athletic scholarship as a way to get an education and to make it to the NBA. After all, if I could get a free education, play basketball at a high level (i.e. in the NCAA), why wouldn't I pursue this dream? – especially, when there were examples of great players like Mugsy Bouges, Allen Iverson, and Damon Stoudemire who, like me, may not have been the tallest or the strongest but were still phenomenal players.

On the way to the camp at the University of Kentucky, our van of early to mid-teenage boys stopped in Windsor, Canada, to meet Jamal Magloire, the Toronto native who won an NCAA championship at that university. He was one of the few and most recent (at the time) Canadians to make it to the NBA. He gave us some autographs and offered words of encouragement. The University of Kentucky was like nothing I had ever seen or experienced before. The campus was large and sprawling. Although my memory is fuzzy, I clearly remember the dorm rooms, the large cafeteria, the large practice gym and the bus, which would shuttle us in between the main practice facility and one of the other large gyms on campus. Though we didn't see it, it was explained to us that players had a "team house" all to themselves, with all the accoutrements. It was an incredible experience. Aside from watching high school recruits scrimmage against current University of Kentucky players and the campers getting the chance to go one-on-one against the players, we also got a chance to visit the players' change rooms, the U of K sports hall of fame, and the enormous arena in which they played. We even got to take pictures and sign autographs with Tubby Smith and other players, some of whom eventually made it to "the league" (NBA). Suffice to say it was a great sport development experiences and a heck of a showcase that could surely convince any youth that being a college athlete was an exciting and a seemingly lavish lifestyle. This experience made the dream of getting a scholarship and going to the league all the more attractive. It re-enforced my scholarship dreams and contributed to my strong commitment to training – sometimes doing as many as three workouts a day and travelling for over an hour each way for practice at my club's gym.

I attended a uniform-wearing, Catholic High School that was well known for academics and athletics – specifically volleyball, cross country, and track and field which were in keeping with the middle class image the school tried to project. And while like Sam, I participated in various sports in high school (volleyball, cross country, curling, and track and field), I mainly played basketball. But more importantly, I concentrated on my academic work – much of which had to do with encouragement or enforcement from my parents, club coaches (no homework = no practice), and the expectations I had for myself. In high school, I was known equally for my academic and athletic performance. In grade three, I was identified for an enrichment program which meant that from grades 4 to 8, once a week I went to a different school where I would participate in enriched academic programming with other so-called "gifted" students. As a result of these expectations, supports, and challenging projects, I was able to build my identity not only around sports but academics as well. This designation became part of my student record which followed me throughout my time in the education system. I cannot be certain, but I assume that this designation influenced the expectations that my teachers had of me.

At the end of grade 10, given my interest and successes on the basketball team, one of the coaches suggested I move to a school that was better known for basketball. I contemplated the benefits of doing so. However, my parents were not in favour of this idea since, for them, academics came first (see Harris, 1994). Furthermore, I had my own doubts about how academically challenging the school would be. Would I get the kind of education I could fall back on if I ever got injured? What would happen to me if I did not have the necessary education? The idea of having education to fall back on was one message that got through to me mainly from my parents. My thinking about a backup plan may have been in part due to the fact that I was a smaller player (5'9"), had already sustained some injuries, and was not a "jump-out-the-gym" athlete. For this reason, I felt I had to be realistic in preparing for alternatives. Also, I was quite aware due to my success in academics, I had other possibilities. So I stayed at the school I was already attending.

When by grades eleven and twelve, I was not receiving a river of letters from scouts, it was pretty clear I would not be making it to the NBA or even the NCAA. Nevertheless, with encouragement from a coach, I still entertained the idea of attending a prep school in the US or a college in Quebec, Canada. But this was overruled by my parents who wanted me to attend university. So in coming to this realization that my athletic scholarship opportunities were limited I had to rely on my academic capabilities to make it to university. Also, I always thought an athletic career can only last so long, and if anything were to happen that might end my playing career, I would need my education. So because I did fairly well academically I figured I could work somewhere in sport – maybe as an athletic therapist. Furthermore, inspired by my physical education teacher and his grade 12 Exercise Sciences course on how the body worked (and not getting what I needed from my training), I came to think of taking Physical and Heath Education or Kinesiology at university and become an athletic trainer thereby combining my interest in academics and athletics. Besides, I had the financial means to attend university without a scholarship which made the desire (or need) to win a scholarship less dire.

Looking back, I would attribute where I am today to the fact that the structure of schooling made it easier for my parents to advocate for me. We could learn and figure out the system. Conversely, in basketball, while my parents were supportive and I was determined, the lines for advancement were less clear and less easy to navigate. My parents did what they could by sending me to camps and ensuring I was able to get to practices, but they clearly believed school should come first. Further, my fair skin (being biracial – how I identified myself growing up) made it difficult, in my view, for me to identify as simply Black or White. Over time, certain signifiers of "Blackness" including my participation in basketball – which is widely perceived as a "Black sport" – contributed to my identification (particularly by others) as Black (see James, 2012). But while I cannot be certain of the way my body was read by others, it is possible that my 'ambiguous appearance' may have expanded my horizon of possibilities such that sport was not provided to me as my only option to educational and career success.

Contrary to Sam, when I was growing up, I always played basketball on club teams away from my community and with people who had a similarly intense commitment to sport. This likely has to do with the demographics (largely White and middle class) of the community where I grew up. The areas of the city where I played basketball had high concentrations of immigrant and racialized people; similarly my basketball teammates at school were mainly other racialized youth. In fact, in high school, I did not have peers who were, like me, putting in extra hours of training. The fact my school did not have a strong basketball team may be related to the fact it did not have a reputation of churning out NCAA-bound ballers.

CONCLUSION

The narratives of Sam and Desmond are illustrative of many of Toronto's young people – then and now – who perceive that the postsecondary education they seek can best be attained through athletic scholarships. What is significant here is the pivotal role that sports have played and continue to play in their lives as well as account for how they construct and think about their future. Interestingly, both Sam and Desmond were identified during their elementary schooling as students who should be in enrichment programs. It seems early support from teachers for them to be placed in enriched middle school programs was particularly helpful in setting an educational trajectory for them in which sport did not become the one or all-consuming means of engaging school (Messer, 2009). This suggests both Sam and Desmond who were very interested in sports, and regularly played, managed not to be defined by athletics. Hence they were able to avoid the stereotype of the "Black student athlete" (James, 2012). So while they, like many other Black Toronto youth, aspired to win athletic scholarship to US university, and someday be on a NBA team, the fact they were not "only" athletes – and they saw themselves in that way – helped them to think of the "what ifs" – what if they got injured and were unable to play? Desmond said that was an important lesson he learned; and Sam did get injured – something which made him think of the important of a back-up plan.

Elsewhere (James, 2005), I have written of young athletes insisting that having a back-up plan would be admitting that they are not "good enough" eventually to attain their educational and career goals. While coaches, teachers, and sports journalist understand the value of a "back-up plan," they do not help to counsel students about putting their efforts into playing. Take the case of Sam's teammate who was failing his English course. The advocacy of his coach made the teacher change the grade to a mere passing grade. While such interventions of coaches could be interpreted as "helping out the student," too often doing so is more in the interest of the coach and the school, and less about the student. Recall Sam's account of how his team was celebrated when they won the cross-country competition which gained much publicity. And Desmond's mention of the fact his school "did not have a reputation of churning out NCAA-bound ballers" signals how much the athletic output of students is tied to the reputation of a school. When students are unable to find a school with the required reputation of sending students south to colleges in the US, they opt to complete high school in the US. Today, a popular website which tells about high school basketball in the Greater Toronto Area reports that at least 48 athletes, most of them racial minorities, from the city are currently playing on teams that participate in the NCAA (Hooptown GTA, 2011).

Further, at the time of writing this chapter, the *Toronto Star* (Feschuk, June, 2012, S1; 7) ran an article which mentioned three Canadians attending high school in the US. Among them was 17 year old Torontonian, Andrew Wiggins who was described as "gifted" and "the highest-rated basketball player in North America." Currently attending high school in West Virginia, Wiggins is said to be "coveted as a first round selection after he fills his league-mandated year as a collegian" (p. S1). Interestingly, but not uncommon, reference is made to Wiggins having "genetics on his side" – specifically his father, a former NBA player, his mother an Olympian, and his brother who "recently signed" to attend a Division 1 school. With profiles and successes like these, it is understandable how Toronto students and their parents can become caught up in the hype, allure, and possibilities that sports provide. In fact, a recent Canadian Broadcasting Corporation [CBC] documentary "Fast Break" (March 3, 2012) reported on "the dream of thousands of young Canadians" wanting "a shot at basketball superstardom by breaking in to the NBA." The documentary which featured two teenage Canadians told of parents putting "everything on the line – one of them going so far as to sell the house – to help their children chase the dream." And as the by-line for the documentary read: "There is no shortage of other Canadian kids – and parents – willing to do anything to follow in their footsteps. Pro-basketball is a billion-dollar business, and with stakes that high, the search for new talent is beginning earlier and earlier: it's predicted the game's next great player will be spotted in elementary school."

Ultimately, winning that supreme athletic award – a scholarship to a US postsecondary institution – is as much a product of individual agency, ability, skill, determination, and hard work. But as the stories of Sam and Desmond indicate, despite these individual qualities and efforts, as well as the support of parents and teachers, there is no guarantee that athletes will realize their aspirations. Attainment of the dreams many young Black Canadian basketball players seek is as much a product of their attributes, as it is about (and at times more so) having coaches who are as committed to their academic performance as the coaches are their athletic performance. It also necessitates having teachers, principals, and coaches who do not define them by their athleticism, but by their educational potential – students who do not wish to reproduce their social situation. The point is, there is an interrelationship between students' sense of self, responsibility, and their potential as well as the educational, economic, social, cultural and athletic structures they must navigate and negotiate to attain their aspirations. Contrary to the commonsense logic of neoliberalism, these structures, buttressed by the apparatus of inequity sustained through classism, racism, discrimination, and gendered expectations, mediate individuals' opportunities and attainments. So students' failure to realize their aspirations cannot simply be attributed to their failings, or be seen as 'their fault' – especially if the social and cultural capital they bring to their schooling is not recognized. Teachers and coaches have a role to play in helping students understand how structures operate to affect the opportunities provided to them, and in turn, the choices they are able to make.

REFERENCES

Bhattacharjee, A. (2003). *Paying the price: The human cost of racial profiling*. Toronto: Ontario Human Rights Commission.

Braddock J. H. (2005) Athletics, academics, and African American males. In O. S. Fashola (Ed.), *Educating African American males: Voices from the field* (pp. 355-383). Thousand Oaks, CA: Corwin Press.

Cable News Network. (2012). *CNN presents: The real march madness.* Aired April 7, 2012. Retrieved May 1, 2012 at http://edition.cnn.com/TRANSCRIPTS/1204/07/cp.01.html

Canadian Broadcasting Corporation (CBC) (2012). *The fifth estate, Fast break*. Aired March 2.Retrieved March 3, 2012. http://www.cbc.ca/fifth/2011-2012/fastbreak.

Codjoe, H. (2006). The role of an affirmed black cultural identity and heritage in the academicachievement of African-Canadian students. *Intercultural Education, 17*(1), 33-54.

Dei, G. S., Holmes, L., Mazzuca, J., McIssac, E., & Zine, J. (1997) *Reconstructing "drop-out": A critical ethnography of the dynamics of black students' disengagement from school.* Toronto: University of Toronto Press.

Eitzen, D. S. (2009). The big-time college sports plantation and the slaves who drive it. In D. S. Eitzen (Ed.), *Sport in contemporary society* (pp. 243-254), Boulder: Paradigm Publishers.

Feschuk, D. (2012). Basketball phenom focused on The Show, not showboating. *Toronto Star*, Saturday, June 9. Section S 1,7.

Gregory, M. (2001). Curriculum, pedagogy, and teacherly ethos. *Pedagogy: Critical Approaches to Teaching Literature, Language, Composition, and Culture, 1*(1), 69-89.

Harris, O. (1994). Race, sport, and social support. *Sociology of Sport Journal, 11*, 40-50.

Harrison, L, Sailes, G., Rotich, W. K., & Bimper, A. Y. (2011). Living out the dream or awakening from the nightmare: Race and athletic identity. *Race, Ethnicity and Education, 4*(1), 91-103.

Harvey, D. (2005). *A brief history of neoliberalism.* New York: Oxford University Press.

Henry, F., & Tator, C. (2010). *The colour of democracy: Racism in Canadian society*. Toronto: Nelson Education.

HooptownGTA. (2011). *NCAA Watch – Men.* Retrieved December 2011, http://wwwhooptowngta.com/ncaaWatchMen.php.

Howard, T. C. (2008). Who really cares? The disenfranchisement of African American males inprek-12 schools: A critical race theory perspective. *Teachers College Record, 110*(5), 954-985.

James, C. E. (2005). *Race and play: Understanding the socio-cultural worlds of student athletes.* Toronto: Canadian Scholars Press.

James, C.E. (2011). Why is the school basketball team predominantly Black? And what that says about educators' role in 'leveling the playing field.' In S. Tozer, B. P. Gallegos, A. Henry, M. Bushnell Greiner, & P. Groves Price (Eds.), *Handbook of research in social foundations of education* (pp. 450-459). New York: Routledge.

James, C. E. (2012). Students "at risk:" Stereotypes and the schooling of Black Boys. *Urban Education, 47*(2), 464-494.

James, C. E., & Taylor, L. (2010). The making of at risk students: How youth see teachers thwarting their education. In C. C. Smith (Ed.), *Anti-racism in education: Missing inaction* (pp. 123-136). Ottawa: Canadian Centre for Policy Alternatives.

Luxton, M. (2010). Doing neoliberalism: Perverse individualism in personal life. In S. Braedley & M. Luxton (Eds.), *Neoliberalism and everyday life* (pp. 163-183). Montreal: McGillQueen's University Press.

Messner, M. A. (2009). The meaning of success: The athletic experience and the development of male identity. In D. S. Eitzen (Ed.), *Sport in contemporary society* (pp. 323-337). Boulder: Paradigm Publishers.

Raby, R. (2012). *School rules: Obedience, discipline and elusive democracy*. Toronto: University ofToronto Press.

Saunders, D. (2010). Neoliberal ideology and public higher education in the United States. *Journal for Critical Education Policy Studies, 8*(1), 42-76.

Singer, J. N., & Buford May, R. B. (2010). The career trajectory of a Black male high schoolbasketball player: A social reproduction perspective. *International Review for the Sociology of Sport, 46*(3), 299-314.

Smith, A., Schneider, B. H., & Ruck, M. D. (2005). Thinking about makin' it: Black Canadian students' beliefs regarding education and academic achievement. *Journal of Youth and Adolescents, 34*, 347-359.

Solomon, P., & Palmer, H. (2004). Schooling in Babylon: When racial profiling and zero tolerance converge. *Canadian Journal of Educational Administration and Policy, 33*. http://www.umanitoba.ca/publications/cjeap/articles/solomonpalmer.html

Spaaij, R. (2009). Sport as a vehicle for social mobility and regulation of disadvantaged urbanyouth: Lessons from Rotterdam. *International Review for the Sociology of Sport, 44*(2), 247-264.

Staurowsky, E. J., & Sack, A. L. (2005). Reconsidering the use of the term student-athlete in academic research. *Journal of Sport Management, 19*(2), 103-116.

Sukarieh, M., & Tannock, S. (2008). In the best interests of youth or neoliberalism? The WorldBank and the new global youth empowerment project. *Journal of Youth Studies, 11*(3), 301-312.

Tecle, S. (2012). Growing up in a stigmatized community ... and making it. In C. E. James (Ed.), *Life atthe intersection: Community, class and schooling* (pp. 118-122). Fernwood Publishing.

The Institute for Diversity and Ethics in Sport. (2012). *Keeping score when it counts: Graduation success and academic progress rates for the 2012 NCAA Division I Men's Basketball Tournament Teams*. University of Central Florida (UCF).

Toronto District School Board. (2010) *Achievement Gap Task Force Draft Report*. Student and Community Equity Department, May.

Walcott, R. (2009). Reconstructing manhood; Or, the drag of Black masculinity. *Small Axe, 13*(1), 75-89.

Wells, C. J. (2009). *Canadian student-athletes in the NCAA: The experiences of those who stayand those who leave*. University of Toronto (Canada). ProQuest Dissertations and Theses, Retrieved from http://search.proquest.com.ezproxy.library.yorku.ca/docview/305106738?accounti d=15182

Wotherspoon, T., & Schissel, B. (2001). The business of placing Canadian children and youth "at-risk." *Canadian Journal of Education, 26*(3), 321-339.

Yosso, T. J. (2005). Whose culture has capital? A critical race theory discussion of community wealth and race. *Ethnicity and Education, 8*(1), 69-91.

ENCARNACIÓN GARZA, JR.

CHAPTER 10

Academically Invulnerable and Resilient Hispanic Migrant Children

The image of children of Hispanic migrant farm workers has been constructed in a way that locks them in a perpetuating cycle of failure. Consequently, many educators believe these children will never escape this restrictive hold. Sadly, many migrant students have been led to think their fate is to follow this path of hopelessness that has been imposed upon them for generations. The attrition rates among the migrant student population are staggering. Barriers that impede migrant student success are well documented (e.g. Clements, King, Gao, Friend, Picucci, Durón, & Laughlin, 2009; Gouwens, 2001; Romanowski, 1992; Salinas & Fránquiz, 2004).

Who are these young people? In many cases they have been referred to as "invisible children." Being invisible implies they do not have the subjectivity by which they can access rights. In other instances these children are not even acknowledged.

There are however many instructive stories of academic success among migrant students that have not been told. This chapter examines the life stories of three successful Hispanic migrant students. Although the original study was conducted fourteen years ago, the findings are still very significant given not much has changed for migrant children. The attrition rates among migrant students continue to be excessive and sufficient is known about the factors that contribute to their failure. Migrant students continue to do poorly in school and that is why it is important studies like this continue to be shared today. A qualitative, life history approach was used to explore in-depth the lives of young people who were migrant farm workers and/or children of farm workers and successful students. One research question guided the project: why are some Hispanic migrant students academically successful in spite of being "culturally disadvantaged?" This research considers how the interaction between socio-cultural, personal, and environmental factors positively influenced the academic performance of the three participants.

Participants for this study were identified through connections I have with teachers, schools, and the Hispanic community in a large city in Texas. Data were collected through interviews (conducted in English and Spanish) and observations. These took place in their natural settings in the participants' homes, labor camps, schools, place of work, and community. After eighteen months of field work, data analysis, and interpretation, each case took the form of a life history. Teachers, admistrators, counselors, coaches, family members, and peers who interacted with these students along the way were also interviewed. Given the academic success

J. Hall (ed.), Children's Human Rights and Public Schooling in the United States, 175–192.

these students experienced during their formal schooling, in this analysis I further provide updates on what the lives of these individuals look like today. As an hispanic male from this community, it is important to note the participants and I have very similar backgrounds and life experiences. This similarity certainly influenced my interpretation in one way or another, but it also served as a tool to see beyond what was not said or directly observed. As they shared their lives with me, I lived my own all over again. I developed close and personal relationships with the participants which enabled us to reach deep into our thoughts and feelings.

STRESSORS: SOCIO-CULTURAL VARIABLES

Low academic achievement among the general Hispanic student population has been linked to a number of socio-cultural variables, including 1) modest educational level of parents, 2) occupational status of family, 3) family income and composition, 4) ethnic and language minority status, and 5) the absence of learning materials in the home. In addition to these obstacles, the lives of migrant children are characterized by further barriers. Poverty, constant mobility, and the responsibility to care for younger siblings while their parents are working in the fields are main factors that also impact the academic outcomes of migrant children (Chavkin, 1991). Migrant children are the poorest and most malnourished children in our schools today. Though their parents play such a critical role in bringing food to our tables through hard labor in the midst of an abundance of food, it is ironic that many of their children suffer from malnutrition and often go to bed hungry (Shotland, 1989). These children moreover face many other hardships such as deplorable sub-standard housing as they travel from place to place in search of work and as they help in the fields.

While the majority of migrant students struggle academically given the difficulties they encounter every day, it is important to learn from those who somehow successfully negotiate their academic journey. In spite of all these seemingly insurmountable obstacles, not all migrant children experience failure at school. The three participants in this study serve as examples of students who defied the odds. They persevered and succeeded in a system not designed for them. Their ability to overcome barriers depended on their personal resources (attitudes, skills, and knowledge) and the environmental resources in place or which they put in place to provide support (Alva & Padilla, 1995).

ROLE OF THE MIGRANT FARM WORKER

Most of us go to the grocery store at least once a week. We spend some time in the produce section selecting fresh vegetables and fruit. We then make our way to the canned goods section and pick up some canned asparagus, spinach, corn, green beans, etc. We expect to have a wide variety of fresh and canned fruit and vegetables to choose from at affordable prices. We may give little thought to how these goods made their way to grocery store shelves. Yet the multi-billion dollar agriculture industry involves a cycle of production and distribution that is long and complex and dependent on migrant farm workers. Government surveys suggest there are roughly 700,000 to 850,000 hired farm workers on average at any given point during the year in the US (US Department of Agriculture [USDA], 2002).

Fruit and vegetable growth and production have steadily increased over the last few decades. Eighty-five percent of fruit and vegetables grown in North America are hand harvested. Though the role of the migrant farm worker is critical, their wages are meager. The annual wages for the majority of these workers is less than $7,500 (Effland, Hamm, & Oliveira, 1993). In 1988, the average income for a migrant family of 5.3 members was about $5,500 (De Mers, 1988). According to the National Agricultural Workers Survey [NAWS] (2005) conducted by the US Department of Labor (2005), 30% of all farm workers had family incomes below the poverty guidelines. In many cases, children also work in the fields to help the family economy.

THE MIGRANT CHILD'S EDUCATIONAL EXPERIENCE

Constant mobility makes it hard for farm worker children to complete their education. Migrant children typically attend two to three schools a year and are usually behind grade level between six to eighteen months. The median educational level for the head of a migrant family is six years in 1986 (Harrington, 1987). These students have the highest failure and dropout rates (Straits, 1987) and the lowest graduation rate of any population group in public schools. Five times as many migrant students are enrolled in the second grade as in the twelfth grade. The Migrant Attrition Project conducted a study that evidenced a 45% national dropout rate, whereas a study completed twelve years earlier reported a 90% dropout rate (Salerno, 1991).

It is not uncommon for a migrant child to be enrolled in school one week and gone the next. Many parents of migrant students are forced to leave on short notice from the labor contractors or growers. Many students leave school without making the proper withdrawal arrangements. Efficient transfer of student records is a major problem because many times receiving schools may not ever get them or may have to wait three to five months for them. Without this information, very often these students are held back or given inappropriate placement (Ascher, 1991). In many instances school officials refuse to admit these children due to lack of documentation. In spite of the Plyler vs. Doe ruling in 1982, schools in Texas and other states continue to violate such civil rights. This ruling struck down a state policy denying funding for education to illegal immigrant children and prohibited school districts from charging illegal immigrants an annual $1,000 tuition fee to compensate for the lost state funding. The court ruled that the law violated the Equal Protection Clause of the Fourteenth Amendment. The ruling stressed that education was crucial to ensuring future membership among those in society (Romero, 2012). In the context of the complexity of all issues discussed thus far, the following narrations reveal how three students were successfully able to negotiate their academic lives.

SCHOOL LIFE AND EXPERIENCES OF PARTICIPANTS

Belinda Magallán

Belinda is an intelligent and highly motivated young woman. She has lived a life full of experiences that have helped her mature into a very confident and responsible person. She is quiet, but very articulate. She is respectful of others, and expects the same in return. She is willing to work hard, and is determined to be successful. Belinda is the fifth child of a family of six, and second of three girls. She was born in La Casita, Texas on May 18, 1975. This was just five days after her parents came to the US. She was born at home, and delivered by a neighbor who happened to be a midwife.

From the start, Belinda was an excellent student, and she remembers doing well in elementary school. As she says, Head Start was her most memorable year because her mother won the attendance award for PTA meetings:

> I remember my mother taking me to Head Start the first day. That's the only year I remember my mom attending PTA meetings. My teacher had a chart on the wall with the names of our parents. She would put a star each time parents went to a PTA meeting and my mom had the most stars on the chart. She won the attendance award for my class. My mom was very involved that year, and my dad was usually at work.

Belinda liked going to school when very young, although as she reflects, aspects of it were painful. One thing she remembers about kindergarten is someone took her to the store and bought her a jacket for winter. "They would take us to Antonio's. It was just the migrant kids that went. That year my neighbor, Bertha and I both got jackets. I didn't like the jacket my teacher had chosen for me. I liked Bertha's and she liked mine so we traded." According to Melinda, nobody told the migrant students why they got the jackets, but everyone knew why. Belinda was aware other children knew why migrant students were getting jackets. "I didn't feel too good because there were some kids that made fun of us. They knew it was the poor kids getting the jackets. We knew we were the poor kids, and it was like they wanted us to know that."

By first grade it was clear to Belinda that students were grouped by language, and the English-speaking children were considered the "smart kids." She wanted to be in the "smart class" but she was labeled limited English proficient [LEP] and placed in the bilingual classroom. She recalls how she always wanted to be in Ms. Reyes' class because "that's where the smart kids were." She says even her teacher would tell them the other class was the smart group. Belinda seemed to have all the labels. She was migrant, immigrant, economically disadvantaged, female, LEP, Hispanic, and "at risk." Though her ability was questioned, she refused to believe she was not capable. She took her academics as a challenge, and was even more determined to prove all wrong. In first grade, she remembers getting lots of awards, including honor roll, perfect attendance, and recognition for the highest scores in a health competition.

As Belinda recalls, the first day of each school year was always full of anticipation to see who her teacher was going to be. Without fail, this anxiety would turn to disappointment. She consistently hoped to be placed in the "smart" class, but says her name was always on the other list. Her pain is evident as she speaks of that experience:

> In second grade I was embarrassed because I was placed with the bilingual kids. I wanted to be with the smart students, the ones who spoke English. Everyone thought we were the dumb ones. There was always the class for Spanish speakers and the one for English speakers. It was the dumb class and the smart class. I could see the smart class was for kids of the high class. The ones who were always well dressed. The ones who had the nice satchels, and huge boxes of crayons. I was aware at that young age. It doesn't make sense; the kids that needed the most help always seemed to get the worse teachers.

Looking back, Belinda says those who knew the system got the best of it. Some parents demanded certain teachers for their children, and their demands were honored. Belinda says back then her parents never knew they had choices. They did not know they could advocate for their children.

Belinda then went to Redfield Elementary. It was the only school in town for fifth graders and consequently, there were many more students and more competition to get the "best" teachers. Belinda found herself again in the same kind of classrooms she had always dreaded. As she recalls, "Oh, I remember my fifth teacher. He was very mad at us. He told us if we would be smart we would be downstairs with the smart kids not up there with him. We were not seen as smart because all the smart kids were in the GT [gifted and talented] class downstairs."

After Redfield Elementary she went to Redfield Intermediate. As a sixth grader she continued to do well, but says she was still unchallenged. She wanted to be in the band that year, and since she still had her brother's clarinet, she took it to the band director who told her she could get her in. Unfortunately her parents did not let her because they needed her to watch her younger siblings at home after school while they worked. Next she went to junior high, and seventh grade was not much different. In a matter of four years she had been in four different campuses. Her test scores kept her from qualifying for the GT program. The expectations were higher for those students.

Due to her persistence, Belinda however somehow found a way into this track in the eighth grade. In junior high, she again wanted to be in the advanced and honors classes because she wanted to prove she could do just as well. She wondered if it "was because I didn't have the money or I didn't wear the nice clothes? It wasn't fair. If you had money you were with one group, and if you didn't you were with the other. I remember telling Mr. G. I wanted to be in his science class, and he told me to go talk to your counselor." The class Mr. G. taught was a science class for

GT students, but he still put Belinda in despite her test scores. He says he knew back then she was talented and capable.

According to Belinda, eighth grade turned out to be a great year. That is when she started participating in a literary competition. Mr. G. encouraged her to try out for the impromptu speaking team. Belinda accepted the challenge and made the team. She had never competed in anything like this before. As she describes, she prepared for two events, impromptu speaking and spelling:

> I was in spelling and impromptu speaking. There was a conflict in schedules with these two events for the district meet. I remember both of my coaches were arguing because both of them wanted me. I ended up doing impromptu and that was the turning point of my life. I won the district championship; I couldn't wait for the next day. The principal announced the results at the awards assembly. After the assembly everybody congratulated me. It felt so good. That's when I was convinced I could do anything I really wanted to do.

Belinda worked hard, and won the district championship. She had a lot of self-discipline and she was determined. She told her coach, "Sir, I'm going to win the district championship. I don't care how long we have to practice. I don't care what we have to do sir. I want to win."

Belinda remembers during this time period she was suddenly popular, and acknowledged by her teachers and peers. The principal selected her as the main speaker for the promotion ceremony. She was honored, and she could hardly wait to tell her parents. She said it was indeed a turning point in her life, but it was also a painful experience. Her parents shocked her back to reality when they told her they had to leave to go work in Minnesota again. She says she was angry and resentful for being the daughter of migrant farm workers. Just when she was beginning to feel good about herself, she remembers she was abruptly reminded school and success were not congruent with her way of life. She could not understand why her parents would not postpone their departure. The principal offered to pay her airfare if her parents would let her stay with a relative. She knew her parents would never allow it, but she still asked only to be disappointed again. They needed her to watch her younger siblings. It was a big letdown for Belinda, but she transformed this seemingly traumatic episode into another life inspiring experience.

As Belinda was going through this disappointment I had been planning to present at the National Migrant Education Conference sponsored by the National Association of State Directors of Migrant Education [NASDME]. The purpose of this conference is to bring together educators from all over the country who serve migrant children in an effort to share effective practices to improve services for migrant students. Each year, this conference is held in a different state. Many teachers, including Belinda's current and future high school teachers and administrators attended each year. Most of the sessions focus on the "deficiencies" of the migrant lifestyle. These researchers and educators typically fail to look at the system, and most blame the victims and their families. As I planned my presentation, my goal was to prompt educators to look within themselves for solutions and to look at the system critically. I wanted to show them how the system was not designed to address the needs of migrant students and families. Most importantly they needed to understand they were the only ones in positions to redesign the program.

Belinda's experience helped me realize no one could tell their stories better than the students themselves. Me and another teacher got a group of migrant children together and asked them to write their stories. The students worked for months and produced scripts that combined their experiences into five mini-dramas to share their stories. Belinda was one of fourteen migrant students who participated in the presentations at the state and national migrant conferences. The children mesmerized the audience with their stories. As they now recall, they were on an emotional roller coaster during this experience: screaming with laughter and then struggling in vain to hold back tears. They confronted the audience boldly with issues and strong emotions. Belinda contends her participation in impromptu speaking was a training ground for those presentations. Belinda said her participation in the presentations gave her a feeling of accomplishment and confidence:

> It was such a good experience telling other people my story … telling them what I had gone through. Some of those teachers that saw the presentation thought that just because I was a migrant or I was leaving early I couldn't do just as well as anybody else. Just because I was a migrant I was placed in the regular classes. It didn't have to be that way.

Most importantly Belinda contends, "those presentations at the migrant conferences brought closure to my migrant life. That is not to say that I was going to put it behind and out of my mind. On the contrary, I'll never forget it … there's no way. It is part of me and that's who I am." She says that experience made her stronger.

When Belinda went to high school, she remembers most people knew who she was because of these presentations. Belinda and the other student presenters say during that time they got recognition. The teachers who saw them perform had high expectations and supported them. Belinda recalls these feelings were different from her early school years. "I remember in every class the teachers all said something when they saw me in their class. They recognized me in front of the class. They explained to the whole class who I was and what I did. They said they were very proud to have me in their class." Belinda explains she enjoyed high school and made the most of it.

High school was also different because the last year she migrated was her freshman year. After that she never left early, and she participated in many extra-curricular activities. From then on she worked at a dry cleaner during the summer. She shares she was glad she did not have to go work in the fields anymore, although she still gave her mom most of what she earned to help them out. I asked which job she liked more, the dry cleaners or the fields:

> Honestly? I would rather work at the dry cleaner. Working in the fields was hard work. I worried about leaving school early, and not knowing where we were going to live. The housing was always terrible no matter where we went. It was an adventure. We knew we were going to work, but we didn't know if it was going to be a good year. When I was in high school my parents stopped going north because it wasn't worth going anymore.

Everything Belinda had hoped for in elementary and junior high finally became a reality in high school. She no longer dreaded the first day of school or worried about her schedule. She was in the advanced and honors classes. Her teachers supported her and inspired her; she said she was treated fairly in high school. The only thing she resented was not being allowed to take the GT English class. That class was still reserved for students who had certain achievement test scores. Belinda knew those requirements, but she still tried to get in anyway. She shared the following anecdote:

> One of the things I felt bad about was that I wanted to be in GT English. The counselor said I couldn't because of my achievement test scores. I knew I could do just as well as all the students in that class. I had a 100 average in all my four advanced English classes. I kept telling him that I could do GT work and I would show him if he just gave me a chance. He refused.

Belinda could not wait to graduate. She wanted to go on to college. She did not want any celebrations as she did not want her parents to spend money they did not have. She said graduation was a good feeling as it was a feeling of accomplishment. Belinda was accepted to George Washington University and St. Edwards University, where she was eligible for the College Assistance Migrant Program College Assistance Migrant Program [CAMP]. She ended up attending St. Edwards as it was a school closer to home and her family and community. She says she was happy with her decision, as family is always crucial to her.

Belinda graduated from college in May of 1997. She earned a Bachelor of Science degree with a major in Spanish and international business. She lived on campus the first year but moved to an apartment as soon as she could. She got financial assistance but she started working the second semester of her freshman year because she wanted to help her parents. She worked as a cashier at a retail store, as a telephone operator, and as a teller at a bank. Belinda never doubted she would earn her degree, but it was not easy. Whenever she felt pressure and doubt, she recalls she had a professor who helped her out: "I would always go to Dr. García when I was down or worried about something. He would encourage me. He would say you can do it Belinda; don't you get down on yourself. You go forward." When she finished she remembers she did not want to go to her graduation ceremony because her parents were not going to be there. When graduation got close her boyfriend convinced her to go:

> He told me I had worked so hard to earn this degree and that I needed to give it closure. He told me I should go because I would regret it later. So I decided to go, and it was so ugly and sad. At the end everybody turned back and looked up to the upper level to find their parents, family, and friends. I felt so sad especially when we walked out and everybody was hugging their parents.

Belinda drove home to see her parents after graduation. They were very happy; everything was ready for the fiesta. "Mom had bought me a little medallion of the Virgin of Guadalupe for graduation. I could see and feel their pride. They were so proud of me. I am the first one to earn a bachelor's degree in my family."

Belinda worked at a bank in San Antonio for a couple of years and then moved back home when she got a promotion as bank vice-president. She wanted to be closer to her ailing parents to help them out. Today Belinda is a proud mother and continues to work in the banking industry. She and I were invited to be the keynote speakers and the National Migrant Conference held in Denver, Colorado in 2006. We occasionally visit with each other when she comes to San Antonio. She is still the strong, determined, and proud young woman I have always known.

Sonia Rodriguez

Sonia is a mature and resilient young woman who has overcome tremendous obstacles to survive and succeed. Her story is indeed a journey through a life full of challenges. Sonia has been in the migrant life cycle since the moment she was born. She was born in Toppenish, Washington on October 10, 1978 during one of their family trips to work. She is the youngest of six children. The three oldest were born in México, and all have graduated from high school. Sonia has led two lives in two different places. Half the year she lived in Texas and attended her home base school. The other half of the year she lived in labor camps – picking asparagus, berries, and cucumbers, and attended school in the state of Washington. On top of things, Sonia was diagnosed with a severe arthritic condition during her childhood. At the time of the study, one sibling earned an associate degree in electronics, one graduated from college and was a teacher, one was attending college, and two just graduated from high school and were working with their parents.

At the beginning of each school year, Sonia's experiences appeared very similar to those of any other student. When she first attended kindergarten she says she was excited but scared about going. She cried when her parents dropped her off on her first day. "I remember my mom dropped me off, and I was kind of scared and I started crying … I didn't want to be alone with people I didn't know. The next thing I knew she wasn't there. I was crying, but then this little girl next to me told me that nothing was going to happen."

Sonia came back to school late in the fall every year. She says she was never in one place long enough to establish meaningful relationships with her peers. Perhaps that is why she does not have memories of specific friends. Sonia remembers fifth grade because it turned out to be her happiest year in elementary school. She says she thinks it was because she was not moving any more from her home school in Texas. As she remembers, "I was already there, and I had my friends from fourth grade. We had different teachers, but we would still meet outside, and we still had lunch together."

But Sonia in fact was not like most other students. When she went to middle school she recalls it was different. She had to somehow figure out that she had to manipulate the system to make sure she stayed with the more challenging group. It occurred to her the only way to stay with her group was to join the school band, as for some reason all the other students in the class were in band. Sonia ended up playing the drums as it was the only instrument left. Sonia was resourceful when she had to be. She submitted herself to things she really did not want to do (join the band and play drums) as a means to an end.

Though she said she liked all her teachers in high school, a couple of teachers were most inspiring, especially her algebra and geometry teacher, Mr. Avalos. Mr. Avalos said back then he knew Sonia would do well because she had exceptional ability, drive, and was very persistent. Mr. Reyes, her pre-calculus teacher agreed with Mr. Avalos. He described her as well behaved with a strong desire to succeed and an excellent work ethic. Sonia's computer teacher also had nothing but praise for her. "She had extraordinary resolve and self-discipline. She was hard working and never complains about anything in spite of her arthritic condition."

I then met with three of her close friends and classmates. Though their impression of Sonia was analogous to those of her teachers,' their perceptions seemed less generic. They saw her through different lenses. They described Sonia as trust worthy, and someone who expects the same things from herself that she expects from her friends. They also say she is focused and very proud. There was a strong sense of admiration amongst her friends as they spoke of her accomplishments and her potential and determination to succeed. Sonia's parents said they felt she would do well in college as she has always been dedicated to her studies and they never had to tell her to do her homework. They did not want Sonia to go so far away to college, but maintained they were ready to support her decision.

As mentioned, Sonia's home base school had always been in Texas, but she also attended several schools in the state of Washington. Every year she withdrew from school early to make the annual trip with her family to *los trabajos* (the jobs) late in March. Her school records show an early withdrawal date for every year except her seventh grade and senior years. Once I interviewed Sonia at Sunset labor camp in Washington State. Sitting at small kitchen table, I asked Sonia how it felt to leave school early every year. She responded with "It's hard … sometimes I feel angry because I have to leave all my friends. The best things happen at the end of the year, the dances, and the parties. I have never been here for a prom." That is how the school year ended for Sonia every year. Though she may have felt anger, she said she was not bitter or resentful. She also shared she never discussed her feelings with her parents or her siblings, and did not hold it against her parents at all as it is the way for her family to survive. She contends she accepted it because that was the only way she knew how to cope with it.

Each time she arrived in Washington, she was immediately enrolled in school to finish the academic year. She also went to school in Washington in the fall before they came back to Texas. Sonia remembers how there she was placed in segregated classrooms:

> I do remember my first, second, and third grade teachers. I remember them because all the migrants were in one class together. We made friends right there. And we all stuck together. Fifth grade is when they decided to put us with the regular students. But we had made a lot of friends. We were all from Texas … most of us from the valley.

Sonia contends she felt secure with her friends. They were all in a new and strange place and were with teachers and students they did not know:

> We did not interact with the regular students very much. We had lunch together, but we would sit separate. Each teacher and her class sat at a table. The other students would look at us because we spoke Spanish. They didn't understand us, but we understood them; we felt like we had an advantage. We spoke two languages. We've got the best of two worlds.

Sonia says she did not feel inferior or less capable than the "regular students." When her ability was questioned, she recalls she was more determined to show them she was just as capable. These challenges only motivated her. "When they made fun of us we always wanted to show them that … yeah, we can do it. And we are smarter. We didn't feel uncomfortable so we continued to keep good grades."

While migrant students are trying to settle into their new classes they are also trying to learn material and concepts they missed or will miss. Sonia describes how it seems like they are always trying to catch up. Those who refuse to stay behind find ways to earn credits anyway they can. They can earn credits by going to summer school or night school in receiving states. Interstate coordination is vital because one of the main reasons migrant students lose credits due to poor record keeping. Many students also earn credit through correspondence courses, enrolling in distance learning courses, or independent courses through the Portable Assisted Sequence Studies [PASS] program. Whatever program they choose, they likely also work in the fields with their parents. In Sonia's case, she went to night high school when she was older because she had to help her parents. According to her sister, even when they were going to elementary school, they had to wake up very early, work an hour or two, come back to the camp, take a shower, and run to catch the bus with the rest of the youth. By the time Sonia got to school, she had already been working for a few hours. Except for her seventh grade and senior years, Sonia has left early and come back late every year:

> I don't want to go. It's a lot of hard work. I would rather leave early and come back to Texas the first day. You don't have to make up work. You just start with everybody. And well, you get your classes, the ones that you want … right now, I still need one fourth of Spanish II. I'm making that so I can graduate in the advanced program.

Sonia not only kept up, but managed to stay ahead. At the end of her junior year she had enough credits to be a senior. Keeping up with her schoolwork was not the only reason she opted to take course work through the PASS program. She took the PASS courses to help her parents out picking asparagus. She describes how she would go to work for four hours in the morning and then leave for school after lunch. She recalls taking classes through PASS at night. Sonia said, "Sometimes my father would keep us because there was so much asparagus to cut. And it's funny. We would cry if my Dad would not let us go. That was my only social time."

Senior year was different for Sonia. For seventeen years, she made the annual trip to Washington. This was the first time in her life she did not travel to Washington with her parents. She had never experienced a summer in her home in Texas. All her brothers and her sister graduated from high schools in Washington. She was the first in her family to graduate from high school in Texas, and unfortunately also the first not to have her parents present at the ceremony because they were picking asparagus in Washington at that time. As much as they wanted to come, they said they could not afford it and would have lost their jobs if they tried to take a few days off.

Sonia graduated from high school in the top third of her class. She was accepted into the CAMP program at St. Edwards University and enrolled in the fall 1997. She graduated from college in 2002 with a major in elementary education. She became a teacher just like her older sister. I have kept in touch with Sonia and her parents. After seven years of teaching, she had to quit due to her arthritic condition. Even with debilitating health, she is as resilient as ever. She is hopeful and determined to get back in the classroom as soon as she can.

Benito García

Benito is an only child. His father passed away when he was three years old and he and his mother became one. His mother dedicated every living moment to him. All they had was each other and together they began their struggle through a long and difficult journey. Their main source of income while he was growing up was a $40.00 monthly social security check and food stamps. When he turned eighteen his mother no longer received any benefits. To supplement their income, his mother worked in the fields and did odd jobs whenever she could. She took good care of her son. Although they were extremely poor, he was always well clothed and he never went hungry. As his mother remembers, "*Yo le cosía su ropita, hasta sus calsoncillos le enmendaba*" [I would sew his little clothes, and even mend his underwear]. No matter what kind of work she had to do, she was always home when her son came home from school. Benito explained what his mother meant to him in great detail. The following quote illustrates Benito's remarkable relationship with his mother:

> It just never ends. She is just embedded in everything that happens and that I do. All my life when I was growing up, it was just she and I. I knew everything she was doing, and she knew everything I was doing. I always knew where she was. You know, to this day when we are in the same building or same house, sometimes out of instinct I still tell her '*Voy para el baño, ma, ahorita vengo*' [I'm going to the restroom Mom; I'll be right back]. I usually … like when I was going to school, I never left without Mom giving me her kiss, and coming home the same thing.

Benito and his mother lived in a wood frame shack that is about twelve by twenty feet. It is still covered with the same gray simulated brick composition siding. Inside, it is divided into two small rooms. One of these is the kitchen. His mother did not have a stove and cooked over coals until Benito bought her a gas range when he was in college. The other room is a combination living room and bedroom.

Benito is the oldest of the three participants in this study. At the time of the original research, he had successfully navigated the public school system, college, and was a successful attorney. His story is full of obstacles including a blatant lack of support at school from teachers and counselors in later years. Benito recalls how he was scared when he first started kindergarten because he did not speak English. He says he struggled but somehow caught up fast and had a strong grasp of the language. In elementary school students were either in the high, medium, or low group. Benito was always with the high group in elementary. The only teacher he mentioned was his fourth grade teacher, but only because that was the year when all his friends came together, Roland, Santiago, Billy, Elmo, and Gerardo. When they all went to fifth grade, Redfield Intermediate was much bigger. Although he was a good student, Benito remembers he and some of his friends were no longer in the more advanced groups.

In junior high it was more of the same. He says he was never placed in the top section. Rather he was always in the third section. "There were sections 7-1a, 7-1b, 7-2a and so on. I was always in the 2a section. I always felt it was because of who I was; all the 7-1a's and 7-1b's were all the kids whose parents were a little bit better and that sort of thing." In the eighth grade he wanted to take algebra, but was not allowed to take it by his math teacher. As Benito recalls, his teacher, Mr. Pérez said he was just an average student. He purports he never had a chance for a spot because there was only one section and he was three sections down. He remembers the sections were populated with "the superintendent's son, and of course the principal's son, and other people like that." Benito was disappointed. He knew he had better scores than some students who got in. As a freshman he tried to sign up for algebra, but Mr. Pérez again discouraged him. Benito started to doubt himself, and began to think maybe he was right and was just an average student.

Benito explains he did well in high school, although his counselor tried to guide him into the vocational program because "he was not college material." He remembers going to the counselor and telling her he wanted to go to college and she told him he should consider a vocational school. He remembers at that time he did not know any better and he just wanted to go play football.

If there was anything he felt totally confident about, it was his ability to play football:

> That was the one thing I had no doubt about. I knew I could do as well as anyone else. No matter what, I could block anybody. The ones that were my size or smaller I could over power. The ones that were bigger I could out speed because I was very fast, and the ones that were faster and stronger, I would outsmart them with other techniques.

Benito was an outstanding football player and was selected to All Valley and All State teams. Benito says his academic motivation and belief in his scholastic abilities came from athletics, his teammates, his friends, and his coaches. Several coaches made a difference in Benito's life when he was in high school. However, according to Benito, the one who had the most impact on him was Coach Ponce:

> Coach Ponce was the main difference for me. He was like a father to me … he helped me through some personal problems. He did some things that most teachers don't do. Spending his own money, gas, his car, and his time to take me to college. Giving me advice like a father I never had. He turned my life around. He was there at that critical time when I was a teenager getting ready to graduate from high school. That was real important for me.

Benito still keeps in touch with his coach. He even named his second son after him. He contends next in line after his mother, Coach Ponce was the person who made the greatest difference in his life. His coach encouraged him to take college prep courses and he ultimately graduated with an 86.55 average.

Benito went on to play football at Sul Ross State University in Alpine, Texas, and he earned a B.A. degree with a major in English. The university did not offer any scholarships, but they helped him with housing. He lived on campus, but not in a dormitory. Instead, he was allowed to stay at the athletic field house. He decided to quit playing after sustaining a knee injury early in his sophomore year. That spring he moved to a small apartment he shared with Gerardo, a childhood friend. Living off campus was not much better than the field house. They lived in a one-bedroom apartment with barely enough room for their beds. They did not have a kitchen. For almost three years they cooked on an electric hot plate and washed dishes in the restroom sink. They paid $50.00 per month each in rent.

Benito became interested in law school during his junior year in college. On one of his trips back home, he ran into a good friend from high school. Benito said, "Rene cranked me up about law school." He began to think about it seriously when another friend, Roel Blanco, told him about the Council on Legal Education

Opportunities [CLEO] program and encouraged him to pursue it. Upon graduation Benito picked up an application from a college counselor and made arrangements to take the Law School Admission Test [LSAT]. He did not prepare for the test. He simply reviewed the sample questions on the application booklet. According to him, he "didn't know any better so that was the only booklet that I studied. I didn't know at that time there were review courses you could pay money and go for a week or two. I went and took the test based on that little booklet." Benito applied to four law schools and was rejected by all of them. He says he was disappointed and discouraged. He forgot about law school and considered teaching and coaching but went back to Sul Ross to work on a Masters' in counseling.

Benito remembers receiving a letter inviting him to participate in the CLEO program, but he threw it away when he was not accepted to any school. Benito thinks it was fate as he describes he went home one day to visit his mother and heard her struggling on the phone with someone. He says he walked in just in time because it was the Executive Director of the CLEO program, and she wanted to know why he had not responded to the letter. Benito explains he thought the invitation to participate in the CLEO program was contingent upon acceptance to law school. To the contrary, Ms. Rosas said the program was designed for applicants like him. It was for those who had not been accepted, but showed potential. She told him he had been awarded a fellowship but he had to be in Topeka, Kansas within two days. Benito was elated and quickly accepted. In looking back he says within minutes he made a decision that changed the course of his life. "I packed the only pair of pants I had brought with me and drove off to Del Rio, Texas to say goodbye to my girlfriend." Benito was in Topeka two days later. There were about thirty-five participants at the institute. They were all Hispanic and African-American. Benito remembers the welcome:

> You are here because we think you have what it takes to be a lawyer. Some of you are here because you have good GPA's but bad LSAT scores, and some of you have very good LSAT scores but low GPA's. Most of you have not been accepted to any law school. If you get through our program we guarantee you placement in one of the top three schools of your choice, and we'll give you a $1,000.00 scholarship each year.

Benito got through the program and chose to go to the Thurgood Marshall School of Law in Houston, Texas. He graduated from law school and today is a very accomplished attorney. Benito has practiced law for twenty-six years. He is a respected attorney at the local, state, and national levels. He is very involved in the community; he was twice elected as mayor of his hometown. Presently, he is running for judge of the Texas 4th Court of Appeals. He is very proud of what he has accomplished but continues to be very humble. Benito and I have kept in touch. I have followed his political career. He serves his clients and community unconditionally and with great humility. His mother still lives within him.

PERSONAL CHARACTERISTICS: PERSONAL RESOURCES

It is not difficult to understand how the many barriers and obstacles confronted by these students could create a sense of failure and hopelessness. While the Hispanic migrant lifestyle (instead of the educational and economic system) may be blamed for their academic failure, in some ways it is also a source of their success. Students like Sonia, Belinda, and Benito survived the negative effects of these stressors because of lessons learned as members of a migrant farm worker family. They were fighters and knew they may have to find their own paths to success as the official system may shut them out.

Sonia, Belinda, and Benito share an extensive core of values and beliefs. This core includes determination, persistence, a strong work ethic, responsibility, commitment, resourcefulness, cooperation, and a sense of hope. The migrant experience is like a survival training session that for participants helped them develop the personal resources common to the resilient child. Their resilience, coupled with their intellectual potential helped to mediate their reaction to stressful life events and conditions. All the young people in this sample had the personal commitment not to give up and to do whatever it takes to reach goals. For instance, as a middle school student, although she was not really interested in doing so, Sonia joined the school band. She was willing to study the drums because she knew it would keep her in a more challenging academic class. Similarly, when he heard he had the chance to attend a law school program, even with only one pair of pants to take, Benito was willing instantly to move to a different state and city. Even though Benito's teachers were not encouraging, he understood they were wrong and did not let it demoralize him. He listened to the advice from other people in his life he respected.

SUPPORT: ENVIRONMENTAL RESOURCES

A strong support system is a critical factor that impacts the success or failure of children to adapt to their environment. This support system is manifested in the form of the environmental resources available to these young people. Such resources include external sources of information, support, and affective feedback, which, when available, can shape how well youth adapt to their environment (Alva & Padilla, 1995). The environmental resources the students in this study depend on can be traced to two main sources: their families and the schools. More specifically, Sonia, Belinda, and Benito attribute their success to the support they drew from their families, teachers, administrators, counselors, coaches, programs, and/or peers. In some cases, Belinda, Sonia, and Benito were motivated by negative feedback among school personnel. Each of these young people either wanted to prove those downbeat individuals wrong or were strong enough to ignore unconstructive opinions and advice. Unfortunately, when it comes to positive school supports, much of it also depends on having the luck to encounter a caring and motivating adult. Accessing such supports is dependent on being in the right place at the right time. An example of this is when Benito happened to walk in on the telephone call his mother was having with a representative from the law school program.

DEBUNKING DEFICIT THINKING

The family is often blamed for the academic failures of migrant children, but in actuality it must be given credit for their successes. Sometimes teachers and other school personnel were blatantly discouraging or overlooked the ability of participants. A strong sense of family support kept these students from falling through the cracks while they tried to establish alternative support systems among coaches, peers, and so forth. Many children of migrant farm workers have overcome the negative effects of the stress factors associated with their lifestyle. They "beat the system" because of (not in spite of) lessons learned as members of a migrant farm worker family. Their lifestyle provides them with the lessons for survival. These experiences help them develop the qualities and attributes of resiliency. The migrant lifestyle was a natural setting that served to develop social competence, problem solving skills, autonomy, and a sense of purpose and hope (Garza, Reyes, & Trueba, 2004). These young people realize the larger system is making a mistake in how they are being characterized, resulting in them having to carve out their own paths to success. Only those with the fortitude, ability, and supports are able to do so.

Migrant students who have been academically "successful" have been found to take advantage of the opportunities to learn from the real life situations they encountered as migrant farm worker children. Their parents had little formal schooling, yet they valued education highly. They encouraged their children to break away from their way of life without making them feel ashamed. Their parents modeled a strong work ethic as they worked in the fields day in and day out. These young people could make concrete connections between hard work and the food on their tables. They knew where their food, clothing, and shelter came from. Although they were poor, there was always a sense of pride. They learned to respect others, including themselves. This sense of pride helped them cope with the pain when others made fun of the way they dressed, their language, and their family. Their parents were proud and had high expectations for their children. There was never a doubt they were expected to graduate from high school and go to college (Garza, 1998).

This study looked into the lives of three invulnerable and successful Hispanic migrant children. Extensive research exists about the obstacles that impede migrant student success (e.g. Clements, King, Gao, Friend, Picucci, Durón, & Laughlin, 2009; Gouwens, 2001; Romanowski, 1992; Salinas & Fránquiz, 2004). Educators have been overexposed to this research, and often think this is the only path for these students. This is where the problem rests. One of the goals of this study was to incite educators and policy makers to transition from the primary phase of awareness to the more advanced phase of deeper understanding and change. It is most important to use this awareness and sensitivity in a way that changes attitudes and raises expectations about the capabilities and competence of these students.

Fourteen years later, the findings of this study continue to contribute to the body of knowledge that will hopefully improve the current schooling experiences of migrant children. No child should have to experience discouragement in public schools where all students are supposed to have an equal chance to succeed.

REFERENCES

Alva, S. A., & Padilla, A. M. (1995). Academically invulnerability among Mexican Americans: A conceptual framework. *Journal of Educational Issues of Language Minority Students*. [Online], Available: Netscape www.

Ascher, C. (1991). *Highly mobile students: Educational problems and possible solutions*. New York, NY: ERIC Clearinghouse on Urban Education. (ERIC Digest ED 351 426).

Chavkin, N. F. (1991). *Family lives and parental involvement in migrant students' education*. Charleston, WV: ERIC Clearinghouse on Rural Education and Small Schools. (ERIC Digest ED 335 174).

Clements, M., King, C., Gao, H., Friend, S., Picucci, A. Durón, S., & Laughlin, T. (2009, August 13). *Texas Migrant Education Program evaluation: Interim report submitted to the Texas Education Agency*. MGT of America, Inc. & Resources for Learning, LLC.

De Mers, D. (1988, November). Migrant programs meet unique challenges. *National Head Start Bulletin*, pp. 2-3.

Effland, J., Hamm, S., & Oliveira, V. (1993). *Hired farm labor use on fruit, vegetable, and horticultural specialty farms*. Washington, DC: US Department of Agriculture.

Garza, E. (1998). *Life histories of academically successful migrant students*. Doctoral dissertation, University of Texas at Austin. UMI Dissertation Services.

Garza, E., Reyes, P., & Trueba, E. T. (2004). *Resiliency and success: Migrant children in the United States*. Boston: Paradigm Publishers.

Gouwens, J. A. (2001). *Migrant education: A reference handbook*. Santa Barbara, CA: ABC-Clio.

Hunter, J., & Howley, C. B. (1990). *Undocumented children in the schools: Successful strategies and policies*. Charleston, WV: ERIC Clearinghouse on Rural Education and Small Schools (ERIC Digest ED 321 962).

Romanowski, M. (2002). Meeting the needs of migrant students. *Principal*, 8242-45, 47.

Romero, A. (2012, June 11). *School is for everyone: Celebrating Plyer v. Doe*. Retrieved from: http://www.aclu.org/blog/immigrants-rights/school-everyone-celebrating-plyler-v-doe

Salerno, A., & Fink, M. A. (1989). *Dropout retrieval report: Thoughts on dropout prevention and retrieval*. Tallahassee, FL: Florida State Department of Education. ERIC ED 345 915.

Salinas, C., & Franquiz, M. E. (Eds.). (2004). *Scholars in the field: The challenges of migrant education*. Charleston, WV: ERIC.

Shotland, J. (1989). *Full fields, empty cupboards: The nutritional status of migrant farmworkers in America*. Washington, DC: Public Voice for Food and Health Policy.

Straits, B. C. (1987). Residence migration and school progress. *Sociology of Education, 60*(1), 34-43.

US Department of Agriculture [USDA]. (2002). *Farm income and costs*. Washington, DC: Economic Research Service.

US Department of Labor. (2005). Findings from the National Agricultural Workers Survey (NAWS) 2001-2002: A demographic and employment profile of United States farm workers (Research Report No. 9). Washington, DC: US Department of Labor.

SUE BOOKS

CHAPTER 11

Funding the Right to Equal Educational Opportunity: An Overview and Call to Follow the Money

> "We wouldn't play Little League this way," a parent in a wealthy district in Ohio told me when she was reflecting on the inequalities of education funding in that state. "We'd be embarrassed. We would feel ashamed."
> Jonathan Kozol, *The shame of the nation*

On paper, education and equal educational opportunity are rights. In a landmark decision that echoed far beyond the nation, the US Supreme Court in 1954 found that educational opportunity, "where the state has undertaken to provide it, is a right which must be made available to all on equal terms." Writing for a unanimous Court in *Brown v. Board of Education*, Chief Justice Earl Warren affirmed equal educational opportunity as a right and underscored the centrality of education to other rights, given the importance of education "to our democratic society" and the likelihood that no child "may reasonably be expected to succeed in life if he [or she] is denied the opportunity of an education." Although significant segregation on the basis of race, ethnicity, language, and especially family wealth continues to mar public schooling in the US almost 60 years later (Orfield, 2009), *Brown* "inspired movements pursuing equal schooling along lines of gender, disability, language, immigration, class, and even religion and sexual orientation" (Minow, 2010, pp. 31-32).

The Supreme Court's acknowledgement of the central importance of education to individuals and to the nation and its consequent strong endorsement of equal educational opportunity resonates with the American Dream ideology that runs so deep in US culture. Despite the reality that the US "stands out as the advanced country in which it matters most who your parents were, the country in which those born on one of society's lower rungs have the least chance of climbing to the top or even to the middle" (Krugman, 2012, p. A19), faith in the possibilities of social mobility persists.[1] "'Movin' on up,' George Jefferson-style, is not only a sitcom song but a civil religion" (DeParle, 2011, p. A1). As Bill Clinton (1993) insisted throughout his presidential campaign, "The American dream that we were all raised on is a simple but powerful one: If you work hard and play by the rules

---

[1] See Jantti (2006) and the Pew Economic Mobility Project (2011), international comparison studies that support Krugman's comments.

J. Hall (ed.), Children's Human Rights and Public Schooling in the United States, 193–211.

you should be given a chance to go as far as your God-given ability will take you."

In the 19th century, the expansive Western frontier "created a literal level playing field that gave everyone a roughly even start in the competitive race for personal success and advancement" (Rebell, 2011, p. 6) – a place where "hard work, intelligently applied, would usually make the land bloom, and that would support a man and his family" (Jillson, 2004, p. 163). When "the frontier was no more," education arguably succeeded the land as the imagined foundation or guarantor of opportunity (p. 163). Now, "for most Americans the path to economic success lies through the schoolhouse door" (Haskins & Sawhill, 2009, p. 125).

Or so we have been told. The open land of the West never really equalized opportunity. John Steinbeck's (1939) masterful portrayal of the big bank collusion and agricultural mechanization that wrought such devastation on the Joad family during the Depression era comes to mind. Like vast numbers of other sharecroppers, the Joads were pushed from their land in Oklahoma by the profit-demanding "bank" and pulled west by a sinister promise of work that would feed only the profit ledgers of ever fewer large landholders. I fear that education as we know it, the current "ticket" to the American Dream, is functioning in much the same way. Pushed by a fear of not being good enough – which is to say, better than someone else – students are pulled by an elusive promise, through education, of a shot at a good job. However, the job market is much too small, and the purported educational path is linked illogically to property wealth.

The practice of funding public schools largely through property taxes results in the children of families who can afford million-dollar homes receive "a million dollar education" as well (Kozol, 2009). The practice also ensures that those who cannot afford anything close to this, or maybe any home at all, must watch their children cope as best they can with the inequalities they are offered. Cogs in a steadily slowing wheel of social immobility, far too many of these young people grow up hearing in one way or another, "More money (for you) is not the answer."

In the discussion that follows, I provide an overview of school funding disparities today; consider the possibilities as well as limitations of the courts as instruments of reform; and share some thoughts about how we might tip the scales towards more equality in the provision of educational opportunity. That work includes paying more attention to what Alex Molnar has called the "financialization of public education" (Saul, 2011, p. A24) and developing the financial literacy required to understand this transformation.

PUBLIC SCHOOLS, STILL SEPARATE AND UNEQUAL

In finding in *Brown* (1954) that education "is a right which must be made available to all on equal terms," the US Supreme Court overturned the principle of "separate but equal" affirmed in *Plessy v. Ferguson* (1896). Although school districts in the South, where segregation had been a matter of law, drug their feet for many years, significant desegregation of public schools there did occur after 1964 when the Civil Rights Act put federal funding of recalcitrant school districts at risk. Few efforts were made in other parts of the country, however, and schools nationwide have again become segregated to a considerable degree, with the Supreme Court's blessing (Orfield, 2009; Orfield, Eaton, & The Harvard Project on School Desegregation, 1996). After the pivotal US Supreme Court decision in 1974 in *Milliken v. Bradley*, other courts, especially in the 1990s, stopped ordering desegregation plans and began dismantling existing arrangements, both court-ordered and voluntary, with the predictable consequence – namely, schools that more closely reflected patterns of residential segregation along the lines of race, ethnicity, and class.

US public schools also are hampered by persistent and significant disparities in school funding (Baker, Sciarra, & Farrie, 2010a). This reality is well known. The National Committee for Responsive Philanthropy, a watchdog and advocacy group, for example, has urged philanthropists to pay more attention to the systemic nature of funding-based educational injustices:

> While the public schools attended by some US students are among the best in the world, other children are cast off into unsafe, unsupportive, unchallenging, and under-resourced schools where their chances of academic success are minimal. These inequities have not arisen randomly or by happenstance. They are tied powerfully to parental wealth, education, ethnicity, and race, and they persevere from generation to generation. (Welner & Farley, 2010, p. 1)

In a pastoral letter to President Obama, the Governing Board of the National Council of Churches (2010) urged him to address "the cavernous resource opportunity gaps – from state to state and from school district to school district" (p. 4).

A pivotal school funding case, *San Antonio v. Rodriguez,* was decided by the US Supreme Court in 1973. Demetrio Rodriquez – a veteran, US Air Force sheet-metal worker, and parent in the Edgewood schools in Texas – was the lead plaintiff in a class-action suit prompted by inequities in funding for public schools in neighboring districts in San Antonio: Alamo Heights, which could spend $594 per pupil, and Edgewood, which could spend only $356, despite taxing itself at a significantly higher rate than its neighbor. The case raised the question of whether such large disparities in school funding violate the US Constitution and turned on an interpretation of the Equal Protection Clause of the 14th Amendment. By a 5-4 vote, the justices reversed a Texas court and said no. As long as some semblance of public schooling is provided – that is, as long as there is no "absolute [educational] deprivation" – even egregious disparities do not violate the federal constitution. The Court concluded education is not a fundamental right protected by the Constitution and children attending poorly funded schools do not constitute a "protected class." Consequently, a lower level of justification for the acknowledged disparities in funding was required. The Court found that justification in the idea of local control.

Proponents of a system of school funding that relies heavily on property wealth tend to regard local control as an example of the "Piper Link" – the idea that "he who pays the piper, calls the tune" (Shelly, 2011, p. 7). However, as Thurgood Marshall argued in his long and passionate dissent in *Rodriguez*, property-tax-based funding ensures not local control, but inequality:

> Local school districts cannot choose to have the best education in the State by imposing the highest tax rate. Instead, the quality of the educational opportunity offered by any particular district is largely determined by the amount of taxable property located in the district – a factor over which local voters can exercise no control.

In other words, local control is meaningless if localities cannot fund the choices they want to make. The alleged sanctity of local control nevertheless has been used repeatedly to rationalize the predictable disparities that result from linking school funding to a district's property wealth.

'Is School Funding Fair?'

Funding for US public schools comes from three primary sources: state revenues, local property taxes, and federal funds. State revenues constitute, on average, 46.5% of the total pie, and property taxes, on average, 44.4% of the total. The federal contribution amounts to only 9.1% (Baker et al., 2010a). Significant disparities exist at every level – among the states, among the 15,000-plus school districts spread across the nation, and among individual schools within single districts.

In a national study designed to bring more conceptual clarity to the question of fairness in school funding, Baker et al. (2010a) published a report titled *Is School Funding Fair?* and essentially answered no. Acknowledging the strong and repeatedly documented correlation between student and school poverty and the costs of providing equal educational opportunity (e.g., Coleman, 1966; Rebell, 2011; Rothstein, 2004; Ryan, 2010), the researchers used as a key measure of fairness whether states are "providing a sufficient level of funding distributed to districts within the state to account for additional needs generated by student poverty" (Baker et al., 2010a, p. 7). States differ markedly, both in terms of total funding provided for public schools and in terms of the weight given to poverty in the distribution of state revenues. At the extremes, a student in Utah receives less than 38% of the funding a student in Vermont receives – $6,899 versus $18,365, after adjusting for regional differences.[2] Only 14 states provide more funding to high-poverty districts, defined as districts in which the poverty rate exceeds 30%. Fourteen other states have "flat" systems, and 20 states privilege low- or no-

[2] These dollar amounts represent the mean state and local revenues per pupil in 2008.

poverty districts.[3] In terms of sensitivity to the educational significance of poverty, the spread ranges from Utah, where high-poverty school districts receive 151% of the funding of districts with no child poverty, to New Hampshire, where high-poverty districts receive only 65% of the funding of no-poverty districts.

These kind of disparities arise year after school year in large part because so much of the school funding is linked to property wealth. Consider the derivation of property-tax revenues, a function of local property values and local tax effort:

> Imagine that District A has $100,000 of property wealth per pupil, which means that the total assessed value of property within the district divided by the total number of students in the district results in $100,000 of property value for each student. Imagine that District B has only $50,000 of property wealth per pupil. If both districts tax property at 5%, District A will raise $5,000 per pupil, whereas District B will raise only $2,500 per pupil. Now imagine that District A lowers its tax rate to 3% while District B retains its 5% rate. District A will still raise more money – $3,000 per pupil – than District B, despite taxing itself at a lower rate. (Ryan, 2010, p. 127)

This often happens: poorer districts tax themselves at higher rates than wealthier districts.[4] A focus on tax *effort* suggests that poorer communities end up with struggling public schools, at least in part, not because they "don't care about education," as is popularly believed, but rather because, despite an often significant tax effort, low property values do not generate adequate revenue.

Baker (2012) also has revisited the "age-old question" of whether money "matters" in education in a review of the major studies that deny a relationship between increased spending and educational outcomes. In his meta-analysis, which includes re-analyses of James Coleman's 1964 data as well as Erik Hanushek's often cited 1986 paper,[5] Baker (2012) finds that "the available evidence leaves little doubt: sufficient financial resources are a necessary underlying condition for improving quality education" (p. 18) and that "on balance, in direct tests of the relationship between financial resources and student outcome, money matters" (p. iv).

---

[3] Other statistical overviews confirm these patterns. The Common Core of Data report for 2011 showed total median revenues per pupil (local, state, and federal) ranging from $8,323 at the 5th percentile of districts to $23,971 at the 95th percentile for fiscal year 2009 (Cornman & Noel, 2011). The Southern Education Foundation (2010) looked specifically at the situation of children growing up in extreme poverty, defined as a family income no greater than half the federal poverty line, and found that in 2007-2008 the median per-pupil expenditure among school districts with low rates of extreme child poverty (less than 5%) was almost twice that of districts with high rates (10% or more), even including the federal funding that is supposed to ameliorate poverty-related disparities.

[4] A US General Accounting Office (1997) study found that in 35 states, the poorest 20% of school districts were making a greater tax effort than the richest 20%, but still ending up with less.

[5] The "money doesn't matter" argument is perhaps most closely linked with Eric Hanushek, a professor at Stanford University, who often testifies for defendant states in school funding lawsuits.

Thurgood Marshall reached the same conclusion 40 years ago on the basis of sheer logic. As he pointed out in his dissent as well in *Rodriguez*:

> It is an inescapable fact that, if one district has more funds available per pupil than another district, the former will have greater choice in educational planning than will the latter. ... The question of discrimination in educational quality must be deemed to be an objective one that looks to what the State provides its children, not to what the children are able to do with what they receive. That a child forced to attend an underfunded school with poorer physical facilities, less experienced teachers, larger classes, and a narrower range of courses than a school with substantially more funds – and thus with greater choice in educational planning – may nevertheless excel is to the credit of the child, not the State. Indeed, who can ever measure for such a child the opportunities lost and the talents wasted for want of a broader, more enriched education?

Better teachers, smaller classes, better libraries and educational technology, more extracurricular opportunities, more school nurses and guidance counselors, and other in-school and out-of-school supports – all carry a price tag. If some districts can afford much more of these resources than others, the haves and have-mores clearly will enjoy much greater educational opportunity than the have-nots.

Money matters in education in part because teachers, like almost everyone else, respond to financial incentives. Experienced teachers tend to seek positions in more affluent schools, leaving many high-poverty schools with the newest and lowest-paid teachers. A 2011 US Department of Education study found that "more than one-third of higher-poverty schools [schools with poverty rates above the district average] had lower per-pupil personnel expenditures than lower-poverty schools in their districts at the same school grade level" (Heuer & Stullich, 2011, p. 22). This finding confirms what many education observers have long known: "Students in poor neighborhoods are frequently taught by low-paid rookie teachers who move on as they gain experience and rise up the salary scale" (Dillon, 2011, p. A29).

Students and teachers in many high-poverty schools spend their days in ill-equipped classrooms in dilapidated and sometimes dangerous buildings. Kozol (1992, 1996, 2005) has been documenting leaking school roofs, faulty heating systems, broken toilets, cracked windows, and missing equipment in high-poverty schools (in which 75% or more of the students qualified for subsidized lunches) for decades. In a case focused on particularly horrendous conditions, *Williams v. State*, the American Civil Liberties Union and other civil rights organizations in California filed a class-action lawsuit in 1999 on behalf of students attending awful schools. The complaint cited a lack of qualified teachers, libraries, and instructional materials; overcrowding that resulted in staggered classes and a shortened school year; and school conditions so "appalling" that they "shock the conscience" – "filthy toilets and leaky roofs, sweltering classrooms (sometimes said to exceed 100 degrees), falling ceiling tiles, and schoolhouse vermin" (Schrag,

2003, p. 98). Less sensational perhaps, but even more tragic, was the record of academic failure:

> For the prior two decades, California had been well below average in the nation in its per-pupil spending and dead last among the major industrial states. That made the stress particularly acute in a state with a large percentage of disadvantaged students, including the 25% of all students whose native language was something other than English. Ever since the early 1990s ... [California's] academic achievement in math and reading ... was near the bottom among the states, even in interstate comparisons of the same ethnic groups. (Schrag, 2003, p. 98)

Although a trial was scheduled to begin in 2004, the *Williams* case was settled out of court after the state agreed to fund $800 million in school repairs over the next several years, to set standards for instructional materials and facilities, and to intervene in failing schools. Still, concerns lingered that the settlement did not guarantee all school buildings would be repaired or all students would receive textbooks (National Education Access Network, 2011).

A study by BEST: Building Educational Success Together (2006) found, not surprisingly, that "public school facility investment aligns with the wealth of the community" (Filardo, Vincent, Sung, & Stein, 2006). Over the decade 1995 to 2004, high-poverty districts spent an average of $4,800 per student on school construction whereas low-poverty districts (in which fewer than 10% of the students qualified for subsidized lunches) spent almost twice as much, $9,361 per student. Renovations to existing buildings showed the same pattern: funding favoring wealthier districts.

Outside the formal structure of school funding, private donations from parents, alumni, and corporations create a "second layer of disparities" (Kozol, 2005, p. 48). These donations, on the rise in recent years, are funding a wide range of needs and wants for the recipient schools, including equipment, supplies, and artists-in-residence. Of course, many schools have no significant donors. Concerned about the unfairness of this situation, school administrators in Greenwich, Connecticut, capped the amount a single school could receive, but often then waived the caps when large donations were offered. An analysis by the school board a few years later showed continuing disparities: $17,000 for one elementary school compared to more than $50,000 each for eight others. To try to spread the beneficence more fairly, 18 school districts in two counties in New York State joined together in the late 1990s to create a nonprofit foundation. However, the regional foundation faltered when "some of the well-heeled participants expressed interest in creating foundations that catered exclusively to their schools" (Cowan, 2007; reported also in Books, 2010).

Given these inequities, it is no surprise the achievement gap between students in rich and poor families has widened over the last 25 years. In a review of 19 national studies, Reardon (2011) found the gap in achievement between students at the 90th and 10th percentiles of the family income distribution is 30% to 40% larger for the cohort born in 2001 than for the cohort born 25 years earlier. This income achievement gap, which appears to have been growing steadily for at least 50 years, is now more than twice as large as the black-white achievement gap. Fifty years ago the black-white achievement gap was 1.5 to two times as large as the income-based achievement gap. Reardon (2011) attributes the increase in the income achievement gap largely to a strengthening association between family income and achievement. In other words, "a dollar of [family] income (or factors correlated with income) appears to buy more academic achievement than it did several decades ago" (Reardon, 2011, p. 104). The "added value" reflects a tightening link between geography and family income, on one hand, and between school quality and educational opportunity, on the other.

Given the increasing significance of educational advantage, it is also no surprise the gap in college graduation rates between high- and low-income students also has grown markedly. A longitudinal study of two generations of young people (Bailey & Dynarski, 2011) found not only that high-income students are graduating college in much higher percentages than low-income students, but the gap between the two groups is growing. College completion rates increased by 18 percentage points for high-income students born around 1980 compared to their counterparts born in the early 1960s, from about one-third to more than half of this cohort graduating. However, for low-income students born around 1980 compared to their counterparts born in the early 1960s, the increase in college graduation rates was only 4 percentage points, from 5% to 9% (Bailey & Dynarski, 2011).

A ROLE FOR THE COURTS?

The inevitable disparities generated by a property-tax-based system of school funding have long been adjudicated, and cases can be made both for and against continuing to seek redress from the courts. School funding inequities and inadequacies have provoked lawsuits in all but five of the 50 states, and plaintiffs have prevailed in 60% of the cases (National Education Access Network, 2012). Despite these "paper victories," school funding is still inequitable and, in many places, inadequate. Although state courts have tended to find state school funding systems unconstitutional, state legislatures have tended not to follow through and ensure meaningful reforms are implemented. Some scholars (e.g., Rebell, 2011) believe the *Rodriquez* decision could be overturned. Others (e.g., Ryan, 2010) are less inclined to view the courts as instruments of reform and argue that equal educational opportunity will require stronger "ties that bind" in the form of genuine school integration (p. 14). I review both arguments below.

The Case for Comprehensive Educational Opportunity

The pivotal *Rodriguez* (1973) decision changed the focus of school funding lawsuits, but did not stop them. Although the US constitution does not affirm education as a fundamental right, almost every state constitution includes an education clause. New Jersey's constitution, for example, calls for the state to provide a "thorough and efficient education" to all children. Colorado is supposed to provide a "general and uniform" system of education, and the Vermont constitution requires its schools to be "competent." Since *Rodriguez*, reformers have challenged systems of school funding based on these state obligations.

However, the time might be right for a reconsideration of this decision, argues Michael Rebell, lead counsel for the plaintiffs in a long-running school funding lawsuit in New York State[6] and now a professor of law and education at Columbia University. Rebell (2011) cites the national focus on student achievement institutionalized in the federal No Child Left Behind (NCLB) Act of 2001 as well as precedents set in recent state court decisions. NCLB requires all public schools to bring virtually all students up to a high (and assessable) level of achievement, but does nothing to help schools address the educational challenges created by widespread and deepening poverty (Ladd & Fiske, 2011). Given the national achievement mandate, is there not a corresponding national responsibility to ensure that the basic conditions exist under which the mandated achievement is possible – that is, to provide "comprehensive educational opportunity?" (Rebell, 2011, p. 1). As Rebell (2011) sees it, state legislatures, held to account by state and federal courts, must recognize that:

> the critical resources and services that students need, both in school and out of school, to obtain a meaningful educational opportunity are part of a *right* to education and are not merely discretionary services that the state may provide to some children some of the time. (p. 4)

Although the Supreme Court found in *Rodriquez* that education is not a fundamental right under the federal constitution, it did not rule on the question of a right to some minimum level of education. The *Rodriguez* court found significant school funding *disparities* do not violate the US Constitution, but did not address the question of a constitutionally protected floor or funding *inadequacies*. Arguably, the case could now be made that students in many high-poverty school districts are deprived of a constitutionally protected opportunity to acquire a minimally adequate education.

Several state courts have already moved in this direction. The New Jersey Supreme Court, for example, found in *Abbott v. Burke* (1990):

> The educational needs of students in poorer urban districts vastly exceed those of others, especially those from richer districts. The difference is monumental, no matter how it is measured. Those needs go beyond educational needs; they include food, clothing and shelter, and extend to lack of close family and community ties and support, and lack of helpful role models. They include the needs that arise from a life led in an environment of violence, poverty, and despair. ... The goal is to motivate

[6] *Campaign for Fiscal Equity v. State of New York* (2003).

> them, to wipe out their disadvantages as much as a school district can, and to give them an educational opportunity that will enable them to use their innate ability.

In Kentucky, the State Supreme Court in *Rose v. Council for Better Education* (1989) prompted the legislature to revamp the state's system of school funding and to establish an extensive network of family resource centers in or near high-poverty elementary schools, a network of youth service centers in or near middle and high schools, and a statewide early childhood program for children in low-income families. In Washington in *McCleary v. State* (2010), a superior court judge found that the state's current system of school funding is unconstitutional, and elaborated:

> Schools cannot and do not perform their role in a vacuum, and this is an important qualification of conclusion reached in any study of adequacy in education. … The State can – and must – do more. Where there is that absence of support for students outside the school, the schools are capable to compensating, given proper and adequate resources.

These and other court decisions affirm that "students who come to school disadvantaged by the burdens of severe poverty need a more comprehensive set of services and resources," and arguably set precedents for finding failure to provide such services and resources unconstitutional at the federal level (Rebell, 2011, p. 19).

A Counter-Argument: Protecting the Suburbs

James Ryan, professor of law at the University of Virginia, is far less optimistic about the prospects of overturning *Rodriguez* or even of looking to the courts to bring about meaningful school funding reform. Providing more funding for students who now have less will not necessarily alter what Ryan (2010) sees as the overriding objective of school finance legislation: protecting the suburbs. Funding disparities are especially significant between large predominantly minority high-poverty city districts and predominantly white suburban districts, and this city-suburban boundary:

> has been the fault line of public education for half a century, doing more than anything else to define and shape the educational opportunities of public school students. On one side stand predominantly white, middle-income, and relative successful schools. On the other side stand predominantly minority, poor, and relative unsuccessful schools. (Ryan, 2010, p. 3)

When a *New York Times* reporter (Greenhouse, 1972) asked Frederick Shore, superintendent of a suburban school district on the south shore of Long Island, about property tax reform proposals in New York State (in the early 1970s, when reform seemed like a real possibility), he shared his misgivings candidly: "I don't want to be hurting myself in order to help my neighbor" (p. 1) – a sentiment that "pretty much captures the politics of educational funding, if not education politics altogether" (Ryan, 2010, p. 172). Property-rich districts like many of those on Long Island have not in fact been asked to "help neighbors" at any significant cost to themselves. In *Milliken v. Bradley* (1974), the US Supreme Court explicitly prohibited inter-district remedies to persistent school segregation – a decision that, along with *Rodriguez* (1973), essentially assured "separate and unequal" would continue to define public schooling in the US. Since then, no court action has challenged this crippling reality. No court has outlawed reliance on property taxes to fund schools, has required districts to share resources, or has required district boundaries to be redrawn (Ryan, 2010).

School funding litigation has failed to alter a reality of separate and unequal. It also has had the unfortunate consequence of narrowing the conversation about what to expect from schools: not "integration or racial tolerance," which more money cannot buy, but rather "a better academic education," which "money *can* buy, at least in theory" (Ryan, 2010, p. 124). In this way, "if anything, school finance reform unintentionally entrenches segregation by defining the problem as one of resources rather than racial separation" (p. 124). As long as "the poor and politically powerless" are separated in their own schools and districts, equal educational opportunity will remain an easily forgotten dream (p. 304). Still,

> One should never pretend that this separation is not a problem simply because there are no easy or obvious solutions. Indeed, in the field of education law and policy, it was *the* problem of the last half century, and it remains the central problem of the 21st century. (Ryan, 2010, p. 304)

From this perspective, strategies to promote integration in school and society hold far more promise of ensuring equality in educational opportunity than does more school funding litigation.

GIVE BACK AND PAY FORWARD

In fact, there is no need to choose between working to "desegregate[e] the money" (Bell, 2004, p. 161) and to desegregate schools and neighborhoods. In times like ours, there is no shortage of good work to be done, in and outside the courtroom, to try to ameliorate the current injustices in school funding and to unite a nation sorely divided between (the disproportionately white) rich and (the disproportionately of-color) poor. The "99% versus the 1%" may describe the current political reality of the US very well in many ways, but it does not fully capture the plight of those who are born into poverty, who are relegated to the very worst living conditions, who get the worst of the worst the public schools have to offer, and who shore up a system in which the rich grow richer and the poor, poorer.

Schools should be funded adequately and fairly *and* integrated racially and socioeconomically – not because children living in poverty or children of color need to sit beside white or affluent children to learn, but because, as Thurgood Marshall told the nation in *Milliken* (1974), "Unless our children begin to learn together, there is little hope that our people will ever learn to live together." Persistent disparities in funding as well as persistent and worsening segregation along lines of race and class violate some of our most profound moral and political beliefs, including a commitment, on paper at least, to equal educational opportunity. At the heart of this commitment is an understanding of the worth and dignity all humans share, inherently and unconditionally. For many people, this is a spiritual insight ("we are all God's children"); for others, it is the basic foundation of democratic thought and practice (Purpel, 1989).

Inequitable school funding flies in the face of this affirmation of a shared humanity as it is one of the few places where we (the broader society) tell children explicitly what we think they "are worth to us in human terms and in the contributions they may someday make to our society" (Kozol, 2005, p. 44). Justin Hudson, one of a handful of students of color at the prestigious Hunter College High School in New York City, recognized the "great untruth"[7] behind such economic and existential calculations.

When Justin got up to give his graduation speech in June 2010, he opened his remarks by praising the school and explaining how appreciative he was to have made it to that moment. Then he shocked his audience: "more than anything else, I feel guilty," Mr. Hudson . . . told his 183 fellow graduates. "I don't deserve any of this. And neither do you." They had been labeled "gifted," he told them, based on a test they passed "due to luck and circumstance." Beneficiaries of advantages, they were disproportionately from middle-class Asian and white neighborhoods known for good schools and the prevalence of tutoring (Otterman, 2010, p. A1). The deeply institutionalized and cleverly rationalized unfairness of separate and unequal schooling affords some children but robs others of a chance to spread their wings and to explore their minds, imaginations, and world.

We owe them more. As Elizabeth Warren (2011) told an audience during her bid for Massachusetts senator, education is one of the social goods we "pay forward:"

> There is nobody in this country who got rich on his own. Nobody. You built a factory out there – good for you! But I want to be clear. You moved your goods to market on the roads the rest of us paid for. You hired workers the rest of us paid to educate. You were safe in your factory because of police forces and fire forces that the rest of us paid for. You didn't have to worry that marauding bands would come and seize everything at your factory, and hire someone to protect against this, because of the work the rest of us did. Now look, you built a factory and it

[7] I borrowed this phrase from David Smith's *Trying to teach in a season of great untruth* (Sense Publishers, 2006).

> turned into something terrific, or [had] a great idea – God bless. Keep a big hunk of it. But part of the underlying social contract is you take a hunk of that and pay forward for the next kid who comes along.

Someone funded our education, so we should fund the next generation's, without strings or regard for property wealth. "But we can't afford it," rings hollow as an excuse (Kozol, 2005; Rebell, 2011). We educate children as citizens of the US, not as citizens of Philadelphia or of Chicago or of the Mississippi Delta, and so should fund public schools out of the national wealth (Solomon, 2005). However, short of this, significant reforms arguably could be made to the existing system of funding (Gillespie, 2010; Rebell, 2011). At the same time, economic integration plans – like those implemented in Wake County, North Carolina; Cambridge, Massachusetts; LaCrosse, Wisconsin; and St. Lucie County, Florida – could be adopted by more school districts as a way to deconcentrate school poverty and simultaneously bring about more racial and ethnic integration (Brown, 2010, p. A18).

The problem is not that there are no "solutions," but rather there is no political will to create more equal educational opportunity. Let me return to *The Grapes of Wrath*. In telling the story of the Joads' physical trek across the land, Steinbeck (1939) also chronicles the development of a political consciousness among the great mass of dispossessed people, rendered surplus in a profit-driven world:

> One man, one family driven from the land; this rusty car creaking along the highway to the West. I lost my land, a single tractor took my land. I'm alone and I am bewildered. In the night one family camps in a ditch and another family pulls in and the tents come out. The two men squat on their hams and the women and children listen. Here's the node, you who hate change and fear revolution. ... For here "I lost my land" is changed; a cell is split and from its splitting grows the thing you hate – "we lost our land." The danger is here, for two men are not as lonely and perplexed as one. And from this first "we" there grows a still more dangerous thing; "I have a little food" plus "I have none." If from this problem the sum is "we have a little food," the thing is on its way, the movement has direction .... This is the beginning – from "I" to "we." (p. 206)

Today, we too need urgently to think in terms of "we" and to say, together, no, this is not who we are. We will not tolerate inequities and inadequacies in school funding based on accidents of birth – a politics of geography over which poor students and families have no control. We will not isolate poor children, disproportionately children of color, in substandard schools that offer them crumbs of an education. We will not shirk our responsibilities to the next generation or make helping others contingent on gaining something ourselves. Instead, we will honor our commitment to equal educational opportunity and make real this right for all children because we can.

CONCLUSION: FOLLOW THE MONEY

I would like to add a coda to this argument. Taking to heart the adult generation's responsibility to provide equal educational opportunity for all children requires not only making the necessary moral, political, and legal commitments, but also doing the hard work of trying to understand the economics involved. State budget crises jeopardize public funding of schools and invite ever more creative private "solutions." In at least 30 states, state education funding in 2011 was less than in 2008 (Baker, 2012). Without public – and publicly funded – education, equality of educational opportunity is not possible.

In talking with undergraduate and graduate students, I find many know very little about how US public schools are funded. Most are familiar with the pervasive anti-tax sentiment of these times, but do not understand how and why inequities arise – and I suspect the general public understands even less. Take property caps, for example. New York passed a 2% property tax cap in 2011, over the objections of educators, school district officials, and unions, among others, including *The New York Times*. An editorial published before the vote warned that a cap would further devastate low-income communities, already suffering from drastic state budget cuts to schools and communities (Reject the tax cap, 2001). Still, the cap passed. "It's popular because somebody comes up to you and says, 'Hey, we're going to put a cap on your property taxes,'" John Whiteley, who helped found the New York State Property Tax Reform Coalition, told *The New York Times*. "Who's going to say no? They don't bother to explain really what it is because it's a sound bite, it's not sound policy" (Hu, 2011, p. A19).

What happened in California after Proposition 13 was passed in 1978 should have informed the conversation in New York. After the California Supreme Court found in *Serrano v. Priest I* (1971) and *II* (1976) that the state's school funding violated both the state constitution and, in the first decision, the federal constitution, the state legislature discouraged property-tax-based revenue increases in high-wealth districts and sought gradually to raise state aid to poor districts. However, before this could happen, voters passed Proposition 13, which rolled back local tax assessments, allowing them to increase only when property was sold, and capped the tax rate at 1% of that reduced value:

> Overnight, therefore, the state became the major source of school funding. … That made it fairly easy to equalize California's school spending … but instead of leveling it up, it was effectively leveled down, and dramatically so, sinking from the top ten among the states in the 1960s to the bottom ten 30 years later. … The results were the largest class sizes in the country; deep cuts in counseling staffs, nurses, and music and arts programs; and in many districts, including the suburbs, rotting buildings and overcrowded classrooms graced by little except emergency maintenance. (Schrag, 2003, p. 78)

At least a dotted line can be drawn from the tax-cap maneuver in California to the conditions that the *Williams* lawsuit documented and contested 22 years later and to the state's current student achievement levels. In a recent report on student achievement, *Education Week* ranked California 46th among the 50 states and the District of Columbia (Hightower, 2011).

The public also needs to understand better what looks like corporate extortion – accomplished through tax breaks for "job creators" that do not create good jobs or sometimes any jobs at all, but do contribute to budget shortfalls that strap states and municipalities and therefore constrain school funding. A 2011 study of state economic development subsidy programs by Good Jobs First, a nonprofit research organization, found these deals cost states and cities $11 billion a year in lost revenue and many states lack safeguards to ensure the subsidies create long-term, well-paying jobs (Mattera, Cafcas, McIlvanine, Seifter, & Tarczynsky, 2011). A wage standard was included in fewer than half the 238 deals Mattera et al. (2011) reviewed – tax credits for "job creation," capital investment, or research and development; cash grants; low-cost or forgivable loans; establishment of enterprise zones; and reimbursement for worker-training expenses. Fewer than a fourth of the deals required the subsidized companies to provide health insurance for workers. Not surprisingly, the researchers expressed concern "about whether states are getting something for their money" (Mattera et al., 2011, p. ii).

Pennsylvania was not. The state found in a legislative report that many businesses in its Keystone Opportunity Zone program were neither creating jobs nor generating capital investment. New Jersey found in a commissioned study that $2.17 billion invested in its Urban Enterprise Zone program over six years had had limited economic impact. New York changed its Empire Zone program, designed to create jobs in high-poverty areas, after auditors found some businesses took their tax breaks but cut jobs while others hired in low-poverty areas (Cooper, 2011). In North Carolina, "people are still smarting from the departure of a Dell factory that put nearly 1,000 people out of work just five years after the state spent close to $2 million on training" (Rich, 2011, p. A1).

In addition to what property tax caps, tax credits, and other business "incentives" mean for public schools, the general public needs to understand better how, even within the public system, for-profit "alternatives" are turning public tax dollars into private profits. Online charter schools are now educating more than 200,000 full-time students and are "spreading quickly across the country" (Troubled, 2012, p. A26). A *New York Times* expose of K12 Inc. and other online charter schools found student test scores are low, online class sizes are high, and teachers are poorly paid at these taxpayer-subsidized schools:

> A look at the company's operations … raises serious questions about whether K12 schools – and full-time online schools in general – benefit children or taxpayers, particularly as state education budgets are being slashed. Instead, a portrait emerges of a company that tries to squeeze profits from public school dollars by raising enrollment, increasing teacher workload and lowering standards. (Saul, 2011, pp. 1, 24)

A National Education Policy Center study (Miron, Urschel, Yat Aguilar & Dailey, 2011) found that only 27% of the privately managed online schools met the NCLB achievement targets in 2010. Because high-poverty districts in some states receive larger state subsidies, they are particularly attractive to companies like K12, which foresees a $15 million market for its schools. "What we're talking about here is the financialization of public education," Alex Molnar told *The New York Times*. "These folks are fundamentally trying to do to public education what the banks did with home mortgages" (Saul, 2011, p. A24). The public needs to understand better "what the banks did with home mortgages"; the role that financial opacity rooted in an ethic of greed played in the recession of 2008 and the near-jobless recovery ever since; and how, as Molnar points out, a similar opacity and greed are reshaping public schooling.

Gloria Ladson-Billings (2008) has urged us to reconceptualize the "achievement gap" as an "education debt" – a shared responsibility, broadly owed:

> When we think of what we are combating as an achievement gap, we implicitly place the onus for closing that gap on the students, their families and their individual teachers and schools. But the notion of education debt requires us to think about how all of us, as members of a democratic society, are implicated in creating these achievement disparities.

The debt made evident by the persistent income and racial achievement gaps ought to be understood literally as well as figuratively. What are the actual numbers – that is, what would equal educational opportunity cost, taking into account the profound educational significance of poverty and especially of concentrated poverty? Who is doing the math? What formulas are being used, and based on what assumptions?

In his advocacy work as the lead counsel in the long-running New York State school funding case, Rebell often remarked no more than ten people truly understand how the state's complex school funding formula works and he is not sure he is among the ten. His humility aside, the point is well made: the fight for fairness must include not only a sense of solidarity, sustained through compassion and a feeling of "we." It also must include the hard work of educating the public about the economics that divide and conquer.

Court Cases Cited

Abbott v. Burke 575 A.2d 359, 400 (N.J. 1990).
Brown v. Board of Education 347 US 483 (1954).
Campaign for Fiscal Equity v. State of New York 100 60%N.Y.2d 893, 801 N.E.2d 326, 769 N.Y.S.2d 106
McCleary v. State of Washington, 84362-7 (2012)
Milliken v. Bradley, 418 US 717 (1974).
Plessy v. Ferguson 163 US 537 (1896).

Rose v. Council for Better Education, 790 S.W.2d 186
San Antonio v. Rodriguez 411 US 1 (1973).
Serrano v. Priest, 5 Cal.3d 584 (1971) (Serrano I)
Serrano v. Priest, 18 Cal.3d 728 (1976) (Serrano II)

REFERENCES

Bailey, M. J., & Dynarski, S. M. (2011). Gains and gaps: Changing inequality in US college entry and completion. In G. J. Duncan & R. Murnane (Eds.), *Whither opportunity? Rising inequality, schools, and children's life chances* (pp. 117-132). Russell Sage.

Baker, B. B., Sciarra, D. G., & Farrie, D. (2010a). *Is school funding fair? A national report card.* Newark, NJ: Education Law Center. Retrieved from http://www.schoolfundingfairness.org/National_Report_Card.pdf.

Baker, B. B., Sciarra, D. G., & Farrie, D. (2010b). *Is school funding fair? A national report card, 2008 update.* Newark, NJ: Education Law Center. Retrieved from http://www.schoolfundingfairness.org/ SFF_2008_Update.pdf.

Baker, B. B. (2012). *Revisiting the age-old question: Does money matter in education?* Washington, DC: The Albert Shanker Institute. Retrieved from http://www.shankerinstitute.org/images/doesmoneymatter_final.pdf.

Bell, D. (2004). *Silent covenants: Brown v. Board of Education and the unfulfilled hopes for racial reform.* Oxford University Press.

Books, S. (2010). Why and how poverty matters in schooling. In G. S. Cannella & L. D. Soto (Eds.), *Childhoods: A handbook* (pp. 157-172). Peter Lang.

Brown, R. (2010, February 27). District may end N.C. economic diversity program. *The New York Times*, p. A18.

Clinton, B. (1993). *Remarks to the Democratic Leadership Council – Bill Clinton speech – transcript.* Retrieved from http://findarticles.com/p/articles/mi_m2889/is_n48_v29/ai_14891633/

Coleman, J. S., Campbell, E. Q., Hobson, C. J., McPartland, J., Mood, A. M., Weinfeld, F. D., & York, R. L. (1966). *Equality of educational opportunity.* Washington, DC: US Department of Health, US Government Printing Office.

Cooper, M. (2011, December 14). With states desperate to keep jobs, companies have upper hand, report shows. *The New York Times*, p. A23.

Cornman, S. Q., & Noel, A. M. (2011, November). *Revenues and expenditures for public elementary and secondary school districts: School year 2008-09 (fiscal year 2009).* NCES 2012-313. Washington, DC: US Department of Education, Institute of Education Sciences, National Center for Education Statistics. Retrieved from http://nces.ed.gov/pubs2012/2012313.pdf.

Cowan, A. (2007, June 3). School's deep-pocketed partners. *The New York Times.* Retrieved from http://www.nytimes.com/2007/06/03/nyregion/nyregionspecial2/03Rschool.html?fta=y.

DeParle, J. (2011, January 5). Harder for Americans to rise from economy's lower rungs. *The New York Times*, p. A1.

Filardo, M. W., Vincent, J. M., Sung, P., & Stein, T. (2006). *Growth & disparity: A decade of US public school construction.* Washington, DC: BEST (Building Educational Success Together). Retrieved from http://www.ncef.org/pubs/GrowthandDisparity.pdf.

Gillespie, L. N. (2010). The fourth wave of education finance litigation: Pursuing a federal right to an adequate education. *Cornell Law Review, 95*(5), 989-1029.

Greenhouse, L. (1972, December 19). Property tax reform enthusiasm lags. *The New York Times.* Retrieved from http://query.nytimes.com/mem/archive/pdf?res=F50913F73F59107A93CBA81789D95F468785F9.

Hanushek, E. A. (1986). Economics of schooling: Production and efficiency in public schools. *Journal of Economic Literature, 24* (3), 1141-1177.

Haskins, R., & Sawhill, I. (2009). *Creating an opportunity society*. Washington, DC: Brookings Institution Press. Retrieved from http://www.brookings.edu/~/media/Files/events/2009/1027_opportunity_society/1027_opportunity_society_presentation.pdf.

Heuer, R., & Stullich, S. (2011). *Comparability of state and local expenditures among schools within districts: A report from the study of school-level expenditures*. Washington, DC: US Department of Education. Retrieved from http://www2.ed.gov/rschstat/eval/title-i/school-level-expenditures/school-level-expenditures.pdf.

Hightower, A. (2011, January 13). Weighing states' school performance, policymaking. *Quality Counts 2011, Education Week*. Retrieved from http://www.edweek.org/ew/articles/2011/01/13/16stateofthestates.h30.html.

Hu, W. (2011, January 23). Unlikely allies fight Cuomo's plan for property tax cap. *The New York Times*, p. A19.

Jäntti, M., Bratsberg, B., Røed, K., Raaum, O., Naylor, R., Österbacka, E., Björklund, A., & Eriksson, T. (2006, January). *American exceptionalism in a new light: A comparison of intergenerational earnings mobility in the Nordic countries, the United Kingdom and the United States*. Discussion Paper No. 1938 (January). Retrieved from http://ftp.iza.org/dp1938.pdf.

Jillson, C. (2004). *Pursuing the American dream: Opportunity and exclusion over four centuries*. Lawrence, KS: University Press of Kansas.

Kozol, J. (1992). *Savage inequalities: Children in America's schools*. New York: Harper Perennial.

Kozol, J. (1996). *Amazing grace: The lives of children and the conscience of a nation*. New York: Harper Perennial.

Kozol, J. (2005). *The shame of the nation: The restoration of apartheid schooling in America*. New York: Crown.

Kozol, J. (2009, September 6). *In depth: Jonathan Kozol*. Video clip and transcript. C-Span2, Book TV. Retrieved from http://www.c-spanvideo.org/appearance/574374262.

Krugman, P. (2012, January 8). America's unlevel field. *The New York Times*, p. A19.

Ladd, H., and Fiske, E.B. (2011, December 11). Class matters: Why won't we admit it? *The New York Times*, A23.

Ladson-Billings, G. (2008). *A letter to our next president*. Forum for Education and Democracy. Retrieved from http://forumforeducation.org/our-team

Mattera, P., Cafcas, T., McIlvanine, L., Seifter, A., & Tarczynsky, K. (2011). *Money for something: Job creation and job quality standards in state economic development subsidy programs*. Washington, DC: God Jobs First. Retrieved from http://www.goodjobsfirst.org/sites/default/files/docs/pdf/moneyforsomething_noappdx.pdf.

Miron, G., Urschel, J. L., Yat Aguilar, M. A., & Dailey, B. (2011). *Profiles of for-profit and nonprofit education management organizations: Thirteenth annual report – 2010-2011*. Boulder, CO: National Education Policy Center. Retrieved from http://nepc.colorado.edu/publication/EMO-profiles-10-11

National Council of Churches. (2010, May 18). *An alternative vision for public education: A pastoral letter on federal policy in public education: An ecumenical call for justice*. New York City: The National Council of the Churches of Christ in the USA. Retrieved from http://www.ncccusa.org/elmc/pastoralletter.pdf.

National Education Access Network. (2012). New York: Teachers College, Columbia University. Retrieved from http://schoolfunding.info/

Orfield, G. (2009). *Reviving the goal of an integrated society: A 21st century challenge*. Los Angeles: The Civil Rights Project, UCLA.

Orfield, G., Eaton, S. E., & The Harvard Project on School Desegregation. (1996). *Dismantling desegregation: The quiet reversal of Brown v. Board of Education*. New York: New Press.

Otterman, S. (2010, August 4). Diversity debate convulses elite high school. *The New York Times*, p. A1.

Pew Economic Mobility Project (2011). *Does America promote mobility as well as other nations?* The Pew Charitable Trusts. Retrieved from http://www.economicmobility.org/assets/pdfs/CRITA_FINAL.pdf.

Purpel, D. (1989). *The moral & spiritual crisis in education: a curriculum for justice & compassion in education*. New York: Bergin & Garvey.

Reardon, S. F. (2011). The widening academic achievement gap between the rich and the poor: New evidence and possible explanations. In G. J. Duncan & R. Murnane (Eds.), *Whither opportunity? Rising inequality, schools, and children's life chances* (pp. 91-116). Russell Sage.

Rebell, M. (2011, October). *Providing comprehensive educational opportunity to low-income students.* New York: Campaign for Educational Equity, Teachers College, Columbia University. Retrieved from: http://www.tc.columbia.edu/i/a/document/18661_1rebell.pdf

Rich, M. (2011). Private sector gets job skills; Public gets bill. *The New York Times*, p. A1.

Rothstein, R. (2004). *Class and schools: Using social, economic, and educational reform to close the black-white achievement gap*. Washington, DC: Economic Policy Institute.

Saul, S. (2011, December 13). Profits and questions at online charter schools. *The New York Times*, pp. A1, A24.

Schrag, P. (2003). *Final test: The battle for adequacy in America's schools*. New York: The New Press.

Shelly, B. (2011). *Money, mandates, and local control in American public education*. Ann Arbor: University of Michigan Press.

Smith, D. (2006). *Trying to teach in a season of great untruth.* Rotterdam: Sense Publishers.

Solomon, D. (2005, September 4). School monitor: Questions for Jonathan Kozol. *The New York Times Magazine*. Interview. Retrieved from http://www.nytimes.com/2005/09/04/magazine/04QUESTIONS.html.

Southern Education Foundation (2010). *The worst of times: Children in extreme poverty in the South and nation*. SEF Research and Policy Report. Retrieved from http://www.southerneducation.org/pdf/TWOT-Extreme%20Child%20Poverty%20Rpt-Final.pdf.

Steinbeck, J. (1939). *The grapes of wrath*. New York: Viking Press.

Troubled Online Charter Schools. (2012, January 11). Editorial. *The New York Times*, p. A26.

United Nations. (1989). *Convention on the rights of the child*. New York: Office of the United Nations High Commissioner for Human Rights. Retrieved from http://www2.ohchr.org/english/law/crc.htm.

US General Accounting Office. (1997, February). *State efforts to reduce funding gaps between poor and wealthy districts*. Report: GAO/HEHS-97-31. Washington, DC: US General Accounting Office. Retrieved from http://www.gao.gov/assets/230/223749.pdf

Warren, E. (2011, September 18). Elizabeth Warren on debt crisis, fair taxation. YouTube video. Retrieved from http://www.youtube.com/watch?v=htX2usfqMEs.

Welner, K., & Farley, A. (2010). *Confronting systemic inequity in education: High impact strategies for philanthropy*. Retrieved from http://www.ncrp.org/files/publications/Confronting_Systemic_Inequities_in_Education_lowres.pdf.

CPSIA information can be obtained at www.ICGtesting.com
Printed in the USA
BVOW08s0825210716

456241BV00002B/25/P

9 789462 091955